TOURISM IN WESTERN EUROPE
A Collection of Case Histories

TOURISM IN WESTERN EUROPE
A Collection of Case Histories

Edited by

RICHARD VOASE

University of Lincoln, Lincoln, UK

CABI *Publishing*

CABI *Publishing* **is a division of CAB** *International*

CABI Publishing	CABI Publishing
CAB International	10 E 40th Street
Wallingford	Suite 3203
Oxon OX10 8DE	New York, NY 10016
UK	USA

Tel.: +44 (0)1491 832111	Tel: +1 212 481 7018
Fax: +44 (0)1491 833508	Fax: +1 212 686 7993
Email: cabi@cabi.org	Email: cabi-nao@cabi.org
Web site: www.cabi-publishing.org	

A catalogue record for this book is available from the British Library, London, UK.

Library of Congress Cataloging-in-Publication Data

Tourism in Western Europe: a collection of case histories/edited by Richard N. Voase.

    p. cm.

    Includes bibliographical references (p.).

    ISBN 0-85199-572-1 (alk. paper)

    1. Tourism––Europe, Western––Case Studies. I. Voase, Richard N., 1954-

G155.E85 T685 2001

338.4'791404––dc21

        2001032585

ISBN 0 85199 572 1

Typeset by Wyvern 21 Limited, Bristol
Printed and bound in the UK by Biddles Ltd, Guildford and King's Lynn

Contents

Contributors

Nacima Baron-Yelles is a *maître de conférences* at the Université de Marne-la-Vallée, France.

Julio Batle is a lecturer in the School of Tourism at the University of the Balearic Islands, Palma, Mallorca.

Solveig Böhn is a lecturer in tourism planning and development at Dalarna University, Sweden.

Patricia East is a lecturer in the Faculty of Tourism, Fachhochschule München, Germany.

Jörgen Elbe is a lecturer in marketing and organizational theory at Darlana University, Sweden.

Mick Finn is a lecturer in tourism at the Lincoln campus of the University of Lincoln, England.

Alison Lewis is a lecturer at the Lincoln campus of the University of Lincoln, England.

Kaija Lindroth is a lecturer in languages and tourism at the Helsinki Business Polytechnic, Finland.

Martin Lohmann is managing director of the Institut für Tourismus- und Bäderforschung, Kiel, Germany.

Kurt Luger is Professor for Intercultural Communication, University of Salzburg, Austria.

Kevin Meethan is a lecturer in sociology at the University of Plymouth, England.

Nigel Morpeth is a lecturer in tourism at Leeds Metropolitan University, England.

Jörn Mundt is Professor for Business Studies with Tourism at the University for Co-operative Education/Berufsakademie Ravensburg, Germany.

Marco Antonio Robledo is a lecturer in the School of Tourism at the University of the Balearic Islands, Palma, Mallorca.

Tuovi Soisalon-Soininen is Assistant Principal of Helsinki Business Polytechnic, Finland.

Richard Voase is a lecturer at the Lincoln campus of the University of Lincoln, England.

Preface

The last 20 years have seen a proliferation of the term 'tourist destination'. Improbable places, such as industrial cities and isolated rural environments, have acquired legitimacy as places for vacational purposes. At the same time, traditional tourist destinations, such as coastal resorts, have seen their fashionability eroded and challenged.

These case histories, drawn from a variety of western European regions, examine these issues. They include an examination of the choices facing decision-makers and communities, and of marketing, planning and product-development practices. Each study is woven around the central theme of change, whether social, cultural, environmental, economic or political. A key feature is understood as a shift from an 'old' to a 'new' tourism.

Each author, drawing on primary information, writes about tourism in a locality where he or she has worked or has had close connections. As such, this collection presents the reader with an unrivalled assemblage of original material. The lively national differences in presentational style are as varied as the regions represented.

The introductory chapter offers a context for interpretation. By applying the social scientific concepts of liminality, myth, ideology and discourse, the shift from 'old' to 'new' tourism is revealed to be more than a change in patterns of consumer behaviour. It is a changed ideological context, by which tourist experiences have been subjected to re-valuation.

Additionally, the contributions have been arranged in three thematic sections in which political, economic and sociocultural factors are respectively dominant. Each part is prefaced with a short introduction, which identifies threads of commonality and disparity revealed by a comparison of the cases.

The reader will complete a consideration of these chapters with a broadened insight into how and why the 'new tourism' has developed in western Europe. Initiatives concerning the planning and development of destinations are revealed to be as much influenced by ideologies and changed cultural valuations, as by the changed patterns of consumer behaviour to which such initiatives intend to respond.

Acknowledgements and Dedication

Particular thanks are due to my friend and colleague Vivienne Cuthill. Her assistance and advice at a key stage in this project was crucial to its progress, and I am deeply grateful. I also acknowledge the help of David Raines for his valued technical assistance in the production of the electronic version of the text. I also thank Eileen Voase for her original painting used as the cover illustration.

Finally, on behalf of all contributors I dedicate the book to those of our students who, through European exchange programmes, have acquired a knowledge of, affection for and understanding of another European country. It is also dedicated to all those students who will enjoy such an experience in the future; and may there be many.

Richard Voase
Lincoln, England
April 2001

Introduction:
Tourism in Western Europe:
a Context of Change

Richard Voase
University of Lincoln, Lincoln Campus, Lincoln, UK

Introduction

The study of tourism is necessarily an interdisciplinary pursuit that exists as a single subject in university and polytechnic institutions across Europe. It also subsists as a specific field of enquiry within disciplines as diverse as business and management, sociology, cultural studies, anthropology and others. For this reason, it is not an easy task to settle on a useful introduction to a collection of case histories of such thematic diversity, and from authors of diverse geographical and cultural backgrounds. One interpretive paradigm, which may be a useful starting-point, is drawn from the discipline of marketing. This is the 'PEST' analysis, which involves an examination of the political, economic, socio-cultural and technological environments external to the tourist product, and into which the product is placed for purchase and consumption. This is established theory in marketing texts (Seaton and Bennett, 1996: 11–14; Horner and Swarbrooke, 1996: 236). It is perhaps open to the charge of being too general a model for effective analysis of this collection of material. My contention, however, is that the model is suited to the purpose, for three reasons:

1. The 'tourist product' is a peculiar kind of 'product': it is simultaneously a 'product' *and* the environment in which the 'product' is located. For example, the politics of a tourist destination and its capacity to favour or disfavour the well-being of the tourism industry must just as readily feature in the SWOT (Strengths, Weaknesses, Opportunities, Threats) analysis of the destination, as in the PEST analysis (Voase, 1995: 96).

2. All manner of cultural, discursive and ideological investigations are possible under the catch-all cachet of the term 'sociocultural'. Indeed, the later part of this chapter explores some key themes relating to the ideological preconditions which are arguably salient in the course of events explored in a number of the contributions in this text.

3. One of the initial aims of this text was to produce a collection which could constitute useful material for interpretation by either a 'business' or a 'cultural' paradigm. While it became apparent that an attempted synthesis of these approaches was a project of a scale inappropriate for a collection such as this, it does no harm to introduce the notion of such an approach, even if its full exploration must be left to the self-authoring activities of the reader.

Therefore, this introductory chapter sets out on a concise exploration of three themes: first, comment will be made on the nature of contemporary tourism; second, reference will be made to the contributions in this text in terms of the PEST analysis model advanced above; and third, observations will be made regarding the discursive and ideological preconditions which, as shall be seen, can be identified as active agents in a number of the contributions.

Contemporary Tourism: the 'Old' and the 'New'

There is a sense, at the simplest level, in which we can speak of an 'old' and a 'new' tourism (Poon, 1989). As Meethan observes in his chapter on tourism in the south-west of England, the 'new' tourism, whose growth might be identified with a range of cultural effects in society which are referred to as 'postmodern', involves changes and fragmentations in the spatial and temporal distribution of vacational tourism. Such changes include a diversification away from the beach, to include inland rural areas and cities; a shortening of the average length of a holiday, brought about by a dramatic increase in the popularity of the 'short break' of 2–3 nights; and qualitative changes in the experiences sought on vacational tourist trips from, broadly speaking, the passive to the active (Euromonitor, 1992: 3). Accompanying these changes is a de-differentiation of the traditional seasonality of vacational tourism, as mobility into different climatic zones is made possible by the growth of overseas tourism. Coupled with the eclecticism of destination choice and seasonality associated with the short break, vacational tourism has become the subject of spatial as well as temporal diversification. Additionally, the qualitative changes can be associated with other societal changes. Lohmann and Mundt's chapter concerning the qualitative evolution of the German outbound market links such changes with increased levels of education. The impact of such changes in market demand is a crucial influence on the development of destinations, especially in the case of Germany, which accounts for one third of outbound European tourism (CAB International, 1992: 113).

One way of interpreting such changes is to regard them as a consequence of a shift from 'Fordism' to 'post-Fordism', as represented by an increase in independent travel, customized vacational packages and efforts on the part of tour operators to tailor products to specifically segmented markets (Poon, 1989: 94). This might be termed a producer-perspective, and it is important to remember that cultural changes are manifested first in market behaviour.[1] It is important to understand that the postmodernization of tourism is not a transformation as such, but rather an intensification of certain thematic traits which have complemented, rather than replaced, the 'old' forms of tourism. As Voase points out in his chapter on the Isle of Thanet in south-east England, the seaside holiday, while having declined substantially in absolute terms during the 1980s, had retained a stable position relative to other forms of domestic tourism. What is more, the growth of Spain and, more recently, of other Mediterranean countries as beach destinations, merely recreates the north European beach holiday in more favourable climes. The growth of overseas vacational beach tourism in this respect remains resolutely 'modern' in character. This need not surprise us; the apostles of theories of postmodernity seldom make the claim that the postmodern represents some kind of dichotomy in relation to the modern. Lyotard (1984: 79), author of the seminal work entitled *The Postmodern Condition*, suggests that the postmodern is 'undoubtedly part of the modern'. Urry (1990: 87) underlines the paradoxical nature of tourism in relation to the cultural condition by pointing out that contemporary tourism is, in its varieties, simultaneously 'prefiguratively postmodern' and 'minimally modernist'. The old tourism – mass tourism – is far from extinct: in fact, it is thriving. The new tourism, however, is the bearer of a range of ideological meanings in which, to use the words of St Paul as used by Althusser (1992: 54), we 'live, move and have our being'. This shall receive more attention later in the chapter.

The External Environment: the PEST Analysis

The political environment

One of the problems of analysing the phenomenon of tourism is the ubiquitous presence of a plethora of media discourses surrounding the field. For example, in the United Kingdom, televisual programmes devoted to the exposition of holiday destinations, and to the examination of consumer complaints regarding holiday experiences, appear to be on the increase in equal measure. The practitioner or academic is thus surrounded by a range of media stories which are repeated and recycled, not because of their representative basis in fact, but because of their suitability to the discourse: they comply with audiences' preconceptions, and with producers' requirements to service those preconceptions (Bourdieu, 1998: 47). The practitioner or academic who wishes to understand a particular circumstance must therefore adopt a rigorous objectivity complemented by the active rejection of recycled conventional wisdom. One piece of writing, for example, which perhaps

---

[1] This is not to say that supply-side activity does not influence and shape consumer expectations. Clearly, market behaviour is in part a response to the purchase opportunities available, rather than to those that are not. Nevertheless, few marketeers would disagree with the suggestion that their art is principally one of identifying and responding to demand, rather than leading it.

failed to achieve such objectivity, attempted to compare and contrast the experience of regenerating UK and Spanish seaside destinations, and was emotively titled 'Seaside Resorts – Spanish Progress and British Malaise' (Curtis, 1997). The author was attempting a brief commentary on regeneration efforts in a seaside resort area in England known as the Isle of Thanet, and in various Spanish destinations including the resorts of Palma Nova and Magalluf, Mallorca. This example is mentioned because, coincidentally, two contributions in this collection encompass the same destination areas. The storyline was that somehow the Spanish resorts were getting it right, and the British had been getting it wrong. The note from Robledo and Batle in this volume regarding the tourism regeneration policies introduced by the government of the Balearics indicates that, despite the comprehensive nature of the legislation enacted to achieve a suitable regeneration of the developed coastal zones of the island of Mallorca, its passage has been far from smooth. As with any mature destination, a range of diverse political and economic interests act as an inhibitor to effective destination redevelopment. Its 'progress' has been somewhat bumpy. This is no less true in Voase's examination of the consequences of economic and social change and its effect on the politics of the Isle of Thanet as a mature destination. In this case, in contrast with the Balearic example, the tourism industry was no longer perceived as a major economic contributor. This was largely due to a national sociocultural context in which the 'seaside' was viewed as an anachronistic reminder of an industrial past characterized by collective values, in contrast with the individualistic values of the post-industrial present. A local culture of entrepreneurialism was ideologically set against publicly led regenerative efforts. To describe this as 'malaise' is to ignore the fundamental processes at work. What is apparent from both these British and Spanish contributions is that, in mature destinations, there is what this author has termed elsewhere a 'conflicting interest in the common environment' (Voase, 1995: 140) and this, it is suggested, should be the focus of study when an analysis of the politics of a mature destination is to be attempted.

This, however, is but one dimension of the politics of the destination: at the point of inception, an infant tourism industry can be the beneficiary of uncritical political acclaim. Beginning in the early 1980s and continuing to the present day, urban communities across the developed world have looked to tourism as an instrument of regeneration. Faced with the challenges posed to traditional economies by the rapid decline of traditional primary and secondary industries as providers of employment, tourism as an instrument of regeneration promised three effects: the creation of low-skill jobs to replace those lost in the former industries; usage of redundant commercial and industrial buildings to create tourist attractions; and the image benefits of the latter, enabling a positive (middle-class) image of the city to be mediated by those cultural intermediaries known as the *service class* (Urry, 1990: chapter 5)[2]. Morpeth's contribution within this collection is a polemic which argues

---

[2] The problem with this attractive package is, of course, that the replacement jobs provided by tourism were frequently part-time and casual or seasonal, and required a different skills base from (say) working on the docks; and the cultural renaissance of these cities did little to satisfy the requirements of their erstwhile blue-collar inhabitants; see for example Boyle and Hughes, 1991; Harvey, 1988.

that the instrumentality of tourism exceeds its utility as set out above. His argument is that the government of the day, in the United Kingdom, actively encouraged the development of tourism in what at first sight were areas with unpromising tourist resources, such as the town of Middlesbrough which is Morpeth's case example, as part and parcel of the accelerated disassembly of the manufacturing infrastructure of the country. What is intriguing is that the representatives of manufacturing industry offered little or no apparent resistance (Leys, 1985). Academic appraisal of the role of politics in tourism is often confined to a juxtaposition with the planning and development functions, and oriented toward the identification of rational good practice. The contribution of Morpeth indicates that there is a case to answer for investigating tourism as a vehicle for socioeconomic engineering.

There are two other respects in which the relationship between politics and tourism are highlighted within this volume. The first could be styled the politics of the 'composite zone'. Meethan's appraisal of tourism marketing in the south-west of England reveals the problems which arise when a destination is defined as a region, as opposed to the autonomous politico-geographical areas from which the region is composed. When it is, in marketing terms, advantageous to define a destination as a region as opposed to its component resorts, a commonality of approach will not arrive easily. This is also the case in Mallorca, as Robledo and Batle point out: one municipality (Alcudia) offers to implement a governmental tourism policy with rigour, but the attitudes of the other 37 vary on a continuum from compliance to hostility. The second political manifestation which deserves mention is that of the political aversion to good practice. There are two examples of this, in the contributions by Voase and by Böhn and Elbe. In the former case, the problem is attributed to an interaction of local culture and national change which made ambivalence almost inevitable. In the case of the Böhn contribution, the implied rejection of a tourism practitioner and his discovery of relationship marketing *avant la lettre* is intriguing. Böhn's contribution is located in Sweden, but the 'tourism manager' at the centre of the case, and his success based on personal drive and charisma as opposed to formal qualification, would seem to have a rapport with a particular cultural circumstance found in the United Kingdom, namely, the approval ascribed to the 'gifted amateur' and the creativity which such individuals, unrestrained by formal and professional structures, can introduce to a business. It is salutary to reflect on the retrospective thoughts of one Thomas Cook, when writing about the beginning of his company in the mid-19th century:

> That moment . . . was the starting point of a career of labour and pleasure which has expanded into . . . a mission of goodwill and benevolence on a large scale (cited in Brendon, 1991: 5)

Cook's biographer went on to point out that 'tourists often became friends. This is not to suggest that Cook was an incompetent entrepreneur, merely that he was not just an entrepreneur' (Brendon, 1991: 99). The parallels with Böhn and Elbe's 'tourism manager' are striking. In consideration of the wider implications of this, one question which those of us working in higher education in tourism must ask ourselves is whether our courses encourage the release of creativity, or whether they

risk stifling innovation by presenting tourism as a structured system whose parameters must be observed.

The economic environment

One of the problems of the PEST analysis is its working assumption that it is
possible to identify separate elements which fit neatly into respective categories.
This of course is fundamentally flawed, since politics, economy, technology and
sociocultural life are interlinked to produce a cybernetic system which we call 'society'. The problem is no more obvious than when considering that element of the
economic environment which features so prominently in the contributions of Lewis
and of Lindroth and Soisalon-Soininen, and is said to provide 'new hope' in the
epilogue of the chapter by Voase: European Union funding. Whether this is a
feature of the political or the economic environment is itself dependent upon the
perspective taken of the European Union. Founded in 1958 as a 'common market'
and naming itself European Economic Community, its original economic objectives are now being superseded by an aspiration for closer political ties. The symbolic
change of name to 'European Union' (EU) is perhaps indicative of this. Certainly,
structural funds to support economic and social regenerative projects have been the
lubricant for the emergence of many newer tourist destinations, not least the industrial cities referred to earlier. The importance of the EU to the developments discussed in Lindroth and Soisalon-Soininen's contribution is clear. Lewis offers us an
insight into the byzantine nature of the system of policies and subventions which
are needed in order to achieve an equitable balance between the need for a template
policy which is applicable throughout the EU, the not inconsiderable power of
non-rural countryside visitors to lobby for the countryside to be maintained in an
idyllic rather than practical form, and the actual and aspired requirements of
countryside residents. In this respect, the concept of 'think global, act local' is
exposed as a somewhat glib phrase which masks a range of problems of ponderous
complexity.

     This subvention to the supply-side to fund destination development is only
one part of the equation; there is also the question of the growth of the whole
market for tourism, whether of the domestic or outbound variety. It was noted
earlier that Germany is Europe's most vigorous outbound market: in 1970, some
40% of Germans took a holiday of 4+ nights; by 1989, that figure had risen to c.
68% (Euromonitor, 1992: 9). The family leisure budget of Germans was said to
have quadrupled between 1965 and 1982, and one-third was expended on holidays
(Krippendorf, 1987: 91). In the United Kingdom, in the early 1990s, 94% of
employees enjoyed a holiday entitlement of 4 weeks or more; as recently as the late
1970s, such an entitlement was rare (Central Statistical Office, 1993: 140–141).
In short, rising disposable incomes and holiday entitlements in the affluent west
were an engine for growth of tourist destinations. Consumption, the economic
feature said to be defining of postmodern society (in contrast with the modern era
whose defining feature was production), itself provided the economic motor for

new industries, such as tourism, to replace old ones. Coupled with qualitative changes from the 'old' to the 'new' tourism, rising affluence provided a growing market for new destinations, and new varieties of destinations.

The technical environment

The proliferation of the jet aircraft has done for international tourism what the railway did for domestic tourism a century or so earlier. In the United Kingdom, for example, between 1840 and 1850, a railway network covered the country and spawned the growth of seaside resorts as tourist destinations. Railways were the means by which small coastal communities, some already enjoying a tourist trade but limited to those with the means to travel to them by horse and carriage, were turned into mass tourist destinations. Similarly, the jet-powered aircraft has democratized travel between nation-states. Perhaps the arrival of computer reservation systems has facilitated a further expansion by making the process of booking and through-ticketing easier, but it is the mechanical rather than the electronic innovation which has made the principal difference.

In a sense, the intricacies of funding systems for tourism development from bodies such as the EU could also be regarded as part and parcel of the technical environment. Such subventions are not in principle dependent upon political patronage, although to win the advance confidence of the fund-giver is naturally politic. Rather, the disbursement of EU structural and related funds is based on the fulfilment of elaborate sets of criteria, and on the successful modelling of projects to match the desired objectives of those funds. Therefore, developing a destination in an area which carries the entitlement to apply for such monies requires an expertise in the technicalities of the fund's criteria. Fundgivers' expressed criteria may also reflect certain ideological aims, as shall be seen shortly.

The sociocultural environment

This category is left until last because, perhaps more so than the other three categories of environmental influence, it is very important. Its importance becomes apparent when the nature of tourism itself is considered. As this author has argued before, many of the misunderstandings in tourism, including those which are discussed in the contributions in this anthology by Böhn and Elbe and Voase, arise out of the perspective taken: is tourism an *activity*, or an *industry*? (Voase, 1995: 5–6). People working in the supply-side of tourism are apt to take the latter view, because their experience of it is as a means of gaining income and providing employment. However, tourists themselves are unlikely to think of themselves as self-conscious consumers, except on those occasions when they wish to complain in respect of service entitlements which have not been delivered to their satisfaction. It is arguably safer to regard vacational tourists as seeing themselves more in the role of guests. To gain further insight into this tourist disposition, we can refer to MacCannell's theorized trajectory of discovery, whereby the tourist is engaged in a constant search to look beyond the 'staged' for the 'real' destination and 'authentic' social relations (MacCannell, 1976: 41–42, 92, 94; see also Selwyn, 1996: 7–8). We can also refer to qualitative studies which reveal that the discourse surrounding satisfactory tourist experience appears to revolve around success in uncovering the 'real'. The three comments which follow are minor extracts from material from 200 interviews, but represent, arguably, the existential satisfaction of finding oneself 'backstage':

> I felt wanted, not alone or an oddity.
> It was a fantastic experience to get to know them and they even refused to let us help pay for the gas.
> Our hostesses were so charming it was like visiting old friends.
> (Source: Pearce, 1982: 127)

Note, in the first example, the respondent is *socially* rather than commercially included; in the second example, the experience is validated once it is relocated *outside* the supply–demand relationship and contractual consumption; and in the third, the charm of the hostess was valid because her manner *transcended* the requirements of being paid to be polite. In this way, tourists define their activity as being outside consumption, despite it being within consumption. The search outside is for an otherness, which in the words of Selwyn (1996: 21) is an 'imagined world which is variously pre-modern, pre-commoditized or part of a benign whole'. In other words, tourism is in its various guises a quest for myths in various forms. The mechanics of delivering this experience may take the form of an industry, but the tourist experience, and hence tourism itself, is culturally generated (Roche, 1992; Urry, 1994). The remaining part of this introduction aims to show how, in various ways, both producer and consumer activity is constituted by cultural forms and the ideologies which lie behind them. The exposition will involve reference to the concepts of liminality, myth and discourse, and will be related to the contributions in this text.

Tourism and Liminality

'Liminal' is a term related to the English word 'limit' and the Latin *limes*, meaning boundary or frontier. Its early use is credited to the anthropologist Arnold van Gennep, who in his seminal work *Rites de Passage* (1909) used it to refer to transitory phases in life during which new experiences were encountered. Such phases, such as adolescence, were regarded as being of ritual and/or sacred significance, during which behavioural protocols are suspended or amended. By extension, liminality can be defined spatially as well as temporally: a beach, for example, can be regarded as a liminal zone in which normal dress and behavioural protocols are suspended (Fiske, 1989: 43–44; Shields, 1990); the urban waterfront in a post-industrial city becomes a liminal zone as commercial use gives way to leisure usage, in which the cultural tastemakers of the *service class* are simultaneously its producers and consumers (Zukin, 1988: 438–439). Indeed, the proclivity of some vacational tourists to expose themselves to demanding activities to which they are unaccustomed, such as bungee-jumping, and to engage in ephemeral sexual relationships with strangers, can lead one to theorize that tourism itself can be regarded as a liminal state 'in which conventional calculations of safety and risk are disrupted' (Urry, 1992: 19). Tourism can be regarded as the result of, to quote Urry (1990: 11) again, a 'basic binary division between the ordinary/everyday and the extraordinary'. Related to this theme is Bakhtin's concept of 'carnival', definable as a spectacle in which all present are participants, rather than divided into performers and spectators. Hence, a crowd on a British seaside promenade, equipped with 'Kiss Me Quick' hats and other ludic objects, and eating food such as sticks of rock and candy floss, consumed for their garish appearance rather than nutritional value, is carnivalesque in the true Bakhtinian sense (Thompson, 1983: 133; Shields, 1990: 51). The inclusive popularity of carnival can be contrasted with contrived official spectacle, which can be labelled 'festival' and which involves the introduction of the binary divide between performer and spectator. The transition from carnival to festival is frequently the effect which ensues when popular events are commodified for tourist purposes (MacCannell, 1992: 231–234).

Applying these theoretical constructs to the contributions in this collection yields some insights. Finn's charting of the progress of the McDonaldization of football can be regarded a transition from carnival to festival. The traditional stadium was considered a sacred place and a location for popular expression (Bale, 1993: 65). As such, its status was liminal, a site for the authentically carnivalesque in which, despite the player/spectator divide, all were in a sense participants united by spatially defined allegiances. The dawn of the all-seater stadium in the early 1990s, equipped with sponsorship boxes and enhanced merchandizing capabilities arguably transformed the experience from one of carnival to festival, and as such eroded the liminal status of the stadium. What had been a site of relatively unrestrained popular expression was now a place of conditioned reaction. The augmented televisual mediation of football eroded the spatially defined social bond between team and supporters. As Finn explains, spectators are now expected to respond on cue to a range of predetermined aural and visual stimuli which complement the game itself: a picture of commodification complete.

Other contributions present a picture of the destination as a liminal zone for popular expression, resistance, and myth. The Pointe du Raz, as Baron-Yelles tells us, became a site of resistance to official versions of environmental concern. Lohmann and Mundt show us how the staged musical, in its contemporary form, involves the importation of theme park techniques into the interior of the theatre, resulting in its transformation into a liminal zone where fantasies become alive. While the musical is festivalesque rather than carnivalesque, the transformed theatre simulates, more so than the traditional staged production, incorporation of the spectators into what is, nevertheless, a passive experience. 'Pirate' cruises, in Lindroth and Soisalon-Soininen's contribution, meet the desire of children to journey into a liminal state where a mythical 'other' can be encountered. This demands a closer examination of the concept of myth, which now follows.

Tourism and Myth

'Myth' is a concept familiar to anthropologists, and for which a working summary will now be attempted. This is a necessarily perilous pursuit (though less perilous than attempting a working summary of discourse and ideology, which follows) because full justice can only be done to the topic through detailed examination. It is hoped that the references will offer a suitable starting point for further reading. The commentators most closely associated with contemporary understandings of 'myth' are Lévi-Strauss and Barthes; we look briefly at their contributions in turn. For Lévi-Strauss, 'myths' were not so much the abstract beliefs and legends associated with a society, but an integral part of the structure of language. His suggestion was that, although specific myths will vary greatly from society to society, a commonality of structure can be traced in widely different myths from different sources. Inherent in this structure were binary oppositions, for example pretty/ugly, male/female, which were their building blocks (Lévi-Strauss, 1968: ch. XI). In other words, the function of myth is as a metaphorical linguistic device to convey abstract truths as understood in common by the sender and the receiver of the message, using binary oppositions as a key structuring ingredient. As we shall see shortly, tourist myths can be usefully understood in this way.

Barthes also saw myth as a function of linguistic structure, but elaborated a system of analysis which he applied to all sorts of texts, including advertisements. He followed the Saussurean linguistic distinction between a signifier+signified (word+concept) which together constituted a sign, but drew particular attention to the way in which signs work at two levels; first, at the denotative level; and second, at the connotative level, which he also refers to as the level of 'signification' or *myth* (Barthes, 1972: 114, 117; 1977: 37). Barthes' term for the operation of signification at mythical level is the 'rhetorical system' (Barthes, 1977: 49; Culler 1983: 75). His example is that of a red rose, an image of which denotes a plant, but which at second level is recognizable as a signifier of love: when the rose is given by a man to a woman, a *sign* of love has been generated (Barthes, 1972: 117). The rose, therefore, has a mythical significance beyond its status as a plant. This mythical significance is dependent upon both sender and receiver understanding the second-level significance of the rose; the referent (meaning) which arises is dependent upon a learned relationship between signifier, signified and referent.

There now arises the question as to what, in the contributions in this collection, can be regarded as 'tourist myths'. We could regard Lindroth and Soisalon-Soininen's pirate cruises as a sanitized excursion into an 'evil' 'other', binarily opposed to 'good'; this at any rate is Eco's assessment of the purpose of the 'Pirates of the Caribbean' and other sanitized 'evil' attractions contained within Disney theme parks (Eco, 1987: 57–58). As such, we have a means of investigating exactly how islands, castles and pirates combine to make a worthwhile tourist experience. It is 'obvious' that they do, but the 'obvious' at the most fundamental level frequently eludes us. More shall be said about this in the following section on ideology. Of equally mythical quality is the role of film in creating a tourist destination, as reported by Luger and East in their contribution regarding the impact of tourism in the mountains of Austria. So-called *Heimatfilme* offered an idealized portrayal of rural life in times gone by. This led to the revival and maintenance of former rural traditions. While, for example, the revival of rural privations are not suitable material for a modern myth of the bucolic past, those features which can be regarded both as comfortable and as absent from the present-day can be agreeably recreated, making possible a journey into the pre-modern for the citizenry of the post-modern. Of more global appeal was the impact of the film *The Sound of Music*, cited by some three out of four inbound tourists as the main reason for their trip to Austria. Tourist destinations with less obvious aesthetic appeal have sought to create their own myths by branding exercises using whatever well-known associations are available: therefore, as Morpeth informs us, Middlesbrough has sought, through the designation 'Captain Cook Country', to generate a mythical status which it would otherwise lack. To examine the workings of tourist myth is not the easiest of tasks since, as was observed at the beginning of this chapter, the recycling of these myths through the media is so prevalent that they acquire a primary 'obviousness'. This in itself is significant, and leads us to consider the role of discourse and ideology in forming the cultural preconditions out of which both producer and consumer behaviour in tourism can be argued to arise.

Discourse and Ideology

This section begins with the repeated caveat that a working summary of these concepts, of the kind which follows, is not intended to offer the sum total of knowledge or the full understanding of this author. It is hoped, as with myth, that the references offer a suitable starting-point for acquiring a deeper understanding. I begin by suggesting that 'discourse' and 'ideology' are separate concepts, but which exist in a kind of symbiosis. Following the distinction proposed by Purvis and Hunt, I suggest that ideology, or rather ideologies, are 'forms of consciousness': they are recurring ideas, embedded in culture. Discourses, by contrast, are the 'terms of engagement': that is, they are recurring messages, embedded in communication (Purvis and Hunt, 1993: 476). Put simply, an ideology is a concept, and a discourse is its vehicle. A discourse is therefore a vehicle of change, one which agents of change – individuals, institutions – use to enact and represent; implying, therefore, that there must be a relationship between discourse and social structure (Fairclough, 1992: 63–64). It thus follows that the wherewithal of culture, including the perceptions of liminal status, the carnivalesque and myth, are influenced and shaped by ideologies mediated by discourse. A discourse is not one form of communication: it is a recurring message which is intertextual in nature, that is to say it is identifiable across a range of forms of communication (Barker and Brooks, 1998: 109). So, we may speak of a 'discourse of tourism' that appears in travel brochures, televized travel programmes, tourism degree courses, and so on.

So what, therefore, is the nature of ideologies, these 'forms of consciousness'? They are embedded ideas which are constituted and mediated in the discourses which surround us in our daily lives. As such they have a power over us, the more so for being largely invisible and hence unrecognized. Thompson (1990: 7) suggests ideology to be 'meaning in the service of power' and that its investigation requires scrutiny of discourses, from everyday utterances to the most complex of images and texts; it also requires us to examine the social contexts in which such discourses appear and to ask how power relationships – 'relations of domination' – are sustained. Michel Foucault, whose ideas cannot be discussed here in anything like their full complexity, suggested that power subsists in the interrelationships between discourses and social practices, rather than being consciously exercised by actors (Gordon, 1980: 246). This sits quite comfortably with the writings of his teacher Louis Althusser, who suggested that ideologies work on subjects by a process of *interpellation*. His example is of a person being hailed (interpellated) in the street: the social practice of responding to a greeting in a prescribed way is to be subjected by the 'form of consciousness' which prescribes it. Embedded in the discourse of polite exchange is a protocol by which we 'live, move and have our being'. As interpellands, we are a 'subject' in two senses: first, a free-thinking actor who chooses whether to respond or not; second, we are a subject in the sense of being *subjected* by the protocols of the exchange. In other words, when we are least aware of it, we are subjected by relations of domination (Althusser, 1992).

'Producing the Postmodern'

Moving therefore toward the end of this introduction, we need to consider the ways in which discursive and ideological preconditions can be identified as active agents in some of the contributions in this text. In short, in what ways do discourse and ideology interact to produce 'relations of domination' which can be identified in both consumer and producer activity? In particular, in what ways does the so-called 'new tourism' represent a changed pattern of power relations? This discussion will be necessarily brief and will begin with a summary of three widely accepted facets of the culture of the condition of postmodernity: postmodernism as a culture of signification; the postmodern preoccupation with 'the past' in various forms; and the role of the new middle class in mediating ideology through discourse.

First, we consider postmodernism as a 'regime of signification' (Lash, 1990: 11). It is a regime because it dominates and governs; one and the same as the relations of domination mentioned above. Second, its identifying feature is not what is denoted, but what is connoted: a regime of 'signification'. The critical insight is that objects and services are increasingly consumed, not so much for their use-value, but for their sign-value. Naturally enough, producers respond to this increased consumer demand for symbolic consumption by imbuing products and services with increased sign-value and promoting them in like fashion, resulting in the phenomenon known as 'lifestyle advertising' (Thrift, 1989). Baudrillard suggests the consequence of this postmodernization of culture to be a perceived state of reality, which is so governed by the mythicization of the real that it merits the term 'hyperreal', defined as the 'meticulous reduplication of the real through another reproductive medium'; the 'real' is simulated to produce new 'realities'.

Elsewhere he points out that the process of simulation can happily take place without any 'real' original at all: 'the generation by models of a real without origin or reality: a "hyperreal"' (in Poster (ed.), 1988: 144, 166). Baudrillard has been one of the principal contributors to our understanding of consumption under the postmodern condition (see especially Baudrillard, 1998). Other theoretical constructs such as the *society of spectacle*, originating in the work of Guy Debord (1992), place similar emphasis on form over content and can be successfully synthesized with Baudrillard's approach (Best, 1994).

Therefore, in the contributions in this collection, we see in Luger and East's chapter a notional past, as depicted in fictional film, being used as a basis for the recreation of a bucolic pre-modern 'reality'. In Finn's contribution, we see the aural and visual spectacle which accompanies American football, simulated and reproduced to accompany another medium, that of English soccer, the aim being to transform the game into spectacle rather than sport, with the intended pacification (or is it passivication?) of the fan:

> Spectacle . . . is not a supplement to the real world, its added decoration. It is the heart of unrealism of the real society . . . It says nothing more than 'whatever appears is good, and whatever is good appears' . . . The attitude it requires in principle is this passive acceptance, which in fact it has already obtained by its method of appearing without reply, by its monopoly of appearance. (Debord, 1992: 64–65)

It is not surprising, therefore, that whether the object of study is football as a destination attribute, or the destination itself, consumers expect (and producers produce) a mythicized product: Morpeth's 'Captain Cook Country' being one of the more obvious examples because of its clumsy mythicization; the mountains of Austria being less obvious because of the acceptance, by three out of four visitors, that Austrian mountains as seen in *The Sound of Music* are real, and the von Trapp family was based on a 'real' (as opposed to fictional) prototype. Ascribing historicity to 'real' film images is of course a slightly risky business, as many potential visitors to Scotland found when, having seen a typical Scottish landscape in the film *Braveheart*, they discovered that it had been filmed in Ireland.

Second, we consider the preoccupation with the recycling of motifs of the past, which is a repeated hallmark of postmodern production and consumption, particularly noticeable around the time of writing, for example, in the music of Oasis and in the designs of recently launched prestige cars by Jaguar and Rover. This preoccupation with the past is arguably linked with the regime of signification as discussed above,the connection being pithily summarized by Baudrillard:

> *When the real is no longer what it used to be, nostalgia assumes its full meaning.*   There is a proliferation of myths of origin and signs of reality; of second-hand truth, objectivity and authenticity. (in Poster (ed.), 1988: 171, my italics)

Once sign-value replaces use-value as the primary product attribute, 'the past' becomes an emporium of images and styles to be annexed, recycled and reduplicated through a variety of media: from reproduction Victorian toilet seats to Agatha Christie Murder-Mystery weekends in full 1930s costume. Once the shackles of the 'real' have been shaken off, 'nostalgia assumes its full meaning'. This searching of the past for meaning is also connected, arguably, with a crisis of confidence in the future: technological progress has not solved all problems of the human condition, and indeed has created some new ones. In an age when progress is perceived as creating more problems than it solves, the conviction arises that there was a time, in the past, when certain issues were better understood. The 'grand narratives' of modernity are being challenged and replaced by a range of *petits récits* which see desirable culture as local and sustainable rather than global and progressive (Lyotard, 1984). Therefore, Lewis' contribution examines in detail a range of structural efforts to marry progress in the form of increased recreational demand with farming practices, which, though not in the vanguard of progress in 'modern' farming practice, are those suited to the locality and its sustained vitality as a place to live and a place to visit: an intended process of de-commodification and re-authenticization.

The third facet of postmodern culture is linked with the second, just as surely as the second emanates from the first. It concerns the means by which the symbolic meanings which attach themselves to objects and services are circulated through society. Thrift (1989) links the preoccupation with the imagery of the natural and built environments of the past, in the United Kingdom, with the emergence of the new fraction within the middle class termed *service class*. The postmodernization of advanced economies, by which many former manual tasks are taken over by mechanico-electrical means, has created societies dominated by service industries. Many of these new service-industry jobs may be casual, undemanding and non-unionized, as described by Morpeth in his contribution. But there has nevertheless been the emergence of a growing group of well-qualified knowledge workers in creative industries whose employment involves the mediation of information. The members of the *service class* as described by Thrift are cultural tastemakers, placing a high valuation on the imagery and practices of 'the past' as objects of symbolic consumption, and, crucially, are in a position to mediate their values throughout the rest of society by virtue of their jobs. Bourdieu (1984: 325, 359), through his exhaustive research in France, has identified the same group and styled them the *new petite bourgeoisie* or 'new cultural intermediaries'. As such, the range of experiences which have earlier been referred to as the 'new tourism' can be ascribed to the mediating influence of this group, and of those whom it successfully evangelizes, in particular, service-class-staffed public and quasi-public bodies including government departments, tourist boards, and municipal councils.

The role of the service class is argued, in Voase's chapter on the English seaside, to have established a national context of unfashionability for domestic coastal tourism, eclipsing the argument that the British coastal resort's decline is attributable to the weather. Similarly, we are tempted to speculate on the extent to which the desire to turn Loviisa in Finland into an historic destination, as ably explained by Lindroth and Soisalon-Soininen, can be regarded as a response to similar social and cultural processes taking place in the countries of the Baltic region; and the extent to which the intended re-fashioning of Mallorcan coastal resorts, as discussed by Robledo and Batle, is a response to indigenous concerns or to changed cultural valuations emerging in the United Kingdom, one of Mallorca's primary markets. We can also speculate as to the extent to which the qualitative changes in the German outbound market, as discussed by Lohmann and Mundt, have influenced the character of destinations. One such example, concerning German environmental influence, can be seen in the remarkable assemblage of environmental management policies pursued by *Grecotel*, the largest hotel management company in Greece. The leading German tour operator TUI is a major shareholder in the company, and it would be intriguing to know the extent to which TUI perceived these policies to be a necessary attribute to maintain credibility with its customers (Horner and Swarbrooke, 1996: 551–554). Finally, Baron-Yelles shows us the way in which, over a sustained time-period, the discourse surrounding a particular tourist destination, the Pointe du Raz, has a cumulative effect in defining the destination and critically, as she points out, adding symbolic value to it; in short, creating a myth.

Conclusion

It must be stated very clearly, before closing this chapter, that the analysis offered in the preceding paragraphs barely touches on the potential for which it, and the eleven contributions in this text, are together intended to offer. I have suggested that both producer and consumer activity in respect of tourist destinations is influenced by a range of ideological preconditions, connected with the technological, societal and cultural changes which have been referred to as postmodern. The initial means of analysis is the PEST analysis derived from marketing theory, but the actual preconditions require an additional level of scrutiny involving cultural analysis. In the end, we can theorize the 'new tourism' to be less a body of products than an ideological construct. Imbued with symbolic connotation, the 'new tourism' is the ideological context in which we as tourists 'live, move and have our being' and whose primary characteristic is its invisible 'obviousness' (Althusser, 1992: 54). Its presence, I suggest, is identifiable in different ways in all of the contributions in this text.

References

Althusser, L. (1992) Ideology and the ideological state apparatus. In: Easthope, A. and McGowan, K. (eds) *A Critical and Cultural Theory Reader*. Open University Press, Buckingham, pp. 50–58.

Bale, J. (1993) *Sport, Space and the City*. Routledge, London.

Barker, M. and Brooks, K. (1998) *Knowing Audiences: Judge Dredd: Its Friends, Fans and Foes*. University of Luton Press, Luton.

Barthes, R. (1972) *Mythologies*. Vintage Books (edition 1993), London.

Barthes, R. (1977) *Image, Music, Text*. Fontana, London.

Baudrillard, J. (1998) *The Consumer Society: Myths and Structures*. Sage, London.

Best, S. (1994) The commodification of reality and the reality of commodification: Baudrillard, Debord and postmodern theory. In: Kellner, D. (ed.) *Baudrillard: a Critical Reader*. Blackwell, Oxford.

Bourdieu, P. (1984) *Distinction: a Social Critique of the Judgement of Taste*. Routledge, London.

Bourdieu, P. (1998) *On Television and Journalism*. Pluto Press, London.

Boyle, M. and Hughes, G. (1991) The politics of the representation of 'the real': discourses from the Left on Glasgow's role as European City of Culture 1990. *Area* 23 (3), 217–228.

Brendon, P. (1991) *Thomas Cook: 150 Years of Popular Tourism*. Martin Secker and Warburg, London.

CAB International (1992) *World Travel and Tourism Review 1992*. CAB International, Wallingford.

Central Statistical Office (1993) *Social Trends 23*. HMSO, London.

Culler, J. (1983) *Barthes*. Fontana, London.

Curtis, S. (1997) Seaside resorts: Spanish progress and British malaise. *Insights* 9, C9–C18, September. English Tourist Board, London.

Debord, G. (1992) *Society of Spectacle and Other Films*. Rebel Press, London.

Eco, U. (1987) *Travels in Hyperreality*. Picador, London.

Euromonitor (1992) *The European Travel and Tourism Marketing Directory*. Euromonitor, London.

Fairclough, N. (1992). *Discourse and Social Change*. Polity Press, Cambridge.

Fiske, J. (1989) *Reading the Popular*. Unwin Hyman, London.

Gordon, C. (ed.) (1980) *Michel Foucault: Power/Knowledge: Selected Interviews and Other Writings 1972–1977*. Harvester Wheatsheaf, London.

Harvey, D. (1988) Voodoo cities. *New Statesman and Society*, 30 September, 33–35.

Horner, S. and Swarbrooke, J. (1996) *Marketing Tourism, Hospitality and Leisure in Europe*. International Thomson, London.

Krippendorf, J. (1987) *The Holiday Makers: Understanding the Impact of Leisure and Travel*. Butterworth-Heinemann, London.

Lash, S. (1990) *Sociology of Postmodernism*. Routledge, London.

Lévi-Strauss, C. (1968) *Structural Anthropology*. Allen Lane, London.

Leys, C. (1985) Thatcherism and British manufacturing: a question of hegemony. *New Left Review* 151, 5–25.

Lyotard, J.-F. (1984) *The Postmodern Condition*. Manchester University Press, Manchester.

MacCannell, D. (1976) *The Tourist: a New Theory of the Leisure Class*. Schocken Books, New York.

MacCannell, D. (1992) *Empty Meeting Grounds: the Tourist Papers*. Routledge, London.

Pearce, P. (1982) *The Social Psychology of Tourist Experience*. Pergamon Press, Oxford.

Poster, M. (ed.) (1988) *Jean Baudrillard: Selected Writings*. Polity Press, Cambridge.

Poon, A. (1989) Competitive strategies for a 'new tourism'. In: Cooper, C. (ed.) *Progress in Tourism, Recreation and Hospitality Management*, Vol. 1. Belhaven, London.

Purvis, T. and Hunt, A. (1993) Discourse, ideology, discourse, ideology, discourse, ideology . . . *British Journal of Sociology* 44 (3), 473–499.

Roche, M. (1992) Mega-events and micro-modernization: on the sociology of the new urban tourism. *British Journal of Sociology* 43 (4), 563–600.

Seaton, A. and Bennett, M. (1996) *Marketing Tourism Products: Concepts, Issues, Cases*. International Thomson, London.

Selwyn, T. (ed.) (1996) *The Tourist Image: Myths and Myth Making in Tourism.* John Wiley and Sons, Chichester.

Shields, R. (1990) The 'system of pleasure': liminality and the carnivalesque at Brighton. *Theory, Culture and Society* 7, 39–72.

Thompson, G. (1983) Carnival and the calculable: consumption and play at Blackpool. In: Bennett, T. (ed.) *Formations of Pleasure.* Routledge and Kegan Paul, London.

Thompson, J. (1990) *Ideology and Modern Culture.* Polity Press, Cambridge.

Thrift, N. (1989) Images of social change. In: Hamnett, C., McDowell, L. and Sarre, D. (eds) *The Changing Social Structure.* Sage, London.

Urry, J. (1990) *The Tourist Gaze: Leisure and Travel in Contemporary Societies.* Sage, London.

Urry, J. (1992) The tourist gaze and the 'environment'. *Theory, Culture and Society* 9, 1–26.

Urry, J. (1994) Cultural change and contemporary tourism. *Leisure Studies* 13, 233–238.

Voase, R.N. (1995) *Tourism: the Human Perspective.* Hodder and Stoughton, London.

Zukin, S. (1988) The postmodern debate over urban form. *Theory, Culture and Society* 5, 431–446.

Part 1

The Political Context

Introduction:
The Political Context as Dominant

Richard Voase,
University of Lincoln, Lincoln Campus, UK

Politics in an apparently *dominant* role is the context which these first four case histories share. The purpose of this introductory note is to underline some salient specifics and interesting commonalities about these four contributions.

The first, by Meetham, introduces the concept of the 'old' and 'new' tourisms as they appear, both as emerging markets and as marketing targets, for tourism businesses in the south-west of England, an established and still buoyant tourist destination region. Politics makes its appearance when the exigencies of targeting new or newly-defined markets demands a re-alignment of existing umbrella organizations representing the industry, and the formation of new coalitions. The second contribution, by Morpeth, takes as its subject matter an entirely different region. Teeside, in the north-east of England, is a little-known tourist region in the throes of creating a nascent tourist economy from improbable beginnings. Morpeth's account links the right-of-centre politics of the central government of the United Kingdom of the 1980s with active attempts to engineer a change in economic base from primary and secondary industry to tertiary. In this respect, the fostering of tourism is seen, overtly, as a means of creating a new economy to replace the old; covertly, as a means of social and economic engineering. The same central government politics are cited by Voase in the third contribution. Here, the local circumstance provides a further contrast: the three resorts of Margate, Broadstairs and Ramsgate, formerly vigorous seaside destinations located on the peninsula known as the Isle of Thanet, south-east England, are seen to experience difficulties in achieving consistent resort regeneration strategies, owing to ideological aversion to municipal intervention in tourism and to the paradoxical necessity of such intervention to guarantee the success of regenerative efforts. Finally, Robledo and Batle's note on the POOT regeneration policy on the island of Mallorca, intended to frame the improvement of resort fabric, illustrates how regenerative efforts can be delayed or hindered by regional and local ideological and economic interests.

Of common interest in all four cases are the following three factors:

1. *The role and interplay of central and local tiers of government in the formulation and implementation of policy.* In south-west England, where the tourism industry was established and relatively buoyant, the political interplay was between emerging re-alignments of businesses and organizations. The direct influence of central or local government was barely present. In north-east England, where tourism was negligible and nascent, the role of central and local politics in subventing and supporting the creation of a tourist economy was crucial. In south-east England, the rapid decline of a formerly buoyant tourist economy attracted (until very recently) no interest from central government, and was the object of constant attention but inconsistent action on the part of the local authority. In Mallorca, a centrally inspired plan for regulating the built environment of the tourism industry was seen to be delayed and inhibited by major economic interests, and by ambivalent commitment on the part of some municipalities.

2. *Politics is seen as a vehicle for the promotion and management of economic interests.* Thus, the issue at stake, in Meethan's contribution, is how best particular organizations, defined spatially as well as economically, might align themselves to achieve the optimal promotion to defined target markets. In Morpeth's contribution, the issue is more concerned with creating a tourism industry from scratch, and creating the symbolic associations by which tourism destinations are recognized: hence branding exercises such as 'Captain Cook Country' and the acquisition of physical icons such as the large sculpture known as the *Angel of the North*. In Voase's chapter on the Isle of Thanet, the dialectic between the desire to maintain the tradition of municipal support for tourism services, 'intervention', and the wish to identify with and adopt the central government ideology of *laissez-faire*, resulted in an inconsistent approach in which the old economy (tourism) was seen in opposition to the new economy (residential care) taking root in the decaying fabric of tourism. In Mallorca, the public initiative known as POOT sought to benefit the overall island economy by means of setting standards for the development of public space and the built environment, while necessarily inhibiting the freedom and economic interest of individual developers.

3. *The powerful influence of sociocultural factors in each case.* In Meethan's contribution, the sociocultural dilemma is the identification of target markets using new criteria which accurately reflect the features of those markets; former methods of classification are argued to be progressively unusable. In Morpeth's contribution, the sociocultural issue is, as Morpeth argues, the question of social and economic engineering: creating a new economy which, unlike the old, is less collectivist in nature, less unionized in character, and hence easier to manage in terms of an intended *laissez-faire* paradigm for economic development. In Voase's contribution, the dilemma facing the declining resort group demands not simply the implementation of well-constructed destination marketing strategies, but the abandonment of a communal mentality that views with distaste the whole question of public intervention in private industry. In Robledo and Batle's note on Mallorca, the contributors' own choice of language indicates an awareness that the island, as a tourist destination, needs to conform to the middle-class view of fashionable tourism outlined in the introductory chapter of this volume. 'Chaotic ... tourism development', it is said, has served Mallorca and its target markets well for 30 or so years. A new discourse, associated with a 'new' tourism, demands a new approach.

Selling the Difference: Tourism Marketing in Devon and Cornwall, South-west England[1]

1

Kevin Meethan

Department of Sociology, University of Plymouth, Plymouth, UK

Introduction: Out with the Old and In with the New?

This chapter will examine some recent marketing strategies in Devon and Cornwall, in particular, the role of local authorities and associated agencies in creating a definable image and product of both the two counties and selected subregions within them. At a macro level, the developments outlined here are taking place within the wider context of changing patterns in leisure and tourism consumption which have been variously described as 'post tourism' (Urry, 1990), 'postmodern' (Rojek, 1993) or 'new tourism' (Poon, 1993). There is little to be gained here by raking over these often contentious labels; what is germane to the argument is the fact that an overall decline in standardized mass tourism, especially within the domestic market, has been matched by the emergence of more individualized and specialized holidays. For the sake of convenience, the former will be referred to here as old tourism, and the latter as new tourism.

In terms of the regional and local level, an important development has been the increasing involvement of county and district authorities in the tourism industry, which is giving rise to new forms of institutional arrangements, in particular, the development of public–private partnerships and marketing alliances. As the economic importance of tourism receives due recognition, local and county government is becoming a key player in deciding the overall strategic direction of tourism (Meethan, 1998). Regions and localities where tourism has been established for a

---

[1] The data for this chapter was gathered as part of a wider research programme within the Department of Sociology at the University of Plymouth and involved interviewing economic development, planning and tourism officers in all 16 districts and the two county councils.

number of years, such as Cornwall and Devon, are facing a dual threat of increasing competition from both overseas mass tourism and new tourist destinations. Both the industry and policy makers are thus faced with the problem of how to respond to these wider changes if they are to maintain their markets and avoid terminal decline.

A further aspect to be considered is one that is fundamental to tourism, namely, that a locality is the product; what is sold and consumed differs from other forms of production and consumption because it is spatially fixed. Localities contain the consumer as well as being the object of consumption itself (Ashworth and Voogd, 1994: 43). In this sense, tourism involves the commodification of place, a process which isolates environmental and cultural aspects of localities and regions as definitive and essential characteristics, ordering them into a coherent and authoritative narrative (Meethan, 1996), which frames people's expectations. What is sold is the idea of a place and the activities that can be pursued within it. The creation of such narratives is, in turn, the result of interactions between the broader political economy and cultural values which are becoming increasingly mediated through the policy directives of supra-national, national, regional and local governments (Meethan, 2000).

The fact that structural changes are leading to the emergence of new tourism is not in doubt. What is less certain is the way in which such changes will impact on current patterns of demand and supply which have relied on mass markets and mass products; how such changes are to be managed and controlled; and how marketing strategies can help or hinder this process. The examples presented here will show how the counties of Cornwall and Devon, and more localized areas within them, are responding to a complex situation which involves firstly, changing patterns of consumer demand and preferences such as the rise of new tourism; secondly, increasing control by local administrations over the strategic direction of tourism; and thirdly, how the tourism product – the idea of place – is being redefined to accommodate such changes.

Tourism in Cornwall and Devon

Together, the counties of Cornwall and Devon (see Fig. 1.1) rank as one of the most popular tourist destinations in the country, with an estimated 8 million visitors per year, the majority of which are UK domestic tourists from London and the south-eastern counties (Griffiths, 1995). In economic terms, these visitors contribute an estimated 24% to the GDP of Cornwall, 18% to the GDP of Devon, and employ a workforce of 60,000 (Bell, 1995).

Historically, the tourism industry within the two counties has relied on the traditional seaside-based family holiday, or old tourism. Although established as a destination region by the turn of the century, visitor numbers only began to increase rapidly in the post-war years, and more especially from the 1960s, until they peaked in the mid to late 1970s (Thornton, 1997). Despite the overall decline in mass domestic tourism in the UK, in the south west this has been less marked.

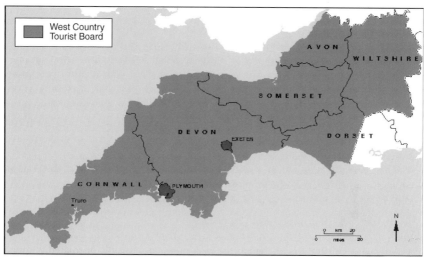

Fig. 1.1. Map showing location of Devon and Cornwall.

In part, this is due to the capacity of the region to adapt to the changing demands of the tourist market. As increasing specialization leads to market fragmentation, difference becomes a necessity for continued survival. One of the reasons why the tourist industry in Cornwall and Devon has not spiralled downwards – although many of the smaller traditional seaside resorts, such as Ilfracombe in North Devon, have been hard hit by the decline in visitor numbers – has been its capacity to accommodate change. In recent years, there have been attempts to shift tourism away from the dominance of the coastal resorts to a more diverse resource base which underlines the increasing importance of new tourism which, although not entirely replacing old tourism, is none the less making its impact felt.

No doubt one of the major strengths of the region is the variety of landscape features from moorland to coastline, and a corresponding variety of places, from 'traditional' farming and fishing villages to the resort conurbation of Torbay. Another overall advantage is its remoteness from urban areas and, apart from the china clay mines in Cornwall and the city of Plymouth, the absence of any large-scale industry and large-scale urbanization. The Tate Gallery, St Ives, an outstation of the nationally funded Tate Gallery in London, offers the attraction of 'high' culture, while Newquay is a popular surfing destination. In addition, recent years have also seen the proliferation of purpose-built attractions which are less reliant on the bucket and spades of the coastal fringe. Tourist accommodation is equally diverse, ranging from top hotels to farmhouse bed and breakfast to caravan and camping sites and other forms of self-catering accommodation.

The tourism industry in the region nonetheless faces problems which are both general and particular, such as seasonality, with its associated problems of lack of local employment during the slack months and crowding during the peak of the summer months. Recent evidence, however, suggests that, in Devon, the season is actually extending (Devon County Council, 1996: 14) and, although no comparable data exists for all of Cornwall, such evidence that exists indicates that more people are taking spring and autumn breaks (Atlantic Consultants, 1997: 7).

Another problem concerns the high number of small and medium enterprises within the two counties, especially in the accommodation sector, many of whom close down after the peak season. A further problem here relates to the cost of marketing, as small-scale enterprises often lack the resources for both national and international marketing campaigns and therefore have to rely on marketing consortia in order to achieve economies of scale.

The perceived remoteness of the two counties, which on the one hand can be a strength, can also be a problem, more so for Cornwall than Devon, yet despite the problems of seasonal traffic congestion caused by the majority of tourists arriving by car, the region is perceived as a good location for touring (MEW Market Research, 1989b: 30–31). This factor in itself allows for greater flexibility in the pattern of tourist behaviour for, as Thornton *et al.* (1997) have noted, tourists are now more mobile and less inclined to stay in one location for their entire holiday.

Tourism and Public Policy

It is within this context, which is in part the historical legacy of old, that local and regional governments have in the past few years been playing a more proactive role in promoting tourism as an economic development strategy (Hall and Jenkins, 1995; Charlton and Essex, 1996; Meethan, 1997, 1998; Wanhill, 1996). The Cornwall County Council economic plan for 1996/7 outlines four key themes for regional economic development including 'Improving the physical appearance, confidence and internal and external perceptions of the County', which is to include overseas promotion, UK marketing and niche market tourist promotion (Cornwall County Council, 1996: 8). The same themes also inform the Devon tourism plan which outlines the following specific objectives:

> To raise the profile of Devon as a year-round destination, to increase the number of visitors and visitor spend; to reposition the traditional Devon holiday image by identifying and promoting the variety of holiday product to niche markets; to improve year round occupancy levels.
>
> (Devon County Council, 1996: 3).

This recognition of the strategic economic importance of tourism, and the proactive stance adopted at a county level, is matched by administrative arrangements at a district level; tourism is viewed not as an extra to both local and regional economies, but rather as a central and integral component. In turn, this concern to incorporate tourism more fully into county and regional economic policies reflects changing attitudes at a central government level (Department for Culture, Media and Sport, 1999: 8–9).

The importance of the industry in regional terms is underlined by its economic peripherality. Under the European Union Regional Development Funding (ERDF) programme of 1994–1999,[2] the whole of Cornwall and approximately half of Devon qualified for grant aid as an Objective 5(b) declining rural area, while Plymouth qualified as an Objective 2 declining urban area. Such designations, and the funding that was made available under them for tourism-related developments, were crucial in the formation of new public-private marketing alliances which sought to redefine the overall tourist product of the two counties.

Although the two counties are therefore well equipped in terms of facilities and attractions to develop new tourism, and, through ERDF funding, the means to achieve this, in order to compete with an ever increasing number of destinations, both domestic and overseas, the two counties need to be marketed as distinct and unique destinations in their own right.

'The Westcountry is Devon and Cornwall'

One of the key problems facing the marketing of the two counties is defining them as a distinct geographical location. The fact that together they comprise a peninsula and show similar physical properties is clearly a factor, yet there are significant differences between Cornwall and Devon, in particular the existence of a distinct sense of Cornish culture and identity (for example see Payton, 1992). The two counties also form part of a wider regional grouping of counties known as the West Country, or Westcountry. Of importance here are not only the county and district administrative boundaries, but also the boundaries of the regional tourist board (Fig. 1.2).

As can be seen from the map, the West Country Tourist Board (WCTB) area includes six and a half counties which, in itself, was seen as problematic, not only because of the cultural differences between the counties mentioned above, but also because the majority of tourists to the region visited Cornwall and Devon, or as one informant aptly summed it up: '. . . the west country exists on the back of Cornwall and Devon.' This statement appears to be borne out by the results of a survey carried out in 1989, which addressed holidaymakers' attitudes towards the region and reported that:

> Devon, Cornwall and Somerset were generally identified with the West Country, but only about two thirds linked the latter with Avon or Dorset and only about one third connected Wiltshire and the West Country. Devon and Cornwall constituted the 'real' West Country, in terms of holiday destinations, but people were willing to accept the concept of a wider West Country for marketing purposes (MEW Market Research, 1989a: 5)

This latter point is of particular interest here, as the concept of the wider Westcountry grouping for marketing purposes was to lead to friction between the WCTB

---

[2] In 1999 under the new ERDF programme, Cornwall was granted Objective 1 status, qualifying for the highest rate of grant aid available.

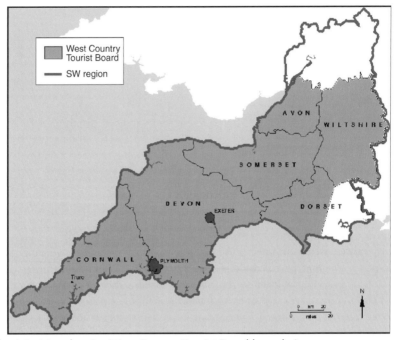

Fig. 1.2. Map showing West Country Tourist Board boundaries.

and other interests. On paper it may appear that the WCTB is best placed to coordinate marketing across the two counties and within the wider regional grouping, yet the WCTB was viewed negatively as an organization that was remote and out of touch for a variety of reasons, in particular its regional basis and its marketing policy.

There was a widespread view that the distinct identity of the two counties, and Cornwall in particular, was in danger of being subsumed under a wider and nebulous geographical entity – the Westcountry – which, it was thought, did not correspond to tourists' perceptions of the region. Secondly, as a private sector and non-statutory body, the WCTB charges an annual membership fee and also has to act in the interests of all its members, not just a sub section of them – the two counties. 'We find it difficult to say we get value for money and that is a pretty general feeling' was one respondent's summary of the situation. The overwhelming opinion among those interviewed was that the WCTB was in danger of being superseded, the question being, who should be responsible for selling the region?

Marketing Alliances

As noted above, the number of overseas visitors to the two counties is relatively small, and this is a market into which the counties wish to expand. In order to achieve this aim, a new marketing alliance – the Devon and Cornwall Overseas Marketing Consortium (DACOM) – was formed in 1995. It grew in part from the frustrations with the WCTB outlined above but, more importantly, because ERDF funding was made available. Membership consists of both county councils, all 16 district authorities as well as Prosper (formerly the Devon and Cornwall Training and Enterprise Council), and the objectives are as follows:

- Increase overseas visitors by 13% by the year 2000.
- Increase economic impact from overseas by £50 million per annum.
- Help to sustain and create 5000 jobs.
- Create business development opportunities for 1000 individuals involved in the tourism industry (DACOM, 1997).

Attitudes towards, and perceptions of, DACOM were invariably positive, and contrasted with the perceived shortcomings of the WCTB: 'We've stepped back from them with DACOM . . . we're pulling further away.' As far as county and district tourism officers were concerned, DACOM offered value for money, a factor contrasted with the perceived shortcomings of WCTB, no doubt aided by the fact that it is in effect subsidized from Brussels. Another important dimension was the perception that DACOM represented a new start and the way forward for marketing that bypassed, if not actually solved, the problems of regional representation that seemed to sour relationships with the WCTB.

So far, the discussion has outlined the broad context and institutional arrangements that are shaping the form of tourism strategy within the two counties. The increasing incorporation of tourism policy as economic policy by local administrations, and their ability to access ERDF money, has undermined the position of the regional tourist board, and led to the formation of marketing alliances viewed as being more responsive to both the current market and the specific needs of the two counties.

While the two counties were happy to cooperate for overseas marketing, for the domestic market the situation was different, as each county saw the other as its main rival. Cooperation, where it existed, was at a district level and, once more, local government backed by ERDF funding played a key role. Two alliances that cut across district administrative boundaries and involve both public and private sectors will serve as examples, the Falmouth and South West Cornwall Joint Guide Committee (for convenience this will be referred to as FSW) and the North Devon Marketing Bureau (NDMB).

Both of these marketing alliances involve public-private sector partnerships and, like DACOM, were able to access ERDF funding for their marketing campaigns. Target Markets for the NDMB were described in their marketing strategy as follows:

> Core Market: Traditional summer visitors, a large proportion of which are BC1C2 families; heavy use of self catering accommodation and camping and touring sites; An increasing propensity to book late and take holidays of less than seven nights; Probably high loyalty but with renewed interest in UK holidays in the past two years also a good possibility of new business. Shoulder Market: Short breaks/additional

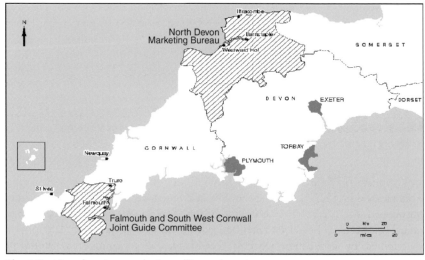

Fig. 1.3. Map showing marketing alliance locations.

holidays; ABC1 couples/families; Late bookers; Within 4 hours travelling time; Growth area so good possibility of new business (NDMB 1996).

The FSW were also directing their attention to similar markets; what we see here is a mixture of both old and new tourism, with the latter being seen as particularly important for the off-season shoulder months.

Before looking at some examples of how such broad changes were translated into specific marketing strategies, it is necessary first to examine the ways in which tourism markets within the two counties are defined. The NDMB strategy document is revealing here as it outlines what is, in effect, a standard approach by which target markets are defined first and foremost by using socio-economic categories as an indicator of consumption preferences; an approach which I shall argue is inherently problematic not only in analytical terms, but also in terms of strategic planning.

'Everyone Would Love to Go Upmarket'

Since the 1980s, there have been a growing number of techniques, such as psychographic or lifestyle modelling, to help identify niche markets and predict consumer behaviour (Gunter and Furnham, 1992; Hawkins *et al.*, 1992; Sleight, 1993; Weinstein, 1994). What they all share in common is an assumption that markets are no longer as mass-oriented or monolithic as they once were, and that successful marketing now relies on the extent to which more specialized consumer demands or lifestyles can be identified and utilized. A second and related element of importance here is the further assumption that, given the apparent decline of old tourism,

Table 1.1. United Kingdom: socio-economic categories.

A:	Higher managerial, administrative and professional
B:	Intermediate managerial, administrative and professional
C1:	Supervisory or clerical, junior managerial, administrative and professional
C2:	Skilled manual
D:	Semi- and unskilled manual
E:	Pensioners, widows, casual and long-term unemployed.

Source: ONS, 1997.

new tourism necessitates a move 'upmarket' towards attracting higher-spending visitors. As Campbell (1995: 113) has pointed out, advertisers and marketers have abandoned socio-economic classifications (Table 1.1) for lifestyle categories because, arguably, it can no longer be taken for granted that consumption preferences are determined by occupation (Mackay, 1997: 5), for as Gunter and Furnham (1992: 20) note, using such gross categories for marketing is 'somewhat simplistic'. In theory, at least, there are any number of ways in which markets can be segmented and divided into discrete categories.

In terms of tourism, the English Tourist Board have identified growth target segments, such as affluent career couples without children (sometimes referred to as 'dinkies', that is, Dual Income No Kids) and 'empty nesters', couples whose children have left home, or who holiday without their children (WCTB, 1991: 5).

Given that this approach is now established orthodoxy within marketing (Weinstein, 1994: 2), and has been recognized at both national and regional level (Department for Culture, Media and Sport, 1999), it is perhaps surprising that, when asked how their target markets were defined, most respondents spoke in terms of socio-economic status or class, often conflating the two. During the course of interviews, one of the key points to emerge was an underlying assumption that to stratify people in this way is a direct and reliable indicator of consumption preferences. For those district authorities whose policy was to move 'upmarket', target niches were defined as the 'AB market segment' or in one case 'ABC1s' (see above). This was often contrasted with what was assumed to be the downmarket 'bucket and spade' preferences of those classified as C2, D and E. Table 1.2 shows the breakdown of the UK population in terms of socio-economic categories. From this it can be seen that when the categories are aggregated, A and B together constitute just over one third of the adult working population, and ABC1 over one half. Although there is perhaps a logic – albeit an implicit one – in viewing these categories as market segments, it is difficult to see, regardless of how one segments the market, how over half the working population of the UK (ABC1) can be described as an 'upmarket niche'.

To classify people in this way for purposes of market analysis is far from clear cut, and involves a series of implicit value judgements as much as methodological problems which cannot be adequately dealt with here (see Ryan, 1995 for further discussion). At one level, all it amounts to saying is that some occupational groups

Table 1.2. UK population by socio-economic group (%).

A:	5.8
B:	28.7 – A+B = 34.5
C1:	21.7 – A+B+C1 = 56.2
C2:	20.0
D:	15.2
E:	5.5 – C2+D+E = 40.7
	(3.1% residual/unclassified)

Source: ONS, 1997: 46.

are likely to have more disposable income than others, and as such can be seen as a judgement based on rational economic criteria. Given the economic importance of tourism within the regional economy, it is hardly surprising that policies should be directed towards extracting the maximum return from the minimum number of people, which is really what the use of the term 'upmarket' implies. Yet even this is subject to qualification as socio-economic groupings only indicate income, not patterns of expenditure. For example, many pensioners, classified as E, can also have high levels of disposable income, and it is also entirely feasible that a couple could be classified as 'dinkies' or 'empty nesters' by one set of criteria, and as C2, D or E by another.

Variables other than socio-economic group are arguably more significant in determining holiday type and choice such as, for example, family structure and age of children (Thornton *et al.*, 1997) and the reciprocal social obligations involved in visiting friends and relatives (Seaton, 1995). In addition, it is also necessary to consider the accessibility of destinations from point of origin and the perceived images of destinations (Selby and Morgan, 1996; Jenkins, 1999). In short, holiday choice is not a simple rational transaction, for, like in other forms of consumption, choice and motivations are complex and perhaps even contradictory and cannot simply be read off from socio-economic position (Longhurst and Savage, 1996: 282).

Although couched in the language of socio-economic categories or class, the existence of other factors was, in some cases, realized. The resort of Newquay is a good example, as one respondent put it: 'The C1, C2 and Ds love Newquay [and within that] . . . there are different markets.' This was explained by the fact that Newquay attracts the 18–30 year olds for surfing and its nightlife; the retired or semi-retired, that is, those aged 60 years and over; and families for the 'bucket and spade' holidays.

In terms of socio-economic groups, it would appear on the surface that Newquay is still catering for a traditional mass clientele, yet if these are broken down into lifestyle groups, a more complicated picture emerges. Clearly, a move to reposition or redefine the resort in terms of moving 'upmarket' would be detrimental, and is certainly not on the agenda for the foreseeable future.

People should not be taken to task for not using the current fashionable phrases to describe their markets, for, after all, it is what is achieved rather than how it is described that is important. Yet despite this qualification, the use of gross classifications can be misleading, especially when evaluation or market analysis is concerned. The conflation of socio-economic group, social class and lifestyle segments, I would argue, is directly related to the ways in which regional and county visitor statistics are gathered. Visitors are classified in terms of economic status and/or 'class' (Griffiths, 1995), which does not take into account the lifestyle factors mentioned, which are more likely to determine holiday preferences.

This in turn, I would argue, is symptomatic of tensions that exist between old and new tourism, evident in the emergence of new marketing alliances. Perhaps it is simply the case that the gathering and use of data in this way is as traditional in the two counties as the 'bucket and spade' holiday, more applicable to old mass tourism than to the diverse and fragmented nature of new tourism. Data gathering and analysis is thus clearly lagging behind developments on the ground as much as organizational arrangements, and policies and strategies based on market segmentation cannot be accurately assessed or evaluated by using these categories.

Despite the methodological problems associated with socio-economic group and social class, and the implicit value judgements that accompany such categorizations, some important facts are less contentious. These concern the size of groups visiting the two counties, the age of group members, and their point of origin. Couples and groups of four – the 'nuclear family'[3] form the largest percentage (Griffiths 1995: 9).

The demographic distribution of visitors to Devon and Cornwall is also straightforward, and surveys show that the pattern is also consistent, with the majority of visitors originating from London and the South-east, and a sizeable contingent from the West Midlands. These factors have remained constant over the years that such data has been gathered (Griffiths, 1995: 9; Devon Research and Intelligence Services, 1996: 7). One group significantly under-represented is that of overseas visitors, who are a small percentage of the total (*ibid.*).

Despite recognizing the importance of more specialized market segments, the two counties still rely on high volume seasonal tourism for families who tend to come from defined geographical areas. These factors caused some informants to doubt that niche marketing could ever make a significant difference: 'you can't live with just niche markets' as one highly placed informant put it, while another remarked that 'buckets and spades will always be popular'.

The value of niche marketing – or indeed, new tourism – lies in the possibilities it offers both to extend the season and to achieve a more-even spatial distribution of visitors, and it is this form of marketing that was viewed as catering for an upmarket clientele. In turn, this also raises the question of what exactly is meant by this term. On one level, it appears to be synonymous with expensive, or at least with the presumed spending capacity of certain sections of the population; as noted

---

[3] The average number of children in UK families has been in the region of 1.8 since the early 1970s – not the 2.4 of popular myth.

above, shifting a product upmarket means extracting more revenue from a smaller number of people. There are thus rational economic criteria which dictate such a policy. A further aspect relates to quality of both services and attractions. If the two counties are to attract an 'upmarket' clientele, then quality becomes an issue, especially in terms of the accommodation stock, where the need to provide better facilities was highlighted by many informants as a problem area. Again, this is a matter of rational economic calculation. However, as with choice, there are less rational and implicit values which also inform such moves.

At another level, the notion of 'upmarket' is indicative of a set of presumed virtues, in that activities labelled as such involve some notion of self-improvement, an idea deeply embedded in western culture (Rojek, 1993: 110–116) rather than the simple idle and aimless pleasures of the beach which, after all, are child's play. There is also some notion of individuality and difference at work, for, in this context, upmarket is not the *undifferentiated* massed 'buckets and spades' of the peak season but the *differentiated* special interest holiday or the off-season second break. In turn, such differentiation is indicative of wider changes in the political economy of consumption and is not restricted either to the two counties, or to the UK as a whole (Meethan, 2001). Strategies based on this approach were more marked in those districts which are seeking to develop tourism from a small or non-existent base – the inland rural areas rather than the traditional bucket and spade tourism of the coast (Meethan, 1997).

As mentioned in the introduction, the process of commodification of place, on which tourism is dependent, involves the identification of environmental and cultural aspects of localities as essential characteristics. It is such narratives of place that are sold; the question that remains is, how does the combination of institutional change and the search for new markets translate into definable images? What narratives of place are being sold to whom?

'The Dream is Real'

With competition between destinations increasing, each has to demarcate itself from the others by emphasising uniqueness and difference, or as the NDMB strategy document states:

> It is important in the promotion of any product to identify a Unique Selling Proposition (USP) to enable that product to stand out from other competitors in the market (NDMB, 1996).

DACOM's contribution to this process is a brochure entitled 'The Dream is Real',[4] which represents the generic attractions of the two counties in the following way:

> Further south and west than anywhere else in Britain, the two counties of Devon and Cornwall point like a giant finger into the Atlantic, their shores washed by the

---

[4] The English language imprint will be referred to here. More-recent editions have not changed significantly.

Gulf Stream. It is an area with an atmosphere all of its own – a north coast with dramatic jagged cliffscapes carved by Atlantic rollers interspersed by safe golden beaches up to 5 km long, tiny cliff hung harbours and great surfing resorts. To the south lies a lush 'subtropical' riviera of time warped fishing villages and sheltered coves, of sophisticated resorts on wide mouthed bays and historic ports in great natural harbours. (DACOM, 1996 p4)

This passage seeks to demarcate the two counties from the rest of the UK by emphasizing their geographical location and relative isolation, while at the same time presenting them as a distinct unit or region. Although the FSW guide is intended for the domestic market, the initial description of place is very similar to that of DACOM:

Falmouth and South West Cornwall has some of Britain's most spectacular coastal scenery – one of the largest natural harbours in the World, wild and towering cliffscapes, small fishing villages, quiet coves, sandy beaches and a fascinating coastal path linking them all together. (FSW, 1997: 2)

The NDMB brochure also emphasizes the natural landscape features of its area but with a difference, for unlike the Falmouth area, the Council for the Protection of Rural England (CPRE) has classified North Devon as an area of tranquillity, the only one in the South West:

Welcome to North Devon – 'England's Green and Pleasant Land' – over 850 square miles of some of Britain's finest coasts and countryside . . . [the CPRE] declared North Devon one of only three areas in the country that could still be classed as 'tranquil'. Tranquillity is defined as a place far enough from development and traffic noise as to be unspoilt by urban influences. (NDMB, 1997: 2)

In all cases, the photographs that accompany the text show panoramic landscapes and beaches, stressing the remoteness and non-urban aspects of the physical landscape; this is a place – or places – to get away from the stresses and strains of industrialized, metropolitan life. The narrative presented for consumption is that of a bucolic idyll where time can be spent in contemplation of nature.

History and Heritage

The two counties are a place apart in other senses as well. As DACOM emphasize, Cornwall is 'an ancient and mystic Celtic Kingdom', while in Devon too, 'There's evidence of early settlements . . . as well as Roman remains in Exeter' (1996: 5). In the Falmouth area '. . . the past is ever present here – Celts, Saxons, Normans, early Christians, Royalists and parliamentarians . . . have all helped shape a distinctive heritage'. The North Devon approach differs from the other two, in that history and heritage are not singled out as a specific theme for the areas as a whole, but are rather dealt with under 11 localized areas, so that Ilfracombe for example boasts an 'ancient harbour' while nearby Chambercombe Manor ' . . . has a 1,000 year history' (NDMB, 1997: 6–7).

The architectural heritage of the two counties is also emphasized: 'The trail of

Great Houses and Buildings takes you through medieval market towns, Cathedral
Cities and even into haunted castles!' (DACOM, 1996: 5). This generic representation is less focused than that presented in the Falmouth guide, which includes
'enigmatic stone circles . . . Iron Age hill forts.. ancient stone crosses' in addition
to the more prosaic industrial heritage of 'pilchard cellars [and] . . . the ivy covered
engine houses and brick topped chimney stacks that are the visible remains of
underground tin and copper mines' (FSW, 1997: 4–5). Although the narratives
stress a nostalgic romanticism, in these postmodern times, where hierarchies of taste
are challenged, there is still room for the '1000 pixies at the Gnome Reserve'; even
kitsch can become a commodified asset (NDMB, 1997: 33).

Culture

The fact that many in Cornwall consider themselves to be culturally different not
only from Devon but also from Britain is notably absent from the DACOM guide,
but assumes prominence in the Falmouth brochure where Cornwall is a 'Celtic
land' with its own language[5] and distinctive history, a place that is 'surprisingly
different!':

> Cornwall is proud of its Celtic traditions. Reflected in the language, customs and
> festivals in its religious relics, Cornwall's celtic roots are obvious. (FSW, 1997: 5)

Although the DACOM brochure features a section entitled 'A Land of Culture',
this emphasizes the visual arts, in particular the Tate Gallery at St Ives (1996: 4)
as well as popular authors such as Agatha Christie, Daphne du Maurier and Rosa-
mund Pilcher, whose popular romantic novels have recently been televised in Germany. This use of both literature and 'recognizable spokespersons' (Dann, 1996:
186) adds a measure of cultural capital to the projected images and also extends to
other media, as can be seen in the Falmouth guide:

> Over the years, many visitors have first discovered the area through television or
> films. In the 1970s and again in 1996, this part of Cornwall played host to . . .
> Winston Graham's historic mining saga 'Poldark'. . . [the] detective series 'Wycliffe' is
> also largely filmed in the Falmouth and South West Cornwall area (FSW, 1997: 3)

Devon cannot claim to have a different and unique culture as Cornwall can,
although in the NDMB there are references to regional literary connections such
as Charles Kingsley's links to the town of Bideford and the resort of Westward
Ho!, and Henry Williamson's 'Country of the two Rivers' which features in the
'Tarka' stories as well as serving as the basis for the Tarka Trail (180 miles of
country walks) and the Tarka Line – the Exeter to Barnstaple railway.

These narratives display common themes that are both generic and particular,

---

[5] Cornish effectively died out as a spoken language in the early 19th C, although the fact that
it exists in a revived form is seen as a mark of cultural distinction.

with the DACOM literature being the most general of the examples. The logic to the texts and the images that accompany them is that domestic markets, having a greater knowledge of the region as a whole, are more likely to be attracted by either special interest holidays, or by marketing which identifies a smaller more defined area within the two counties, whereas marketing for the overseas market needs to concentrate more on the generic attractions of the region. While place is obviously important, so too are the activities that take place within it.

Things to Do

A range of activities are also featured within the three brochures. DACOM features water sports, country pursuits, cycling and walking. Although the bucket and spade element of the region gets a mention – the 'Coastal gems' are '. . . a great attraction for families' (1996: 4), the photographs that accompany the text show very few families and children, the majority of images showing groups or couples who tend to be middle aged. No doubt these are the 'empty nesters', although the cover of the brochure shows a young but childless couple. Clearly, it is not the family market that is being aimed for, an approach that is contrasted to that presented in the other two guides, where holidaymakers to the Falmouth area can 'Choose the convenience of the main family beaches with their full range of facilities, or discover the delightful secluded coves and hidden bays off the beaten track' (FSW, 1997: 7) while those choosing North Devon are advised that 'The area is a great holiday destination for families, with a wide choice of good value accommodation, magnificent beaches and lots of attractions' (NDMB, 1997: 6). Both the Falmouth and North Devon brochures feature pictures of children and adults relaxing on the beach, and although such images also feature in the DACOM brochure, they do not have the same prominence, nor the same frequency of occurrence.

Shopping – a recreational pursuit for many – also features in all the brochures, '. . . great antiques and collectibles' (DACOM, 1996) the '. . . tiny specialist shops' of Truro (FSW, 1997) and the 'traditional Pannier and Craft markets' of Barnstaple. This is not the simple quotidian shopping for necessities in undifferentiated mass retail outlets, but differentiated recreational shopping for curios, antiques, the quaint, the unusual, the souvenir.

The narratives of place and the activities offered within them conform to certain themes that emphasize difference on the one hand, yet unity on the other, yet in many respects there is little to differentiate them. Although there are different emphases, these are of degree rather than of kind. The irony is that, although new tourism appears to demand more differentiation, what it results in is another set of generic images, so that shopping, for example, is always about the quaint, the souvenir, that which is not day-to-day, yet where most differentiation occurs. It is not the activities or places that matter so much as who is portrayed, and what they are portrayed doing.

People

As I have noted, pictures of beaches with children and families feature prominently in both the North Devon and Falmouth guides, and less so in the DACOM guide. In the latter, the dominant images of tourists are couples or groups without children, or to use marketing terminology, 'dinkies' and 'empty nesters'. These generic types also feature on the other two brochures, the Falmouth guide offering a picture of 'dinkies' on mountain bikes silhouetted against a setting sun, and 'empty nesters' contemplating nature, while the North Devon Guide contains comparable images. Children are confined either to the beaches, or to certain specific attractions that cater for their needs. The consumption and contemplation of nature, on the other hand, is entirely an adult affair, as are off-season breaks which do not, as such, feature in the DACOM brochure. The Falmouth guide describes the attractions as follows:

> Spring garden holidays have been popular for many years in Falmouth . . . When sandals and swimsuits have given way to scarves and walking boots, Autumn has arrived . . . its time for those peaceful walks when nature is your best companion. When winter beckons why not treat yourself to a Christmas break in Cornwall . . . Apparelled in Spring, Falmouth and South West Cornwall really shows its colours (FSW, 1997: 11)

While a similar approach was also adopted by North Devon:

> The great diversity of North Devon means that there is a reason to come on holiday at any time of the year. the climate is one of the mildest in the country so you will be pleasantly surprized at how warm it can be, especially in the spring and autumn (NDMB, 1997: 34).

What is of interest here is that the type of holidays being offered for the shoulder markets are not family holidays, but are more tailored for specific market niches. Although the romanticism of nature features prominently, what are also emphasized are

> . . . opportunities to walk, cycle, ride, fish, play golf, surf, sail and canoe . . . hang gliding, diving, bird watching or rock climbing . . . themed breaks where you can play croquet, learn landscape painting or simply experience the best gourmet food (NDMB, 1997: 34)

Here we have the active pursuit of interests and the significant absence of children, for as Rojek (1985: 174) aptly comments 'Only adults have leisure: children merely play'. In effect, what is being offered here is purposeful guided leisure, the notion that certain pursuits are valued as self-improving, and are not simply the idle and childlike pleasures of the undifferentiated mass. There is thus a clear attempt to develop new tourism through the use of imagery and copy that is aiming at lifestyle market segments which are clearly demarcated from old tourism.

Conclusions

I would argue that, in effect, we have a variety of spatial narratives (or images of place) used for different purposes and directed at different markets, which none the less do so under a broader two-county approach which seeks to reconcile internal diversity with outward unity. Such differentiation is in turn associated with overall changes in patterns of consumption, the shift from old tourism to new tourism, and the consequent need for those in the region to adapt to such developments. However, it would be overstating the case to say that the development of new tourism is displacing old tourism. Rather, what the case studies presented here have shown is that the tourism in the two counties is better considered more as a mixed economy in which we find the co-existence of different types of tourism. The task thus facing both policy makers and marketing strategists is how to reconcile the tensions between the two.

The expressed desire to move 'upmarket', seen as a solution to the problem of decline is, I would argue, misplaced. Rather than being evidence of a coherent policy, the usage of this term is ill defined and only serves to confuse a series of complex issues relating to consumer preferences and choice. In turn, this could be seen to be linked to implicit assumptions in the data collection which conflates class, socio-economic status and niche marketing which, by providing the overall analysis of tourism in the two counties, acted as the foundation for strategic planning. In short, although the rhetoric of niche marketing had been incorporated into the discourse of planners and administrators, this had not been matched with corresponding and necessary changes to market analysis. This is an important point, for any attempts to assess and evaluate marketing strategies will need to be clear from the outset precisely who the target markets are; they cannot be simply seen as subsets of categories more suited to the patterns of old tourism.

What these examples also show is that both broad marketing strategies and specific campaigns do not take place in a vacuum, nor can they be reduced to the function of marketing criteria alone. Rather, the context in which they occur involves a complex set of inter-relationships between methodological, social, political and regional factors, some explicit, some implicit, whose combination determines the overall shape and direction of tourism strategy. In the cases presented here, marketing was one aspect of a wider integrated policy which aims to incorporate tourism more fully into the regional economy, and would not have been possible in their present format without ERDF funding, which facilitated the formation of new marketing alliances.

The role of such organizations in both coordinating and creating marketing strategies, and thus providing the overall coherence within which diversity can flourish, is central to the process of redefining or repositioning the tourist product – the narratives of place. The emergence of DACOM and the sidelining of the WCTB can be seen as evidence of the tensions that exist between the desire to reconcile both old and new tourism, and the examples from Falmouth and North Devon also demonstrate how new organizational forms are emerging as a response to wider structural changes.

Since the interviews were conducted for this chapter, there have been some significant developments at both national and regional levels. First, the new tourism strategy introduced by central government in 1999 argues that tourism needs to be more fully integrated into economic planning (Department for Culture, Media and Sport, 1999). In turn, this is partly to be achieved through the new system of Regional Development Agencies (RDAs) which were put in place in April 1999. The RDAs are in turn, responsible for handling applications to the ERDF. Given Cornwall's new Objective 1 status, this may well lead to the County deciding to go it alone, abandoning the strategic alliances discussed here, which were the result of a specific set of circumstances. Finally, the soon to be implemented reorganization of the regional tourist boards may also provide the WCTB with the opportunity to reposition and redefine itself. Although the outcome of all these changes is uncertain, indications are that the two counties, the local councils and other interest groups are about to embark on another round of alliance formation and repositioning, while at the same time attempting to balance the old and the new.

References

Ashworth, J. and Voogd, H. (1994) Marketing and place promotion. In: Gold, J. and Ward, S. (eds) *Place Promotion: the Use of Publicity and Marketing to Sell Towns and Regions*. John Wiley and Sons, Chichester.

Atlantic Consultants (1997) *Falmouth and South West Cornwall Holiday Guide Monitoring and Evaluation Survey*. Atlantic Consultants, Truro.

Bell, M. (1995) *Cornwall and Devon Tourism Development Plan 1995–1999*. Westcountry Development Corporation/Devon and Cornwall Training and Enterprise Council, Plymouth.

Campbell, C. (1995) The sociology of consumption. In: Miller, D. (ed.) *Acknowledging Consumption: a Review of New Studies*. Routledge, London.

Charlton, S. and Essex, S. (1996) The Involvement of District Councils in Tourism in England and Wales. *Geoforum*, 27 (2) 175–192.

Cornwall County Council (1995) *Cornwall Structure Plan – Deposit Draft*. Cornwall County Council, Truro.

Cornwall County Council (1996) *Cornwall Economic Development Strategy and Plan for 1996/9*. Cornwall County Council, Truro.

DACOM (1996) *Devon and Cornwall: the Dream is Real*. DACOM, Truro/Exeter.

DACOM (1997) *Update on 'The Dream is Real' Campaign*. DACOM/Devon and Cornwall Training and Enterprise Council, Plymouth.

Dann, G. (1996) *The Language of Tourism: a Sociolinguistic Perspective*. CAB International, Wallingford.

Department for Culture, Media and Sport (1999) *Tomorrow's Tourism: A Growth Industry for the New Millennium*. Department for Culture, Media and Sport, London.

Devon County Council (1996) *Tourism Marketing and Development Plan*. Devon County Council Economy and Europe Office, Exeter.

Devon Research and Intelligence Services (1996) *Devon Tourism Statistics 1995*. Devon County Council, Exeter.

Falmouth and South West Cornwall Joint Guide Committee (FSW) (1997) *Falmouth and*

South West Cornwall Official Holiday Guide '97. Falmouth and South West Cornwall Joint Guide Committee, Falmouth.

Griffiths, A. (1995) *The Changing Visitor: the First Eight Years of the Cornwall Holiday Survey 1987–1994.* University of Exeter, Exeter.

Gunter, B. and Furnham, A. (1992) *Consumer Profiles: an Introduction to Psychograhics.* Routledge, London.

Hall, C. and Jenkins, J. (1995) *Tourism and Public Policy.* Routledge, London.

Hawkins, D., Best, R. and Coney, K. (1992) *Consumer Behavior Implications for Marketing Strategy,* Fifth Edition. Irwin, Homewood, Illinois.

Jenkins, O. (1999) Understanding and measuring tourist destination images. *International Journal of Tourism Research* 1 (1), 1–17.

Longhurst, B. and Savage, M. (1996) Social class, consumption and the influence of Bourdieu: some critical issues. In: Edgell, S., Hetherington, K. and Warde, A. (eds) *Consumption Matters.* Blackwell, Oxford.

Mackay, H. (ed.) (1997) *Consumption and Everyday Life.* Sage, London.

Meethan, K. (1996) Consuming (in) the civilized city. *Annals of Tourism Research* 23 (2), 322–340.

Meethan, K. (1997) York: managing the tourist city. *Cities* 14 (6), 333–342.

Meethan, K. (1998) New tourism for old? Policy developments in Cornwall and Devon. *Tourism Management* 19 (6), 583–595.

Meethan, K. (2000) *Tourism in Modern Society: Place, Culture and Consumption.* MacMillan, Basingstoke.

MEW Market Research (1989a) *A Survey of Holidaymakers' Attitudes to the West Country: Quantitative Report.* MEW Market Research, London.

MEW Market Research (1989b) *Holidaymakers' Attitudes to the West Country: Quantitative Report.* MEW Market Research, London.

North Devon Marketing Bureau (NDMB) (1996) *Draft Marketing Plan.* NDMB, Barnstaple.

North Devon Marketing Bureau (NDMB) (1997) *Holiday and Accommodation Guide 1997.* NDMB, Barnstaple.

ONS (Office for National Statistics) (1997) *Regional Trends.* HMSO, London.

Payton, P. (1992) *The Making of Modern Cornwall: Historical Experience and the Persistence of 'Difference'.* Dyllansow Truran, Redruth.

Poon, A. (1993) *Tourism, Technology and Competitive Strategies.* CAB International, Wallingford.

Rojek, C. (1985) *Capitalism and Leisure Theory.* Tavistock, London.

Rojek, C. (1993) *Ways of Escape: Modern Transformation in Leisure and Travel.* MacMillan, Basingstoke.

Ryan, C. (1995) *Researching Tourist Satisfaction: Issues, Concepts, Problems.* Routledge, London.

Seaton, A. (1995) The VFR category in segmenting tourism markets. In: Seaton, A. (ed.) *Tourism: the State of the Art.* John Wiley and Sons, Chichester.

Selby, M. and Morgan, N. (1996) Reconstructing place image: a case study of its role in destination market research. *Tourism Management* 17 (4), 287–294.

Sleight, P. (1993) *Targeting Customers: How to use Geodemographics and Lifestyle Data in Your Business.* NTC Publications, Henley-on-Thames.

Thornton, P. (1997) Coastal tourism in Cornwall since 1900. In: Fisher, S. (ed.) *Recreation and the Sea.* University of Exeter Press, Exeter.

Thornton, P., Shaw, G. and Williams, A. (1997) Tourist group holiday decision making and behaviour: the influence of children. *Tourism Management* 18 (5), 287–297.

Urry, J. (1990) *The Tourist Gaze: Leisure and Travel in Contemporary Society.* Sage, London.

Wanhill, S. (1996) Local enterprise and development in tourism. *Tourism Management* 17 (1), 35–42.

Weinstein, A. (1994) *Market Segmentation: Using Demographics, Psychographics and other Niche Marketing Techniques to Predict and Model Customer Behaviour.* Probus, Chicago.

West Country Tourist Board (1991) *Spreading Success: a Regional Tourism Strategy for the West Country.* WCTB, Exeter.

Leisure and Tourism as Political Instruments: the Case of Britain in the 1980s or *One Wedding, a Funeral and a Riot*

2

Nigel Morpeth

*Leeds Metropolitan University,
Leeds, UK*

Introduction

Tourists visiting Britain during the summer of 1981 will have had the opportunity to experience contrasting aspects of British culture. In July of 1981, thousands of people *en plein air* were celebrating the marriage of the Prince and the late Princess of Wales. Later that year, the same tourists might have sensed a different mood on the streets, with civil insurrection manifested through a series of urban riots in major cities, which displayed the heightening social tension and more turbulent aspects of life in Britain in the early 1980s. Beyond the images of Royal pageantry and spontaneous revelry, was a dimension of British life that signalled a nation ill at ease with itself. Storry and Childs (1997: 64) speculate that these riots 'led to violent clashes between police and protesters against the government's race, housing and employment policies'.

This critique explores how the Conservative government of the day advocated the extrinsic use of leisure and tourism policies to ameliorate social cleavages, particularly within decaying inner cities. This raises the issue of what areas of public policy governments should involve themselves in, and also the efficacy, legitimacy and appropriateness of leisure- and tourism-based public policy, as used by central and local government as instruments of urban policy. In particular, Carrington and Leaman (1983: 2) question the hidden agenda of recreation and sports policy as an extension of urban policy, as 'a medium for social work and an instrument of social control' and the use of sport and recreation as a form of 'piecemeal social engineering,' attempting to alleviate the boredom of unemployment and deep-seated structural problems.

© CAB *International 2002. Tourism in Western Europe: a Collection of Case Histories*
(ed. Richard Voase)

These concerns apply equally to public policy related to tourism, in which tourism was perceived, particularly throughout the 1980s in Britain, as a panacea for urban problems through generating economic-based regeneration. The exploration of this particular thesis does not discount the fact that there are critiques which suggest that leisure and tourism should be the legitimate focus of public policy, and, indeed, that public policy is used to promote the intrinsic benefits of leisure and tourism (see e.g. Hall and Jenkins, 1995).

However, this chapter focuses on the ideology that underpinned and dominated the politics of a Conservative-governed Britain in the 1980s, and chronicles the development of leisure and tourism policy, both at national and the local level, as forms of social engineering. In assessing to what extent leisure and tourism policies have the capacity to address deep seated structural problems and the re-orbiting of decaying urban settlements, creating more-attractive environments for residents and tourists, the northern British town of Middlesbrough is used as a case history example. Whilst Middlesbrough did not experience urban riots, it suffered de-industrialization, extreme levels of unemployment, and consistently applied policies of 'recreation as welfare' (Richards, 1995). Local authorities within Middlesbrough and its environs coexisted for a 7-year period from 1987 within the fiefdom of an Urban Development Corporation, a quasi-autonomous institution established by national government in particular areas of developmental need, which involved the suspension and curtailment of the planning powers of locally elected authorities. An assessment is made of the role of the Teesside Development Corporation in the re-imaging of Middlesbrough as an unlikely tourist destination.

Middlesbrough also serves as a useful reference point in exploring current New Labour urban policy manifested through social inclusion policy, a contemporary experiment in urban policy. If the benefits of leisure and tourism to the individual are well documented, the aggregated experiences of leisure and tourism towards the creation of a civil society and the emergence of social capital (Bullen and Onyx, 1998), remains a nebulous yet compelling concept.

Government, the Welfare State and the Spirit of Enterprise

The Benthamite view of 19th-century society with its doctrine of individualism, *laissez-faire*, and minimum state intervention gave way during the next century to an acceptance that 'problems posed by urban industrial society of necessity enlarged the practical activities of the state' (Fraser, 1984: 11). Atkinson and Moon (1994: 65) argue that:

> The British economy had entered a crisis by 1975 and appeared unable to cope with these problems; its role was being questioned, with increasing doubt cast upon the effectiveness of state intervention and in particular the value of public expenditure.

They highlight that with the accession to power of the Thatcher government in May 1979, and throughout the 1980s, 'Thatcherite' policy dominated the political landscape of Britain, and exacerbated 'de-industrialization, the urban-rural shift, and the increasingly conspicuous nature of the so-called 'North–South divide'' (Atkinson and Moon, 1994: 90). Corner and Harvey (1991: 3) identify how politics in Britain 'marked a break with the consensus politics of the mixed economy and the welfare state', and Atkinson and Moon (1994: 208) suggest that the ethic of central government, playing an anchor role of working towards the social well-being of its citizens, was eroded, and, furthermore, there was a challenge to the notion that central and local government should respond to the needs of a 'service-dependent poor'. Riddell (1989: 71) highlights these challenges when he states that:

> The post-1979 approach attempted to revive enterprise and the entrepreneurial spirit by a variety of measures. A common theme of the actions initiated by Sir Geoffrey Howe as Chancellor and taken on by Lord Young and others has been the belief that by removing restrictions and promoting competition, enterprise would be encouraged. This has involved both short-term moves to remove market rigidities as well as longer-term measures to encourage a revival of an enterprise culture.

With the pervasive watchwords of enterprise, entrepreneurship and privatization, local authorities, who were traditionally regarded as guardians of the concept of social responsibility delivering a wide portfolio of welfare provision, had to increasingly subsume these watchwords within restructured public policy. Furthermore, as Crouch (1990: 118) observes, during the 1980s there was a realignment of the balance between national government and local government intervention in public policy, and 'the characteristic development in social policy was for the state to grant first permissive and then obligatory powers to local agencies for the enforcement of regulations'. According to Chandler (1988: 7), central government effectively decides the structure, functions and processes of local government within Britain, and he suggests that during successive Conservative administrations in the 1980s:

> Greater emphasis (was) now placed on the ability of central government to dictate to, rather than bargain with, the local government community. (Chandler, 1988: 7)

Chandler (1988: 8) argues that the expectation is that local government will manage the delivery of local services with central government maintaining a stewardship role. A key element within this relationship is the extent to which central government is willing to fund the service areas of local government, and the degree of centralized power that limits the scope for action by local authorities within the parameters of their statutory powers. The squeezing of local government finance by central government was a *leitmotiv* of the relationship with local government in 1980s Britain. Coupled with this, Atkinson and Moon (1994: 206) emphasize that political power was polarized at the centre, to the detriment of local democracy, and encapsulated by a particularly distinct ideological clash between central government and municipal socialist authorities. What then was the nature of the ideology that underpinned these political changes to the governance of Britain in the 1980s?

Ideological Beginnings

From May 1979 to May 1997, the political landscape of the UK was dominated by the Conservative party which won four consecutive General Elections, spawning one of the most dominant political 'isms' of British 20th century political life: Thatcherism. Thatcherite political and economic policies set in motion a cultural revolution domestically, and proved to be an unlikely invisible export to a variety of nations around the world. The New Right political agenda in Britain mirrored the proliferation of right wing political regimes within the West and arguably was the *zeitgeist* of politics of the 1980s. Atkinson and Moon (1994: 87) characterize Thatcherism as:

> a contradictory articulation of neo-liberalism and neo-conservatism, reconciled, somewhat precariously, on a populist political platform and perhaps best encapsulated in the persona of Margaret Thatcher herself.

Riddell (1989: 2–3), in discussing the nature of Thatcher, identifies that 'Thatcherism is essentially an instinct, a series of moral values and an approach to leadership rather than ideology'. Johnston (1991: 476), describes this philosophy as having great repercussions for the political, economic and social aspects of Britain in the 1980s and maintains that in 'rolling back the state' it 'redefined capitalism and the welfare state, allowing the economy to operate within market forces rather than regulation'. According to Atkinson and Moon (1994: 88) the crucial significance of Thatcher was that she 'was the fulcrum around which the union of neo-liberalism and neo-conservatism moved', essentially a combination of pragmatic elements which were galvanized by more-centralized government. Cockerell (1983: 22) emphasizes the idiosyncratic nature of her style of leadership:

> As she drove a mechanical dumper truck, sorted peanuts on a conveyor belt or operated a microcomputer, it sometimes seemed as if Mrs Thatcher wanted to solve all Britain's productivity problems herself.

In particular, Atkinson and Moon (1994: 96) identify three policy areas given distinct focus, which included: an expanded role for the private sector; property-led regeneration (but with the necessary intervention of the state with infrastructure investment and with subsidies and grants); and the promotion of small businesses.

These policy areas remained central to the Thatcher government's decade of political control and arguably have continued to reverberate in the policy of government in the 1990s. Identifying the sustaining qualities of Thatcherism is helpful in understanding the content and purpose of policy portfolios in subsequent political administrations. John Major, the prime minister who succeeded Mrs Thatcher in 1990, according to Hudson and Williams (1995: 296), was unable to move out of the political shadow of Thatcherism, identifying 'Majorism as no more than Thatcherism without its glorification of strong government', and suggesting also that it was 'a partial decomposition of Thatcherism' (Hudson and Williams, 1995: 40).

Arguably, one of the most enduring legacies of 'Thatcherite' policies which has occupied the minds of successive governments is the North–South divide, which encapsulates 'the economic, social, cultural and political differences within Britain' (Smith, 1994: 1). Smith outlines the North–South disparities in the 1980s which were rooted within economic factors. He suggests a crucial factor was that regional imbalances were allowed to grow unchecked by an absence of government intervention and infra-structural investment was skewed towards the South. By the end of the 1980s (and prior to the recession of the early 1990s) 'the South accounted for 62.7 per cent of GDP and 58 per cent of population' (Smith, 1994: 128).

Additionally, the Conservative government was said to have been heavily criticized for distancing itself from the future welfare of the British industry (Smith, 1994: 126) and did little to address the disparities of regional levels of unemployment. The *Sunday Times* headline of 'Jobless Britain' (Perrott, 1980) states that there was a danger of 'the Eighties bequeathing a legacy as bitter and divisive as the Thirties.' Exacerbating these regional imbalances was the narrowing scope for local intervention, with increasing centralized government power imposing a stranglehold on local government finances. To what extent did national government prevent local authorities from assisting in redressing social and economic imbalances on a local level?

Political Minimalism and Experiments in Social Engineering

Hudson and William's (1995) proclamation that at the heart of Thatcherite ideology was a credo of political minimalism is perhaps best personified by the late Nicholas Ridley. Regarded as one of Margaret Thatcher's chief architects of ideology, he advocated local authorities to adopt an 'enabling role', which in its ultimate form would involve local authorities meeting once a year to award tenders to private firms delivering council services. This concept encapsulates the uneasy relationship between central and local government. Local government throughout the 1980s had to endure a series of reorganizations, marginalization, a fragmentation of their roles and responsibilities, and what Patterson and Theobold (1996) describe as a 'hollowing out' of service delivery.

By the end of 18 years of Conservative administrations, the underlying spirit of preserving a viable system of local democracy in local government had been severely challenged. Arguably, Hanson and Haller's (1976: 224) view of 'common sense limiting the amount of backseat driving that central government was prepared to attempt' evaporated during the Thatcher years, with 'collaboration (being) replaced by antagonism'. Ridley's vision for the restructuring of local government expressed a wider application of an ideology imbued with classical neo-liberal economics, which applied the logic of the market in pursuit of economic rather than social goals. Furthermore, the role of local authorities in urban regeneration was called into question. Viewed by the national government as 'overly bureaucratic and stifling enterprise via planning and rate policies,' their 'participation was to take place within the primacy of private sector-led growth' (Atkinson and Moon, 1994: 208).

The identification of social inequalities within urban areas was particularly highlighted within the latter part of the 1960s with the creation of the 'Urban Programme' which targeted resources towards urban regeneration in areas of special need. Deakin and Edwards (1993: 21) identify the Labour White Paper of 1977, *Policy for the Inner Cities*, as recognizing that local authorities had a special role as service providers who had 'their finger on the pulse of local needs' and could therefore assess the best path of urban regeneration. They highlight how the White Paper advocated a more entrepreneurial and partnership role with the private sector, and suggest that this became a point of leverage for the incoming Conservative administration in 1979 to express a more expansive role for the private sector.

> Once the 1977 White Paper *Policy for the Inner Cities* had put down a marker that the fundamental problem was the collapse of the economic infrastructures of the inner cities, the way was clear for an incoming government, ideologically so inclined, to see economic regeneration as a job for the private sector. Thus there was a neat fit between economic logic and ideological leanings. Clearly, only the private sector could produce the jobs and economic buoyancy that inner cities lacked, and equally self-evident was the superior drive, energy and effectiveness of a private sector increasingly fired by the enterprise culture. (Deakin and Edwards, 1994: 1)

The 1980 Local Government Planning and Land Act provided the Secretary of State for the Environment with the power to create Urban Development Corporations (UDCs), whose main aim was 'to secure the regeneration of the area designated, chiefly in terms of physical renewal of land and buildings' (Deakin and Edwards, 1993: 38). The boards of UDCs were largely composed of local business representatives. UDCs had the powers to circumvent the planning and development functions of local authorities, facilitating development by other agencies (Deakin and Edwards, 1993: 38). Deakin and Edwards (1993: 40) suggest that the ideological underpinning of the work of UDCs was to 'lift the dead hand of socialism'.

They also argue that, despite this ideological vigour, Conservative inner city policy on tourism, education and crime was not part of a coherent strategy, and followed a piecemeal and pragmatic approach. Atkinson and Moon (1994: xi) characterize Thatcherite policy as emphasizing the pre-eminence of the private sector, with the mantra that 'the economic fortunes of an urban area were to be revived by the private sector'; and the market, rather than state planning, was to be the key instrument.

One of the many generations of government-funded urban programmes was the £3 billion 'Action for Cities' project, which included 57 initiatives in inner city areas and was a direct response to the Conservatives' post-1987 election success, for which the manifesto had recognized the need to prioritize the inner city policy. The 1990 Department of Environment-sponsored report, *Inner City Research Programme, Tourism and The Inner City*, which assessed 20 case studies of tourism-based urban regeneration projects, was optimistic about the economic and image-making potential of tourism projects:

> Tourism projects have had a positive net impact on the areas in which they have been undertaken. They have created jobs, resulted in environmental improvements, provided local facilities and helped change the image of an area (Department of the Environment, 1990: 66).

Miles Collinge, the Director of Development at the English Tourist Board, was sanguine about the perceived link between tourism as a tool for urban regeneration, in line with the Conservative policy of 'Action for Cities'. He talked of the potential to transform northern towns and cities through 'Tourism Development Action Programmes', suggesting that:

> ... tourism has an important place in the inner city, but it is no panacea and can help to create an environment which is exciting for the visitor and ultimately one in which residents take pride. ('Tourism: a catalyst for urban regeneration', paper presented to Inner Cities Conference, Sheffield, February 15, 1989)

The five 'Garden Festivals', which were staged in five urban areas between 1984 and 1992 in Britain and followed the German model of staging *Bundesgartenschauen* as an act of reclaiming derelict land, perhaps hinted at the tourism potential of event-led generation. Michael Heseltine, the Government Minister with special responsibility for Liverpool (post 1981 Toxteth riots), launched the first of the festivals in Liverpool in 1984. The temporary nature of these events, with no compulsion for use after the festivals finished, was a major criticism of this form of tourist-driven regeneration.

Subsequent urban programmes, such as City Challenge, City Action Teams and Task Forces, all signalled an attempt by central government to mobilize government departments 'to instil private-sector interest in the inner city' (Lawless, 1991: 17). Whilst the Conservative government would argue that they were not directly involved in creating and implementing these policy initiatives, the usurping of local government roles in this regeneration process, by agencies such as UDCs, was viewed as part of an ideological shift towards the 'privatization of urban policy' (Lawless, 1991: 23).

Policy Arenas for Leisure and Tourism

How is public policy for leisure and tourism applied as a form of social welfare and as a form of economic instrumentality? The notion that leisure is part of the social welfare portfolio (Bramham and Henry, 1985), was embodied within the discourse of national politics during the early 1970s. The Cobham Committee (1973), presenting the findings of the Select Committee of the House of Lords on Sport and Leisure, highlights the need for leisure to be a fundamental part of contributing to the quality of life, while 'the problem of leisure' is one of having to compensate for the scarcity of work. This report proved to be an impetus for the 1975 Government White Paper *Sport and Recreation* which stated that recreation was 'part of the general fabric of the social services' and an every day need of communities. Bramham and Henry (1985: 9) also suggest that it is possible to 'corrupt and pervert' the intrinsic value of leisure if it is used to curb delinquency and other processes in society. Carrington and Leaman (1983: 10) extend this theme by questioning:

> Why has sport been accorded a *particular* role in piecemeal social engineering? Which desirable social propensities could sport be said to cultivate? In general, it can be

argued that sport embodies values and beliefs which legitimate the existing hierarchial arrangements of society and lend support to the status quo.

Clarke (1994: 166) observes that there is 'an odd dualism to be found in the approaches to public sector leisure which combine freedom and facilitation with control and coercion'. Ironic, as Clarke considers that leisure should be an element of people's lives where they could exercise most control.

Travis (1979: 1) argues that the history of leisure provision and leisure-related legislation was about 'growing problems, failures leading to crisis situations and dimensions, before general innovative and remedial propositions were put forward to be tested in individual situations'. He identifies the largely permissive nature of leisure provision by local authorities and the fragmentary nature of leisure provision, with leisure provision emerging within the departments of at least seven Secretaries of State. Travis observes a clustering of functions which emerged around the former Department of the Environment, and suggests that perhaps it was not until the emergence of the Department of National Heritage in 1992 that one might argue that a coherent arena for leisure policy was created.

Traditionally, local authority leisure provision has, according to Travis (1979: 18), had to accommodate 'a lack of planners' understanding of the *range* of substantive issues in leisure provisions, creat(ing) a series of gaps, or shortfalls that grossly inhibit the development of this field':

> Historically separate problem-solving issues, rather than normative bases of action have epitomized the field. Therefore a scatter of separate Government responses led to a multi-sectoral Government response to many separate questions. Local Government has evolved towards functionalist solutions and latterly gone for a comprehensive leisure service approach (in 30% of Local Authorities) so a growing non-fit is evident between central and local government approaches to the field. (Travis, 1979: 32)

In terms of the broader application of ideology on leisure and tourism, Richards (1995: 168) identifies a shift in ideological emphasis in the development of leisure and tourism policy within the UK. This ranges from 'traditional pluralism', with minimum state intervention assisting largely voluntary sector initiatives, to the notion of 'welfare reformism' 'concerned with access for all (and limited attempts at promoting subsidized social tourism in the mid 1970s) and the democratization of culture', to the notion of 'economic realism' and the response of 'recreation as welfare' in using leisure and tourism as a panacea for social problems and inner city decline.

Richards' analysis of leisure and tourism public policy, with tourism viewed as a subset of leisure, might prove to be heretical to schools of thought that do not observe a seamlessness between leisure and tourism. It is beyond the scope of this chapter to dissect their characteristics precisely, but according to Richards as a policy area within national and local provision, tourism would appear to have had a similar history of a 'multi-sectoral and non-fit approach' as has public sector leisure provision. However, Richards identifies tourism policy as an aspect of leisure policy and argues that the historical analysis applied to the development of leisure policy within the UK can also be applied to the emergence of tourism policy. He argues that:

> although tourism is often treated as a sub-area of leisure, it has differed from others
> sectors of leisure in one key respect. Leisure in general has been identified as an area of
> social consumption, where public provision often forms an extension of welfare policy,
> such as swimming baths or libraries. Tourism policy, in contrast, has usually developed
> from a production perspective, aimed at providing jobs and income for local residents
> rather than simply meeting the consumption needs of tourists themselves. (Richards,
> 1995: 157)

He argues that increasingly both sectors are converging and can be 'linked to the wider political, social and economic developments' of post-1980 Thatcherism and that the breakdown of 'social democratic consensus,' led to a greater degree of politicization and provided greater links between policy and ideology (Richards, 1995: 157). This is characterized by the fact that:

> tourism has historically been considered politically as unimportant, and therefore
> often been ignored by national government. In fact, the pattern seems to be one of
> long periods of government inaction interspersed with short bursts of activity. What
> has tended to be ignored in the literature, however, is the fact that inaction can form
> an important ideological and political statement itself. (Richards, 1995: 155)

What then are these periods of activity and inactivity characterized by Richards? The *Development of Tourism Act* (1969) brought tourism into the political arena, although Richards argues that it did not resolve the political coyness of tourism as a policy area for government intervention. Nevertheless, in his view there are clear historical markers that can be identified, which plot national government intervention from the 'Come to Britain Movement' in 1926 to the *Development of Tourism Act* in 1969, and form a statutory framework for the development of tourism contributing to Britain's balance of payments and gaining more foreign exchange expenditure. According to Richards, the 1969 Act

> can be seen as part of a general movement in the 1960s towards greater state
> involvement in social planning and social consumption in general, and leisure
> consumption in particular. The model for such state intervention, as in the case of
> tourism, was the establishment of quangos which would implement government
> policy at 'arms length' therefore preserving the neutrality of the policy areas involved.
> (Richards, 1995: 164)

Richards argues that the instrumental use of tourism for wider economic aims was consolidated by the publication of the official report *Pleasure, Leisure and Jobs* (HMSO, 1985), which spelt out the employment-creation potential of tourism, and the subsequent relocation of ministerial responsibility for tourism from the Department of Trade, to the Department of Employment. Richards (1995: 165) posits that the direct link between tourism and trade, which had existed for 46 years, had come to an end. This was also a clear sign that the balance of payments justification for government intervention had been replaced by wider economic development considerations.

This historical overview positions tourism at the vanguard of the enterprise culture and as part of the creation of wealth and jobs. By 1989, the significant diminution in government funding for tourism quangos meant that they were subject to the same value for money and cost effectiveness yardsticks as those used for local authorities scrutinized by central government. Richards (1995: 197) identifies that the synthesis of functions of the BTA and national tourist boards was one of a residual function to 'fill the gaps left by the market'.

If the emergence in 1992 of a new government department styled 'Department of National Heritage' was a perhaps cynically motivated move to stimulate a 'consumer-driven society' (Richards, 1995: 168), to what extent does that department, re-styled 'Culture, Media and Sport' under the post-1997 Labour government, embrace a more socially driven motive? The language embedded within the latest government strategy document, *A New Approach to Investment in Culture*, outlines policy statements on leisure and tourism that are underpinned by the latest policy buzzwords of 'joined-up government' and 'social inclusion.' In highlighting the crucial role of sport, leisure and tourism in 'the work of social regeneration', Chris Smith the former Secretary of State for Culture, Media and Sport stated that:

> We believe that enhancing the cultural, sporting and creative life of the nation is a vital part of Government. The activities that we sponsor and support as a Department have a fundamental impact on the quality of life for all our citizens. They provide enjoyment and inspiration. They help to foster individual well-being. They help to bind us together as a community. They assist with the work of social regeneration. And in themselves, and with the allied importance of tourism, they form a crucial part of our nation's economy.
> (http://www.culture.gov.uk/TEXTDRSR.HTM)

The central theme of this report is that the Department of State will provide the strategic leadership with a necessary commitment from 'partners,' particularly local authorities (and more than likely the new regional development agencies), who will play a key role in facilitating social regeneration. To what extent have leisure and tourism policies featured in the social regeneration of a specific destination, Middlesbrough?

Message in a Bottle: From Captain Cook to Claes Oldenburg

How does the notion of 'recreation as welfare' and the instrumental use of tourism for economic aims relate to a specific destination? The identified case study town of Middlesbrough was chosen because it is viewed as typical of many towns and cities within the Britain of the 1980s, whose industrial infrastructure was in terminal decline. One of the mainstays of Middlesbrough's economy, British Steel, was the focus of 'streamlining policies' which exacerbated the already high levels of unemployment. Despite an established Eisteddfod which periodically attracted visitors from many world destinations, Middlesbrough was not known as an obvious tourist destination and was a long way from 'the traditional Beefeater and thatched cottage image of Britain' (Smithers, 1991).

Middlesbrough's unique selling point within the 1980s was to employ a strategy of using one of its 'famous sons', Captain James Cook, to market the town as the 'Gateway to Captain Cook Country'. It is a moot point whether this strategy of destination marketing was an original concept, and it would appear to follow a national trend to mythologize destinations. It certainly followed the pattern of other northern urban settlements which had to coexist with Urban Development Corporations.

Lillie (1953: 7), writing in commemoration of a century of 'the municipal and social and industrial progress' of the town of Middlesbrough, wrote that:

> We have never deluded ourselves with any romantic idea that our town is anything but a normal average industrial town, somewhat grey and possessed of no great beauty. We are, however, extremely proud of the craftmanship that has given to the world some of its most beautiful Ships, Bridges and Buildings, and has supplied the tools and the machinery that have helped to make our country prosperous. We are one of the workshops of the country and, as such, take no mean place in its Economy and Prosperity.

This view was later shared by the celebrated travel photographer Nick Danzinger (1996: 66) who observed that:

> In the urban plain of the River Tees there are symbols of continuity and renewal among the deritus of abandoned industry. Dinosaur cranes, cooling towers and billowing chimneys of the steel and chemical works loom everywhere, but above them are the Cleveland Hills. Such a scarred landscape only emphasizes the contrasts of the region, in which a short drive transports you from one of England's ugliest industrial landscapes to some of its most captivating countryside.

Established initially as a coal-exporting town and described in 1862 by the then premier Gladstone as 'the youngest child of England's Enterprise' (Lillie, 1953: 20), Middlesbrough built its early reputation on manufacturing steel from locally mined ore. This steel was used to build one of Sydney's tourist icons, the harbour bridge.

Historically, as a Labour-controlled authority, leisure services provision within Middlesbrough followed a traditional route of a service steeped in horticultural origins, gaining national notoriety through 'Britain in Bloom' competitions, a national kite mark of excellence for horticultural achievement. By the start of the 1980s, the impetus of this policy area was maintained together with an investment in satellite community facilities, built on the notion of leisure policy as 'traditional pluralism', with the authority working with a range of voluntary providers towards responding to the needs of its 143,000 residents. This philosophy of provision was most evident in the Department's 1985 *Community Development Strategy 1985–1995* which stated that:

> Community Development is a service which seeks to act as a bridge between the Local Authority and local communities; it also strives to develop formal and informal contacts between departments and other agencies and to assist local groups to define

and meet their own objectives. The ideology which underlines community work is that whereas Central or Local Government provides and manages services such as education, health facilities and housing, there are many facets of service provision which cannot be provided without at least some community participation. However, because not enough of that type of participation occurs naturally Community Development workers are needed to promote and encourage it. (Middlesbrough Borough Council, 1985: 2)

The commitment towards social welfare in its policies was particularly evident with the Middlesbrough Sport Motivation Project, and later the Action Sport programme, which provided an outreach service mainly targeted at unemployed people and offered a wide menu of indoor and outdoor sports. The then chief officer for leisure services saw this as a way of responding to the structural changes within local employment, which saw a reduction in employment in the steel industry from 28,000 jobs in 1970 to 6800 in 1989 and up to 90% male unemployment in some council wards. This type of initiative was redolent of national 'Sports for All' campaigns through national sports organizations such as the Sports Council (now Sports England), concentrated on urban areas within cities which would be eligible for funding through the 'Action for Cities' initiative. This provided the impetus for local authorities to organize sport and recreational activities which would target people who were traditionally felt to be missing out on sport, with women, people with disabilities, youths, unemployed people and ethnic minorities particularly targeted. Local authorities such as Middlesbrough talked of the need to enrich the quality of people's lives, whilst commentators such as Carrington and Leaman (1983: 5) describe such 'Action for Sport' campaigns as 'forays into social work'.

Whilst trying to maintain policies of social welfare for leisure, by the latter part of the 1980s and into the 1990s, Middlesbrough Borough Council had to respond to the Government's programme for privatization of services through Compulsory Competitive Tendering, and this meant that the leisure services had to operate within stringent financial constraints. This was consolidated by Government funding regimes which impacted heavily on local authorities at the start of the 1990s. The 1990–91 *Leisure Services Annual Report* lamented the fact that:

> Government legislation put tremendous pressure on Local Government Services with leisure squarely in the front line as much as any other Council service. As a result service budgets across the Council had to be cut and Leisure Services were forced to make preparations for budget reductions in 1991/1992 totalling £1.1 million (Middlesbrough Borough Council, 1991: 1).

Furthermore, the government proceeded with plans to dismantle certain municipal authorities in the mid-1990s. With the break up of Cleveland County Council, the county-level authority for the region, Middlesbrough Borough Council underwent a major restructure. Leisure services was subsumed within a larger 'super-department' of Education and Leisure, reflecting perhaps the national vogue for 'joined-up government'.

A key leisure officer with over 20 years service within the local authority, charged with determining the future development of leisure provision within

Middlesbrough, provided an overview of changes in service provision. His main reflections on the evolution of leisure suggest that, as a service area, it has been transformed from 'a Cinderella activity secondary to other service functions,' to a policy area which now underpins many service areas: the local authority reforms introduced by successive Conservative governments during the 1980s were crudely implemented and created a series of enforced changes without flexibility. However, he suggested that the experience made local authorities more entrepreneurial and receptive 'to the game' of identifying new sources of funding and of recognising the potential advantages of working with private sector partners. As a public sector organization, it had 'borrowed' private sector clothing and had added 'customer-orientated services' to the *patois* of community-centred provision. The structure of the local authority had become a fusion of a private sector entity, with managing directors, and a cabinet-style government, replacing the existing committee structure. Power and decision making had been centralized. Somewhat ironically, at a time when local authorities were responding to New Labour's political mindset of 'joined-up government' and social inclusion, the political control of Middlesbrough Borough Council had moved to a less radical, right-of-centre orientation.

Perhaps the legacy of Conservative reform of local government is that local authorities have absorbed, in the words of Deakin and Edwards, 'the language of "enterprise"(which) mines a rich seam of metaphors' suggesting that as

> customers, we are told, are more powerful than mere consumers or supplicants. If the enterprise culture comes to the inner cities therefore, might it be possible too that it will bring with it the power of consumerism, not just in people's relations to the providers of housing leisure, public services and so on, but also in the more visceral sense of bringing the cultural revolution of enterprise. (Deakin and Edwards, 1993: 25)

With respect to the creation of improved leisure provision for Middlesbrough citizens, the interviewed leisure officer is uncertain whether there has truly been an enhancing effect for the tourism potential of the town, apart from some notable exceptions. One such exception is a major installation of public art, *The Bottle*, created by Claes Oldenburg in the early 1990s, which provides a symbolic totem of Middlesbrough's heritage of steel, and a potential tourist icon in the mould of Anthony Gormley's *Angel of the North*.

There is little evidence that the 'Action for Cities' and 'Tourism Development Action Programme' have elevated Middlesbrough beyond the long-standing council marketing campaign of 'Gateway to Captain Cook Country' with its inbuilt logic of deflecting tourist activity away from Middlesbrough towards associated regions. This point was adeptly underlined during the interview, when the leisure officer stated that tourists will potentially visit the Captain Cook museum on the periphery of the town, but will inevitably be attracted to key sites of Cook memorabilia within neighbouring North Yorkshire. (The 1991 *Visitor Profile Information For Middlesbrough* (Cleveland County Research and Intelligence) revealed that, in the sample interviewed, 'Visiting Friends and Relatives' was cited as the main reason for visiting Middlesbrough for first time and returning visitors).

The leisure officer indicated that Middlesbrough's attempts to recognize the redevelopment of 'Middlehaven', a proposed waterfront development in Middlesbrough docks, were limited, amongst other factors, by the non-cooperation between the former Teesside Development Corporation (TDC) and Middlesbrough Borough Council. 'Middlehaven', to date, houses the Riverside football stadium, home of Middlesbrough Football Club, built in a wasteland of dereliction. Established in 1987, the TDC's remit was to engage in the economic regeneration of Middlesbrough, and it might claim to have had a hand in transforming the industrial landscape of neighbouring areas. Specifically, the TDC has funded a marina development in Hartlepool, and a barrage in Stockton-on-Tees, and arguably has recognized the latent demand for a leisure retail park sandwiched between Middlesbrough and Stockton. The TDC, much to the chagrin of neighbouring rural areas upstream of the industrialized section of the Tees, relaunched the area of Middlesbrough and its environs, as 'Tees Valley'. Quite how history will judge the legacy of the TDC and other Development Corporations is a moot point. Tellingly, during the interview it was suggested that the residents in Middlesbrough's outer estates, who were traditionally the target of 'recreation as welfare policies', have realized little direct economic benefit from the TDC.

Revealingly for international arrivals, Middlesbrough remains an invisible destination, with the BTA's promotional document *Britain Welcomes You*, available at the 'Britain visitor centre' in London, omitting Middlesbrough from its tourist map of Britain. It will be interesting to see whether the strategy for tourism emerging from Middlesbrough Borough Council's department for economic development will move beyond Captain Cook and seek to focus on and expose newer symbolic attractions such as *The Bottle*.

Evaluation and Comments

The legacy of 'those inner cities', a priority for the then prime minister Margaret Thatcher on the night of the Conservative election victory in 1987, was communicated as a similar challenge by Tony Blair 10 years later on the night of the Labour election victory in May 1997. Anne Power, Professor of Social Policy at the London School of Economics and a member of the government's Social Exclusion Unit suggests that:

> Many question the success or value of expensive urban regeneration, when poor neighbourhoods continue to be poor, unpopular, and disorder, crime, dirt and noise continue unabated or, according to many, simply get worse. Urban squalor is still with us after 25 years of regeneration. (Power, 1999)

The manner in which governments position public policy to respond to this identified 'urban squalor' remains contentious, and the role of leisure and tourism in that process is an imprecise science. The discretionary nature of local authority

leisure and tourism provision, coupled with the privatization of some of these service areas, has produced a fragmented programme of service provision. The policy
of 'recreation as welfare' has been used widely within Britain as a panacea for
unemployment and lawlessness, and the instrumental use of tourism as a tool for
economic regeneration continues to attract criticism as well as support. Richards
(1995) indicates that tenuous attempts have been made to widen the constituency
of access through social tourism projects, and local authorities maintain that 'Leisure for All' and 'Sport for All' projects enfranchize non-participants. The breakdown of service areas in 'joined-up government' appears to offer the opportunity
for the fusion of service delivery and the fact that these services are now delivered
for the benefit of customers and stakeholders is perhaps the enduring legacy of the
language of the 1980s enterprise culture.

The evidence from contemporary local government is that the discourse of
managerialism is replacing pluralism. The establishment of cabinet-style local government, with 'managing directors' overseeing resources, is redolent of the ideology
of early Thatcherite policy with presentational politics being very much in vogue.
The focus upon managing economic capital during the heady days of the enterprise
culture in the 1980s has now been superseded with concerns for the emergence of
social capital and social inclusion. The personal satisfaction of citizens in having
access to leisure and tourism activities might increasingly be identified as a vital
constituent of social capital, in what Bullen and Onyx describe as 'the pre-eminent
and most valued form of any capital as it provides the basis on which we build a
truly civil society' (http://www.mapl.com.au/A2.htm). Perhaps then, one of the
greatest challenges for politicians and policy makers is to rediscover the potential
for the wider applications of a civil society, a concept deemed to be redundant
during the height of the Thatcher revolution. Roberts (1978: 36) reminds us
that:

> the social construction of recreation tak(ing) as its building materials not only
> physical resources, but also attitudes and values that are invariably rooted in the
> surrounding society.

Does the current New Labour government strategy, *A New Approach to Investment in Culture*, merely recast leisure and tourism as extrinsic elements in social
regeneration and engineering couched in Conservative ideology? As history awaits
the outcome, a new generation of 'those inner cities' continues to occupy the minds
of local and national government policy makers.

Acknowledgement

I am grateful to Tony Duggan, formerly Principal Leisure Officer for the Department of Education and Leisure, Middlesborough Borough Council, for information
provided through interview during the preparation of this chapter.

References

Atkinson, R. and Moon, G. (1994) *Urban Policy in Britain: the City, the State and the Market*. Macmillan, Basingstoke.

Bianchini, F. and Schwengel, H. (1991) Re-imaging the city. In: Corner, J. and Harvey, S. (eds) *Enterprise and Heritage*. Routledge, London, pp. 212–234.

Braham, P. and Henry, I. (1985) Political ideology and leisure policy in the UK. *Leisure Studies* 4, 1–19.

Bullen, P. and Onyx, J. (1998) *Measuring Social Capital in Five Communities in NSW*. University of Technology, Sydney. Available from: http://www.mapl.com.au/A2.htm (Accessed 26 May 1999).

Carrington, B. and Leaman, O. (1983) Sport as community politics: a critique of some recent policy initiatives in sport and physical recreation. In: Haywood, L. (ed.) *Sport in the Community. The Next Ten Years: Problems and Issues*. Leisure Studies Association Newsletter Supplement, Bradford, pp. 1–19.

Chandler, J. (1988) *Public Policy-Making For Local Government*. Croom Helm, Beckenham.

Clarke, A. (1994) Leisure and the new managerialism. In: Clarke, J., Cochrane, A. and McLaughlin, E. (eds) *Managing Social Policy*. Sage Publications, London, pp. 162–181.

Cleveland County Research and Intelligence (1991) *Visitor Profile Information for Middlesborough*. Cleveland County Council, Middlesbrough.

Cockerill, M. (1983) The marketing of Margaret. *The Listener*, 16 June.

Corner, J. and Harvey, S. (1991) Great Britain Limited. In: Corner, J. and Harvey, S. *Enterprise and Heritage*. Routledge, London, pp. 1–20.

Crouch, C. (1990) *Urban Renewal: Theory and Practice*. Macmillan, Basingstoke.

Danziger, N. (1996) *Danziger's Britain: a Journey To The Edge*. Harper-Collins, London.

Deakin, N. and Edwards, J. (1993) *The Enterprise Culture and the Inner City*. Routledge, London.

Department of the Environment (1990) *Tourism and the Inner City: An Evaluation of the Impact of Grant Assisted Tourism Projects*. HMSO, London.

Department of Culture, Media and Sport (1998) *A New Approach to Investment in Culture*. Department of Culture, Media and Sport, London. Available from http://www.culture.gov.uk/TEXTDSR.HTM (Accessed 26 May 1999).

Fraser, D. (1984) *The Evolution of the British Welfare State*. Macmillan, Basingstoke.

Hall, C. and Jenkins, J. (1995) *Tourism and Public Policy*. Routledge, London.

Hanson, A. and Haller, C. (1976) *Governing Britain*. Sphere, London.

HMSO (1973) *Second Report from the Select Committee of the House of Lords on Sport and Leisure*. HMSO, London.

HMSO (1975) *Sport and Recreation*. HMSO, London.

HMSO (1977) *Recreation and Deprivation in Inner Urban Areas*. Department of the Environment, London.

HMSO (1985) *Pleasure, Leisure and Jobs*. HMSO, London.

Hudson, R. and Williams, A. (1995) *Divided Britain*. John Wiley and Sons, Chichester.

Johnston, R. (1991) And the future? In: Johnston, R. and Gardiner, V. (eds) *The Changing Geography of the United Kingdom*. Routledge, London, pp. 200–236.

Lawless, P. (1991) Urban policy in the Thatcher decade: English inner-city policy, 1979–1990. *Environment and Planning C: Government and Policy* 9, 15–30.

Lillie, W. (1953) *Middlesbrough 1853–1953: a Century of Municipal Social and Industrial Progress*. Middlesbrough Corporation, Middlesbrough.

Middlesbrough Borough Council (1985) *Department of Leisure and Amenities – Community Development – Future Policy*. Middlesbrough Borough Council, Middlesbrough.

Middlesbrough Borough Council (1991) *Leisure Services – Annual Report*. Middlesbrough Borough Council, Middlesbrough.

Patterson, A. and Theobold, K. (1996) Local Agenda 21, Compulsory competitive tendering and local environmental practices. *Local Environment* 1 (1), 7–19.

Perrott, R. (1980) Jobless Britain. *The Sunday Times*, 29 June, pp. 20–21.

Power, A. (1999) Pool of resources. *The Guardian*, 3 February, p. 8.

Richards, G. (1995) The Politics of national tourism policy in Britain. *Leisure Studies Journal* 14 (3), 153–173.

Riddell, P. (1989) *The Thatcher Decade*. Blackwell, Oxford.

Roberts, K. (1978) *Contemporary Society and the Growth of Leisure*. Longman, London.

Smith, D. (1994) *North and South: Britain's Economic, Social and Political Divide*. Penguin, London.

Smithers, R. (1991) Britain issues 6m pounds to Beefeater tourist image. *The Guardian*, 13 September, p. 3.

Storry, M. and Childs, P. (1997) *British Cultural Identities*. Routledge, London.

The Sports Council (1980) *Sport in the Community: the Next Ten Years*. Sports Council, London.

Travis, A. (1979) *The State and Leisure Provision*. The Sports Council, Birmingham.

The Influence of Political, Economic and Social Change in a Mature Tourist Destination: the Case of the Isle of Thanet, South-east England

3

Richard Voase
University of Lincoln, Lincoln Campus, Lincoln, UK

Introduction

This chapter seeks to examine the influence of political, economic and social change on municipal decision-taking in the mature resort. Specifically, it seeks to identify the kind of local policy likely to be associated with a particular political circumstance, and to examine the extent to which such a circumstance can be expected to lead to a specific kind of tourism policy and planning. The progress of a tourist destination along the curve of the theorized destination life-cycle (Butler, 1980) inevitably leads to relative changes in the economic importance of tourism to the overall local economy, and also to changes in its *perceived* importance. The extent to which these changes, both real and perceived, have a transforming influence on patterns of economic dependency and economic interest, which in turn feed in to the politics of the locality, will be a key theme.

First, a national context of political, economic and social change during the 1980s will be established, with particular reference to the impact on domestic tourism and on seaside resorts. Second, a British seaside community will be studied as a case example: the Isle of Thanet, located on the eastern coast of the county of Kent in southern England, perhaps better recognized by the names of its component resorts of Margate, Broadstairs and Ramsgate. The research involves reference to municipal documents and publications, media comment, existing published research, and the background knowledge of the author through personal practitioner experience as a resort marketeer in the locality. Third, the case will be analysed in terms of both local factors and the national context of change during the 1980s. By way of conclusion, it will be suggested that the ability of a destination to take optimal decisions during the 'decline' phase of its life-cycle is inhibited by a range of political, social and economic factors. The implication is that the implementation of sound strategy with respect to policy-making and planning for tourism is not simply a matter of researching and implementing best practice.

Political, Economic and Social Change: the National Context

The purpose of this section is to summarize some of the salient political, economic and social contexts and changes observable in Britain during the 1980s, which is the era immediately antedating that in which the case history is set. This is a deliberately brief and selective exposition which will summarize three causes and effects: first, the national political context and its effect on local municipalities; second, changes in the national economy and its outcomes in terms of the nature and culture of business; and third, economic change and its consequence in terms of patterns of employment and related changes in the structure and culture of society. Finally, in this section, the implications at district level for seaside resort management will be considered.

The national political context

In 1979, a Conservative government was elected in the United Kingdom. Its response to the inherited political circumstances of the 1970s, which included the failure of 'consensus' politics as attempted during that decade by successive Conservative and Labour governments, was to adopt a position which can be described as broadly 'authoritarian'. Its response to the inherited economic circumstances, which included high inflation and high public spending, was to use the raising and lowering of interest rates as a vehicle for controlling inflation, and to control public spending through placing restraints on the volume of funds disbursed by local authorities. At the beginning of the decade, roughly 60% of municipalities' spending needs were provided by central government, and roughly 40% raised from local taxation. Quickly, the central government's mechanism for providing this support, the RSG (Rate Support Grant), was replaced by a so-called 'block grant', in which the determination of a municipality's global spending need, and block grant requirement, became the object of the Secretary of State's standard spending assessment (SSA) rather than of local determination. Subsequent measures implemented during the course of the 1980s by central government included penalties for exceeding the Secretary of State's spending assessment (commonly referred to as 'rate capping') and, in the later 1980s, severe restrictions on local authority capital spending and on the discretion to spend the proceeds of the sale of capital assets, such as land and buildings, and the introduction of compulsory competitive tendering (CCT) for a range of local authority services. As a consequence, locally elected bodies were obliged to examine their expenditure in detail and make diffi-cult decisions as to where economies could be made, or if economies were not thought to be possible, where withdrawals of service were to be made. There is evidence that senior officials in local government regarded these pressures, particu-larly the introduction of CCT, to have led to a more businesslike approach and to an improvement in managerial practices (Nichols, 1995: 251). However, it was commonly observed that the orientation of the actual elected bodies, that is the councillors, became increasingly political rather than managerial during the 1980s. Deciding whether or how to make 'cuts' became a charged political process; the role of committee chairpersons became, in the words of one contemporary chief executive, 'increasingly ministerial'. At the same time, the loss of financial discretion and independence by local councils created concerns that this would result in a diminution of the overall quality of people prepared to stand for election (Burgess, 1980).

The national economic context

The key economic change in the UK during the 1980s was arguably the dramatic decline in employment in manufacturing industry and the expansion of the service sector. These had been established trends in the post World War II era and had been marked since the beginning of the 1960s: the proportion of the workforce in civilian employment engaged in manufacturing industry fell from nearly 40% in 1960, to barely 30% in 1980, but the initial years of the 1980s saw dramatic politically-induced pressures placed on this sector (Leys, 1985: 8, 12). The govern-ment's policies, with respect to the use of high rates to control consumer spending and thus inflation, had the ancillary effect of putting additional pressure on manu-facturing companies through making borrowing needs for re-investment expensive, thereby increasing the likelihood of insolvency. The restrictions on public spending also impacted on a range of private-sector industries as public purchasing and the availability of public contracts diminished. During this time, however, certain industries, notably in the service sector, were growing; tourism was one such indus-try. Industrial cities were not slow to recognize the potential. Faced with the con-traction of their traditional industries and seeking new sources of employment, cities such as Bradford embarked on strategies to position themselves as destinations for what during the 1980s was the fastest-growing sector of domestic tourism, the short break (Walsh-Heron, 1988). Sources tended to agree that the cost of creating a job in tourism, estimated at £4000 in the mid-1980s and £5000 in 1990, was only one-seventh of the cost of creating a job in a manufacturing industry (Lumley, 1988: 22; Battersby, 1990). Ostensibly therefore, a seaside resort economy, tradi-tionally dependent upon tourism, was already placed in an industry which enjoyed growth potential in the new 'post-industrial' economy. However, as shall be seen, the 'problem' of the seaside resort was occluded by a range of culturally-induced perceptions which complicated and, arguably, successfully prevented key decisions being taken. The case history to be outlined later arguably illustrates this point.

Social and cultural change

In 1971, 8m people in the United Kingdom were employed in manufacturing industry; by 1990, that figure had contracted to 5.1m. During the same period, the numbers employed in service industries rose from 11.6m to 15.9m (CSO, 1993: 56). Admittedly, many of these new service-industry jobs were low-paid and casual or seasonal, such as working in the hospitality industry or at the checkout in a supermarket, but many others involved part of an expanding, educated sector of the middle class, employed in the so-called 'knowledge industries', such as education, advertising, journalism, government and the creative professions (Urry, 1990: 88–89; Featherstone, 1991: 43; Frow, 1993; Brown, 1995). Though 'weakly formed' as a class (Frow, 1993: 270), the members of this grouping were united in being upwardly mobile, if not in terms of remuneration, in terms of knowledge and educational credentials. 'Service class' has been the term affixed to them (Urry, 1988: 40–41; Thrift, 1989; Frow, 1993: 257–262; Butler, 1995). Bourdieu, in his exhaustive investigations into the nature of taste and social positioning, has identified a similar group, which he terms the *new petite bourgeoisie*. Bourdieu's alternative name for the group is the 'new cultural intermediaries', because they are united by their ability – through their classroom activity, news features, governmental reports and creative advertisements – to mediate information through society (Bourdieu, 1984: 359, 325). Crucially, so the argument goes, the information which they circulate becomes either representative of, or interpreted in terms of, their own class-values, which are reflected in their cultural origins, rejecting perhaps the more lurid aspects of the money-culture of 1980s Britain, but adopting values which can be properly associated with what can be extracted from the culture of the present and the 'heritage' of the past and regarded, very subjectively, to be of 'good taste'. 'Good taste', naturally, enjoys a symbiotic relationship with something called 'bad taste', or 'vulgarity', call it what you will. That which is tasteful cannot appear distinctive unless or until juxtaposed with the un-tasteful. Accordingly, the cultural self-identity of the service class is rooted in individualistic, rather than collective, values (Urry, 1988: 41; Thrift, 1989: 21).

So, a radical change in patterns of employment does not simply have implications for the jobs people do: British people were not just in different jobs, they were different people. The differing cultural values of the white-collar worker and the blue-collar worker, though now perhaps more blurred than they ever have been, nevertheless remain distinctive in a crucial sense. Blue-collar culture has traditionally sought its identity as part of a collective: being in the 'mining community' or the 'textile community', or whatever. Service-class culture, as part of an expanded middle class, is individualistic in character (Henley Centre, 1989; Thrift, 1989: 21). For this individualism to appear fully distinctive, the exercise of taste requires not just the acquisition of the tasteful, whether in job, role, or lifestyle, but the *active rejection* of the un-tasteful. This, it can be argued, is a root cause of the problem of the decline of the domestic seaside: domestic seaside resorts were perceived in the context of the declining industries whose mass workforces, during the 19th century and the first three-quarters of the 20th, had given rise to the resorts and sustained them. To demonstrate 'good taste' is to avoid such places (Urry, 1988: 41, 1996: 103).[1] The common perception that the domestic seaside has been eclipsed by the availability of better weather abroad is thus revealed as an obfuscation. There are plenty of resorts on the European mainland, located on similar latitudes and enjoying similar climates to British resorts, which have maintained fashionability. While the proliferation of the Mediterranean holiday is a factor, the primary reason for decline is purely domestic, in the form of the exclusion of the seaside resort from the canon of fashion, and the concomitant failure of the resorts themselves, the result perhaps of the occlusion of understanding, to take appropriate remedial decisions at the appropriate time.

Implications for seaside resort management

Britton (1991: 458) suggests that there are two identifiable ways in which 'the state' in its broadest sense intervenes in the tourism industry. The first is to provide the service commonly known as 'destination marketing'. Given that the businesses which collectively constitute the 'tourism industry' are diverse in character and, in many cases, number their employees in only single figures, an effective 'corporate' approach to tourist destination marketing is difficult; the locally elected governmental body is the obvious candidate to provide this 'umbrella' service. The second is to provide incentives to development, either in the form of encouragement to existing businesses to improve their facilities and operation, or incentives for new businesses to establish themselves. At national level, the *Development of Tourism Act* (1969) established the English Tourist Board and a network of regional tourist boards to discharge both these responsibilities. Britton observes, tellingly, that agreement on the mode of input of this expenditure, and clear identification of benefits from it, and the distribution of those benefits, is problematic (Britton, 1991: 458). This will be a key issue in our later discussion. Moreover, to Britton's list must be added a third responsibility, associated almost exclusively with the 'lowest' tier of government at district level: the maintenance and running of theatres, visitor attractions, public entertainments, plus secondary facilities such as public toilets, in order to maintain the attractiveness of the destination and service the needs of tourists. As local authorities saw their financial discretion reduced during the 1980s, and found themselves relatively isolated in providing what appeared to be commercial undertakings in return for benefits which to some extent defied empirical measurement, the pressure to reconsider the importance of these roles was considerable. This process of reconsideration was taken in a climate of socio-cultural change associated with the postmodernization of British society during the 1980s, in which the prevailing ethic was one of neo-liberal *laissez-faire*

---

[1] Brighton is an apparent exception, having retained a place in the canon of service-class fashion owing to idiosyncracies of past history. However, closer examination of Brighton reveals an assemblage of social and environmental problems (see Meethan, 1996) identical to those which will be described, shortly, in relation to the Isle of Thanet.

economic policy. Public intervention in commercial undertakings was frowned upon, accompanied by the conviction, in right-of-centre circles at least, that a change from a manufacturing-dominated to a service-dominated economy was not only inevitable, but a worthy objective to be pursued (Leys, 1985: 7).[2]

In simple terms, this was an old economic order being replaced by a new one. Paradoxically, this liberal (in the economic sense) approach was accompanied by illiberal (in the political sense) government: an authoritarian stance was necessary in order to bridle the activity of other elected bodies within the country, principally local authorities. The political outlook and style portrayed in the case which follows can be seen to emulate in some respects the outlook and style at national level. Added to this, there is the changed cultural climate, outlined in the previous section, which created an invisible but none the less powerful, possibly hegemonic ideological context (Thrift, 1989: 22). Resort communities were thus subjected to a sustained media discourse, rooted in service-class values of perceived 'good taste'. Arguably, this contributed to a conviction of having been marginalized from the mainstream of fashionable regard: the small businesspeople who owned tourism undertakings readily embraced the aspirational benefits of taking package holidays abroad. Against such a background of personal preference and practice, maintenance of belief in one's own domestic product becomes difficult.

The Isle of Thanet: a Specific Case History

The parameters of this case history are temporally set during the tenure of the author as a head of division in charge of destination marketing, employed by the Thanet District Council, from mid-1990 to the end of 1991. Reference will be made to events prior to and subsequent to this period where it is appropriate to do so in order to establish a context or pattern, and to historical and external circumstances where required[3]. Detailed studies of the area and its socio-political circumstances were conducted during the second half of the 1980s by researchers from the nearby University of Kent at Canterbury (Buck *et al.*, 1989; Pickvance, 1990). Use will be made of these studies to provide detail and context where appropriate.

---

[2] This is not to say that such a transformation was not in many respects desirable: progress toward full industrialization would inevitably lead to this effect. Perhaps the ultimate validation of the 'Thatcherite' emphasis on private enterprise and entrepreneurialism can be seen in the attitude of the present Labour government in the United Kingdom: at the time of writing (Autumn 1999), the Prime Minister is castigating the 'forces of conservatism', clearly directing his remarks toward mass trade unions and their resistance to change; and the Chancellor of the Exchequer is seeking to encourage 'American-style entrepreneurialism' in his pre-budget measures.
[3] I should point out that my own role as an actor in this case history leads to something of a conflation of subject and object. I have made efforts to report events and interpret them in a dispassionate manner, but the reader should be aware that other interpretations are possible. Local lore in the Isle of Thanet tends to locate responsibility for problems with the local body politic, and with individual politicians. I have attempted to show that the problems experienced in achieving consistent regenerative policies were inevitable owing to the social and cultural make-up of the locality, combined with the national context at the time.

Margate, Broadstairs and Ramsgate

The component resorts of the Isle of Thanet are Margate, Broadstairs and Ramsgate. They are located adjacent to one another on the eastern tip of the county of Kent, in southern England. Their development as resorts, as in the case of the majority of coastal resorts in Britain, is a consequence of the railway boom of 1840–1850. As Urry (1990: 22–23) has pointed out, seaside resorts rapidly segmented themselves to appeal to different markets on the basis of nuances of class distinction; each acquired its particular 'social tone'. Margate became a favoured destination for the working classes of the London conurbation, Ramsgate remained somewhat more genteel, and Broadstairs remained comparatively undeveloped, and hence genteel. In addition, ribbon development along the coast to the west of Margate resulted in the emergence of suburban settlements of 'genteel' character, which have since become favoured retirement locations (Buck *et al.*, 1989: 170). It is probably safe to suggest that the perceived differences between Margate, Broadstairs and Ramsgate, though undoubtedly important in the early days and still referred to in local discourse, are now relatively insignificant in terms of visitor markets. A holidaymaker survey undertaken during the 1991 season showed a comparable socio-economic profile for visitors to all three resorts: the primary market was revealed as persons whose head of household was located in socio-economic classifications C1, C2 and D (clerical, skilled manual and unskilled manual). The majority of C1 tourists were from overseas, so it is probably safe to assume a primary C2 market for the Thanet resorts (TDC, 1991a: 17). This coincides with the national profile for seaside resorts at that time (Travis, 1992).

The differing 'social tone' of the three towns, while being of little, yet lingering, importance in each town's contemporary self-perception, can be illuminated by taking a glimpse at past associations. Resort holiday guides seldom miss an opportunity to use links with famous visitors of the past as a means of celebrity product endorsement. Broadstairs, for example, was the summer retreat of Charles Dickens, to the extent that his chosen place of refuge is now known as 'Bleak House' after the title of one of his works. Open to the public, it contains relics and ephemera from the novelist's visits (TDC, 1992: 9). What is perhaps less well known is that one Johanna von Westfalen, daughter of Prussian aristocrat Ludwig von Westfalen and whose claim to fame was to become Mrs Karl Marx, took holidays in Ramsgate, where she encountered refined and intelligent female company. This pleased Marx, who was concerned that their life of bourgeois penury in London prevented her from mixing with women of similar upbringing (Wheen, 1999: 16). Of more recent origin is the endorsement of Margate by the former Great Train Robber, Ronald Biggs, living in enforced exile in Brazil since the mid-1960s following his escape from prison. In a newspaper interview, his response to the question, 'What is your favourite smell?', was 'Margate'. In similar vein, his favourite journey was from London to Margate by train (Greenstreet, 1994). This particular celebrity endorsement could be expected, of course, to meet with mixed reactions from the people of Margate; yet it conveys some of the sense in which Margate was regarded with affection in the East End of London, and led Margate to attract the epithet 'cockneyfied' (Hill, 1993).

Situational analysis: June 1990

On arrival in June 1990 as head of marketing for the local authority, the author encountered an elected body which was supportive, with some hint of reservation, of maintaining its direct role in supporting and promoting tourism to the three resorts. It was also interested in exploring alternative options for economic development and the creation of employment, and had engaged another officer to undertake this work. As concerns the tourism industry, there appeared to be copious misunderstanding of the importance of tourism to the local economy. There was a need for what might be termed a 'relaunch'. The means for this were to be the classical formula of situational analysis, followed by the formulation of a strategy, to be implemented by means of a marketing plan embracing a range of projects in pursuit of specific targets. The first task within the context of the situational analysis was to assemble such facts about the tourism industry as were available, interpret them and make them known, in order to combat misunderstanding. In partnership with officials in the Economic Development Department of Kent County Council, the county-level body whose area included Thanet, an attempt was made to identify the salient facts.

One method of establishing the value of tourism to Thanet was to take the most recent (1988) county-level figures for visitor numbers and spending, from the *British Tourism Survey Monthly* produced by the English Tourist Board, and disaggregate them to district level, using the proportions revealed in a comprehensive district survey undertaken by the Association of District Councils in 1984, and published in 1987. This was labelled the 'BTSM model'. It suggested 743,000 staying visitors, spending £47.4m (Lawrie, R., 1990 *Economic Impact of Tourism in Thanet*, unpublished, used with permission.) This visitor spend, when uprated to 1990 levels by applying the Retail Price Index, emerged as £55m. The problem with this method was that it assumed the constancy of the proportion of staying visitors as distributed amongst districts within Kent. Mention will be made shortly of later research which suggested this was likely to be a flawed assumption.

An alternative methodology was a Local Impact Model, which used the size of the accommodation base, average percentage occupancy, and average levels of tourist spend to calculate total spend by staying visitors. The spend in this case was suggested to be £38.6m at 1990 prices, somewhat lower than the £55m calculated by the other model. An additional methodology was applied in order to calculate day visitor ('excursionist') activity and spend: it related levels of excursionist activity to a given level of staying visitor spend calculated from a previous study elsewhere. Using the £38.6m from the Local Impact Model as a base, day visitor spend could add from £14m (low impact, representing 1.2m visitors) to £36m (high impact, representing 1.7m visitors) to the figure for staying visitors. An average of the high and low impact estimates suggested a combined total of 1.5m staying visitors and excursionists, spending £64m annually into the local economy. The calculation of the number of jobs supported by the industry was computed by the application of yet another model to this data, based on detailed studies elsewhere, which enabled the accommodation spend data to be translated into employment created. The result was 4650 jobs, excluding those generated by day visits (Lawrie, 1990, unpublished, as cited above.) A consultants' report commissioned by TDC 3 years earlier had suggested that tourism in total, including both staying and day visitors, accounted for 15% of local employment, representing just over 6000 jobs (Bishop Associates, 1987).

To discuss these methodologies and their application in greater detail would be to digress from the central purpose of this study. However, the difficulties of acquiring reliable information on tourism have been ably illustrated. It was decided to adopt the data revealed by the BTSM model as the standard (TDC, 1991b: 4). In the light of subsequent research into the change in bedstock between 1987 and 1991, summarized below, the Local Impact Model should have been regarded as the more reliable, especially since in its amended version it included the excursionist contribution to tourism. As a more general comment, the lack of regular reliable data at district level for tourism volumes and spend was problematic, because it enabled perceptions at political level, governed more often than not by political interest than by science, to become predominant. Furthermore, the national government's SSA (standard spending assessment) of what each local authority should spend took into account the role of temporary visitors in the form of tourists and the public spending which was required to service them. For this reason, there was a need for accurate data. This was observed in the report of a joint industry committee for tourism statistics, for which the representative for district councils happened to be the Director of Finance for TDC (Tourism Society/DoE, 1992: 58–61).[4]

Other research carried out during the phase of situational analysis revealed data which was of greater empirical validity. In three fields in particular, it was possible to assess past performance in discrete areas of marketing activity. For example, it was possible to calculate, with some precision, the volume of business gained from major conferences which held their functions in the Winter Gardens theatre complex in Margate. This venue, a traditional seaside auditorium that opened in 1911 and to which an extension was added in the 1960s, was operated and subsidized by the council for the purpose of municipal entertainments and conference usage. Conference bookings were mediated through the Marketing Office and as such were measurable. The results, which were placed in a report for the scrutiny of the council (TDC, 1991c: 3.8), gave cause for concern (see Table 3.1).

The decline, which appears to begin in the mid-1980s, coincides, significantly,

---

[4] The chairman of the JICTOURS working group reports that their recommendations were endorsed by the government at the time of publication, but subsequent efforts to secure changes in the collection of tourism data had met with inaction from government and tourist boards (Middleton, 1995: A-7).

Table 3.1. Usage of Margate Winter Gardens by major conferences, 1980–1990.

Year	Number of conferences	Number of delegate nights
1980	14	14,470
1981	13	17,405
1982	13	17,835
1983	8	30,195
1984	10	33,850
1985	4	4,370
1986	4	5,500
1987	4	3,220
1988	5	5,100
1989	2	1,550
1990	4	3,840

Source: Voase, 1992: 8.

with the departure of a head of marketing and his non-replacement until 1988. This inaction arguably incurred significant costs to the resort. The English Tourist Board estimate for delegate spending per day at seaside venues, in 1988, was £40 per day. This figure, if adjusted by the retail price index for each year of the decade and used to calculate aggregate spend, reveals that the total 'lost' during the second half of the 1980s, in comparison with the first half, approaches £5m. If hypothetically distributed across trading hotels and guest houses, this averages out at between £3000 and £4000 'lost' per establishment per annum. For some establishments, this figure could be the difference between solvency and insolvency (Voase, 1995: 135).

Unsurprisingly, a study of the accommodation base revealed a substantial contraction, relative to a competing resort of similar size in the same region. In 1984, Eastbourne, located on the coast of Sussex, and Thanet each had a serviced accommodation base of 12,000 beds apiece. By 1990, Eastbourne's base had shrunk to 10,072 bedspaces (Eastbourne Borough Council, 1990: 35), while Thanet's had shrunk, by 1991, to 7398 (TDC, 1991c: Appendix 3). It would of course be wrong to ascribe the rapidity of this contraction solely to the loss of large conference business, though it would be equally mistaken to suggest that the two are unconnected. However, an examination of the promotional budgets throughout the 1980s revealed that attempts to attract general vacational tourists were also less vigorous than those of other resorts. During the first half of the 1980s and moving into the second half, the above-the-line promotional spend, that is, the amount spent on resort advertising aimed at general holidaymakers and a key indicator of promotional exposure, was running at half the rate of comparable resorts. For example, the advertising budget for Thanet in 1983 was £50,000, whereas competing resorts at that time were spending in the region of twice that amount (Voase, 1992). Therefore, what emerged was a picture of failure to maintain a presence in the marketplace for domestic vacational tourism through low (or misplaced) expenditure, and failure to address key market sectors, such as large conferences.

However, it is true to say that well-intended efforts to support the tourism industry were made during the 1980s. In particular, a large volume of special funds was applied to a special event. The council had been approached by a local enthusiast with the suggestion that it adopt an International Cartoon Festival which had hitherto run at a resort on the Belgian coast. This approach coincided with the time, from 1985 to 1988, when the council employed no marketing adviser of senior rank. The council's leisure committee decided to invest £50,000 in this event, supplemented by a guarantee against loss of £100,000. A newly appointed senior marketeer inherited this project on his arrival in 1988 and proceeded with its organization. The event, which consisted of an exhibition of art cartoons displayed in a marquee on a seafront site in Margate, attracted *c*. 3000 visitors, considerably short of the 100,000 projected.

Foresight should have suggested that to place an indoor exhibition of art cartoons on the seafront of an essentially working-class resort, adjacent to the competing attractions of an amusement park, the beach and the sea, was to invite failure. The problem of this event and its attendant financial embarrassment led to internal discord, recrimination, and a spectacle for the local media. For many people encountered by the author on arrival in 1990, this was the defining event of the council's efforts to revitalize its tourism industry during the 1980s. Strangely, as shall be seen later, this negative experience did not seem to deter a prevalent and, in the author's view, mistaken belief that special events, in various forms, offered some form of salvation to the tourism industry.

Marketing strategy and plan

The strategy and plan which was agreed by the council in November 1990 adopted a root-and-branch approach to relaunching the resorts, focusing on known potential markets and involving the deployment of promotional techniques selected for reaching those markets. Any marketing strategy for a domestic seaside would have to take into account the national marketing environment for domestic coastal holidays. Without doubt, there had been a rather dramatic reduction in seaside holidaytaking during the 1980s: an estimated decline from 150 million nights in 1980, to 116 million in 1988, a fall of 23% (Middleton, 1989). However, in other respects the picture looked promising, for four reasons: (i) Nights, trips and spending at the seaside as a *proportion* of overall domestic holiday tourism had remained fairly constant between 1978 and 1990; relatively speaking, the seaside was not declining (ETB, 1992). (ii) In demographic terms, a key market served by the domestic seaside, the family formation group in ages 25–34, was growing by 17% between 1985 and 1995, adding 1.3m adults in that age range to the population. The potential for growth in 'family' consumption was the object of comment in the practitioner press (*Marketing*, 1989). The importance of this group as a target market for domestic seaside holidays had been well researched and documented (MEW Research, 1992; Travis, 1992). (iii) The competition in the form of the seaside holiday in the warmer climate of Spain was beginning to look decidedly shaky; a decline was beginning, variously attributed to jaded resorts, a reputation for excessive behaviour by visitors, and a strong peseta. Whatever the reason, nights spent in Spain by non-resident tourists declined by 11.4% between 1988 and 1989; and Spain's share of travel receipts declined during that same period from 24.6% to 22.7% of the European total (Eurostat, 1992). (iv) The development of the domestic short break, holiday 'snacking' in the form of 2- or 3-night breaks in paid accommodation, grew vigorously during the 1980s, from 12.5m trips in 1980, to 16.9m in 1988. Vitally, the short break was a product which was typically consumed on multiple occasions during the year, and was thus less destination-specific than the traditional 'long' holiday (Beioley, 1991).

In Thanet there had been, as in a number of medium-sized and smaller resorts, a lack of investment in tourist facilities during the 1980s,[5] but the action recommended by a national study commissioned by the English Tourist Board was to break the spiral of decline by the vigorous marketing of the existing product (Middleton, 1991). This was one dimension of the underpinning philosophy of the approach recommended to Thanet District Council. The second dimension was of more managerial nature, but none the less vital: that a successful relaunch required the renewal of the confidence of the tourism industry in Thanet as a destination. This involved showing to the industry, within and outside the district, that a confident team, enjoying the support of its elected employers, was now undertaking a methodical reconstruction of the area as a tourist product. This, as much as spending money on promotion, was regarded as vital to the success of the relaunch efforts.

The tourism strategy recommended to the council by Bishop Associates in 1987 recognized most of the opportunities; it was the implementation, rather than the strategy, which had hitherto been lacking in vigour and consistency. What was proposed, in a Marketing Plan presented to the council's policy committee in November 1990 and in its draft update 1 year later, was a comprehensive package of proposals designed to implement the strategy, forty individual projects in all. The most important included:

- reworked promotional materials to 'speak' specifically to target markets;
- money transferred into the advertising budget to raise it to levels comparable to those of competing domestic resorts;
- a short-break holiday product, directly bookable through the Marketing Office, whose success would be measurable;
- proactive efforts to regain large conference business lost during the 1980s;

---

[5] In fairness to the many private hoteliers in the area who did their best to upgrade their facilities during the 1980s, it should be mentioned that the proportion of serviced rooms with ensuite facilities rose from 13% in 1987 to 36% in 1991 (TDC, 1991c: Appendix 3). While this effect was partly due to the attrition of poor-quality bedspaces, it also represents determined efforts by some hoteliers to match the requirements of the contemporary market.

- the transfer of all enquiries on to a computer database for future marketing usage, and to facilitate identification of new market segments through psychographic analysis;
- active partnerships with other industry operators such as Kent County Council, the English Tourist Board and the Royal Mail.

(TDC, 1990, 1991c)

Without exception, these and a range of other objectives were achieved. Although the author left his position in early 1992, the renewed proactive efforts to regain large conference business were to result in provisonal bookings totalling 16,000 delegate nights for 1993, four times the 1990 total. The short-break product was to generate 1000 bednights in its pilot year, and thereafter the same volume in the first quarter of the following year. The resort advertising campaign was to show year-on-year improvements in responses (see Table 3.2).

Table 3.2. Margate, Broadstairs and Ramsgate: responses to national advertising campaign.

	1990	1991	1992
to 26 March	12,391	18,741	Not available
to 30 April	Not available	20,478	22,137
to 2 November	16,156	26,080	Not available

Source: TDC 1991c: Appendix 5; Voase, 1992.

Some months later, in October of 1992, the relaunch project and its implementation was to attract the endorsement of the Chartered Institute of Marketing. However, this indicative success conceals a picture of ambivalence in the support by local politicians for the work. In fact, the more the renewed vigour with which the marketing of the resorts became apparent, the greater the reservations of some councillors. The widely-believed explanation at the time was that a change in political control following elections in May 1991 led inexorably to such an outcome, but the reality, it will be argued, was more complex. In the next section, the political circumstances will be summarized, and, in the discussion that follows, it will be proposed that the socio-economic culture of the Isle of Thanet, as reflected in local politics and accompanied by entrenched misunderstandings about the importance of tourism to the local economy, made continued ambivalence inevitable regardless of the parties and personalities in power.

The local political context

On the author's arrival in June 1990, the council was 'hung', with Independents as the largest group; the Leader of the Council was an Independent. The Independents were, broadly speaking, supportive of council intervention in tourism, but their confidence had been visibly shaken by the débâcle of the International Cartoon Festival. Many of the Independents were, in fact, conservative with a small 'c' and, in some cases, with a capital 'c', making cross-voting a likelihood on a whole range of issues. There were two Conservative groups, styled 'Official' and 'Reform', with a state of acrimony between them. Understanding the differing political orientations of the two Conservative groups is complex. Pickvance (1990: 180–181) suggests that on the vital topic of direct intervention in support of (for example) the tourism industry, those who were to become the 'official' group were anti-intervention, and those who were to become the 'reform' group were pro-intervention. The present author, from his own experience, sees the distinction as less clear-cut. Anecdotal information gleaned on arrival suggested that the differences between the groups had ceased to rest on policy differences and had become personal in nature. The personal differences are not material to this paper, except inasmuch as their existence in the abstract says something about the individualistic sociopolitical culture of the area, of which more shortly. There was also a Labour group, which had a paradoxical relationship with the concept of intervention. While pro-intervention in principle, this group was known to be opposed in some measure to intervention in support of the tourism industry. Whether this was because it perceived intervention in tourism to be of primary benefit to Conservative-voting business-owners, or whether it was rooted in an aversion to the non-unionized and casual nature of much employment in tourism, was unclear.

A series of key events from June 1990 to December 1991 will now be summarized. The Marketing Plan for tourism was approved by the council's policy committee in November 1990; remaining budgets for the current financial year were earmarked to projects, as were allocations for the following financial year. At the following meeting of the policy committee in February 1991, a surprise amendment moved by a member of the Official Conservatives and supported by some members of that group, and by some members of the Independents, removed 50% of the primary budgets for resort promotion, including the funds earmarked by the same committee 3 months earlier. This was not a 'cut' as such; the funds were moved sideways into a holding fund. The reasons offered by the proposer of this amendment involved the creation of a fund for which bids could be invited for a range of as yet unspecified projects, and the possible privatization of the resort marketing function. The author's response was, in so many words, that the situation in the industry required resolute implementation of the marketing plan, which had already been agreed, and that ideological experimentation was, in the pertaining circumstances, a luxury which could be ill-afforded. In May 1991, local elections delivered a radical change to the political make-up of the council: the Official Conservatives were returned with an absolute majority, the Independents were reduced to being the third largest group, and Labour became the second largest. No Reform Conservatives were returned to office. The councillor who had moved the removal of the marketing budgets 3 months earlier became Leader of the Council.

These circumstances initially looked unpromising. However, an excellent relationship was forged with the new Conservative chairman and vice-chairman of the council's leisure and tourism committee, and, following a series of persuasive presentations to the new Conservative members, the budgets removed under the auspices of that same group were, barely six months later, restored. However, in other respects there were some worrying signs. One of these involved the apparently continued belief, widely held, that conspicuous behaviour in the form of 'special events' was the key to regenerating tourism. Despite the recent failure of the International Cartoon Festival, 'event' ideas were common currency. Pains were taken by the author to explain that events only generated visitor nights for their duration, were costly and labour-intensive to organize, and risked causing long-term image problems if they failed (see Voase, 1995, 37–38 for a full appraisal). Special events had their place, but as a sequel to, rather than a substitute for, the initial process of relaunch and regeneration. The attachment to such ideas ran deeper than logic, and an attempt will be made to explain it in the discussion which now follows.

Local Culture and 'Entrepreneurial' Ideology

Arising out of the paper thus far, are three points which, amongst others, need to be addressed. First, there is the question of the importance of tourism in the local economy, and the misunderstanding which surrounded it. The clearer these facts became, the more uncomfortable the reaction in some quarters. These words are taken from the text of a presentation made by the author to newly elected council members in July 1991:

> I was astounded many times during the final months of the last Council. Making public the facts of tourism was, in the reaction of some members, rather like confronting a vampire with a crucifix. 'We don't want the £55m which we earn from tourism', was one reaction. It was very bold to say that. Well . . . very something.
> (R. N. Voase, Notes of the presentation by Richard Voase, Marketing Manager, at new council members' induction day. July 5, 1991)

It seemed that a greater sense of comfort was offered to some council members by a perception based on misunderstanding, than by the results of best efforts to uncover the meaningful facts. Second, there was the question of the attachment to attention-seeking behaviour in the form of 'special events' despite a highly conspicuous recent failure. Third, there is the apparent inconsistency in policy toward tourism.

To explore these issues and other issues raised by them, it is useful to refer to the work of Pickvance. Having established that the make-up of the local economy was significantly based on small business, and that many in-migrants had come to the area for the purpose of establishing such businesses, he concludes that the culture of the Isle of Thanet is one of individualism in which entrepreneurialism is lauded:

> . . . there is a local culture of individualism, enterprise and weak trade unionism, which is linked to its experience of small businesses (and above average

self-employment) and the lack of large employers.' (Pickvance, 1990: 167) . . . the typicality of non-unionized small firms and the under-representation of public sector employment help make Thanet culturally individualistic, rather than collectivistic. It is an area with a well-entrenched 'enterprise culture'. (Pickvance, 1990: 179)

Anecdotal endorsement of the salience of this entrepreneurial culture of the small-business variety remains in the mind of the author from a particular meeting of the council's leisure committee. Potential operators for a bar and catering franchise at a municipal leisure centre were being interviewed by members. The choice seemed to be between an established firm of locally based operators with collective expertise represented by a number of such interests, and an individual whose career had followed the path of a single self-reliant owner-operator. In the post-interview discussion, one councillor articulated his support for the single individual, 'because he is a small man' who will 'put his shirt on it'. Anecdotes should of course be treated with caution, but as a statement which was transparently ideological it was revealing.

Pickvance's work comfortably establishes the premise that the prevalent culture of Thanet is that of what might be termed the lower middle class, alternatively styled the *petite bourgeoisie*. It is worthwhile to summarize some observations as to what this means in terms of cultural outlook, using the observations of researchers in the field. (It is important to understand that these emerge as general character-istics; it is of course possible for any individual to exempt himself or herself from them by virtue of disposition, beliefs and deliberate choice). First, the personal ideology is typically 'distinctively illiberal'; the personal culture is closer to that of the working class, than to the middle class with educational qualifications, with the exception that the *petite bourgeoisie*, in contrast with the working class, is *aspirational* in disposition (Frow, 1993: 270). For example, typical newspaper reading would involve the right-of-centre mid-market tabloids, rather than the broadsheets favoured by the credentialled middle class, or the popular tabloids read by the working class. Second, the tortuous research of Pierre Bourdieu into tastes, lifestyles and class orientation discloses further dimensions to the culture of the lower middle class. The aspirational nature of this group leads them to

> . . . 'conceive the social world as *will and representation* . . . the petit bourgeois is inclined to a . . . *vision* of the social world, reducing it to a theatre in which being is never more that *perceived* being, a mental representation of a theatrical performance.' (Bourdieu, 1984: 253, my emphasis)

However, the aspirations and 'vision of the social world' of the *petit bourgeois* are not performed on a large stage, but, like the aspirations of the 'small man' in the anecdote, 'writ small' (Bourdieu, 1984: 338). This is accompanied by rejection of the cultivated pursuits of the traditional middle class (the 'professions') and, espe-cially, the 'liberated tastes' of the *new petite bourgeoisie*, mentioned earlier in this paper and styled the 'service class' (Bourdieu, 1984: 350–351). This paradoxical combination of active aspiration, yet active rejection of the cultural adaptations of other middle-class groupings who possess greater educational and professional credentials than themselves, leads to a predilection to opinionation:

> To explain the petit-bourgeois pretension to 'personal opinion', one has to consider
> . . . the specific social conditions which produce the 'opinionated' habitus. It can be
> seen that the claim to the right to 'personal opinion' and distrust of all forms of
> delegation, especially in politics, have their logical place in the disposition system of
> individuals whose whole past and whole projected future are orientated towards
> individual salvation, based on personal 'gifts' and 'merits' . . . (Bourdieu, 1984: 415)

In the light of these observations, one fact becomes immediately clear: it would be impossible to avoid, in the Isle of Thanet, a collision between the culture of the area based on small business and small business values, and the necessity for the local authority to work contrary to those values by intervening economically to ensure the continued health of those very businesses (see Pickvance, 1990: 170). One can speculate that, during the heyday of tourism, the economic interests of the whole community were so clearly defined by tourism that this paradox did not become an issue. However, as the economy of the area has diversified since the 1950s (Buck *et al.*, 1989) and the dependence on tourism has lessened, the *laissez-faire* values of entrepreneurial culture, encouraged no doubt by the political culture at national level in Britain during the 1980s, increasingly challenged the precepts of municipal intervention. It is indeed a valid challenge; the question to what extent municipal funds should continue to be expended to support a declining industry is surely a legitimate issue.

Unfortunately, a rational treatment of the issue was complicated by a number of other factors. First, as mentioned earlier, there was the problem of objectifying the precise nature of the problem: is tourism dead, or is it a national growth industry? If it is growing, can the Isle of Thanet be part of that growth? Second, there was the transformation of tourism into a 'perceived' rather than real world, a stage upon which political rivalries could be enacted, rather than a generator of real incomes for real people. Third, there was the deep suspicion of other middle-class groupings who were equipped with educational and cultural credentials. The answer to the problem of tourism did not lie in the methodical application of tested marketing principles. Rather, the views of persons of claimed business success, however 'writ small', were to be taken seriously: salvation was gained through 'shirt-on-it' inspiration. Hence, it must be supposed, the continued interest in special events, despite past failures. The aspiration of the community as a whole, so it seemed, drove it urgently to seek means of self-actualization. To stage a conspicuous special event, that is to throw a party to convince oneself of one's home area's respectability on the wider stage, says more about the communal psychology of the area than about the merits of special events as useful regeneration tools. Fourth, the culture of the Isle of Thanet was one in which, as has been argued, perceived visions of the social world supplanted reality, and opinion was transcendent. In such circumstances, political populism is a not unsurprising outcome; again, the ubiquitous attachment to the concept of the 'special event' becomes clearer. Six months following the author's departure, this was seen in the pages of *The Stage* newspaper:

> There are fireworks in Thanet this summer – but unfortunately not at the box office.

Pyrotechnics have been introduced because . . . Thanet Council's policy committee (was told) . . . that the state of the area was turning tourists away . . . Hence the free firework displays in Margate and Broadstairs. (Evans, 1992)

Accompanying the introduction of pyrotechnics as compensation for the low quality of the resort environment was an effort to recreate the Isle of Thanet's cultural roots in the form of a 'Cockney Festival'. To see tourism as a vehicle for conspicuous display, in which the concept of activity in the form of visible spectacle becomes conflated and confused with the concept of progress, is a variant of the ancient Roman formula of 'bread and circuses', directed, one could suggest, at locals rather than at tourists.

Agents of ideological paradox

There are three other issues which are arguably of importance in discussing this case: the role of the new 'service' economy in the area, the role of service-class discourse in placing seaside resorts at the margins of fashionability, and the means by which ideologies, as fundamental cultural precepts, are transmitted. They shall be dealt with in turn. An important feature was the development of a new service economy: residential homes for the elderly. Like the optimistic possibilities for tourism directed at the growing family formation group, a study of demographic change revealed residential care to be a similarly promising growth market: the numbers of retired were due to rise substantially as a proportion of the population between 1985 and 1995 (*Marketing*, 1989). Buck *et al.* (1989: 181) show an increase in the numbers in residential accommodation in Thanet, which rose within 4 years from 1654 in 1981 to just over 2000 in 1985. The turnover of this new industry in the mid-1980s was estimated at £20m, of which £7.5m was sourced in public-sector welfare contributions on behalf of the elderly clients. Other new forms of residential accommodation which appeared concurrently were hostels for people with special needs, and for the young unemployed who relocated from the inland conurbations. Crucially, these new industries grew up in the debris of tourism, in that they used redundant tourist accommodation. In one sense, the residential care industry could be said to have a vested interest in the active decline of tourism, because its decline would ensure the release, at favourable prices, of former hotel buildings suitable for the new application. However, the initial pattern of development involved the hoteliers themselves and their attempts to gain an income from otherwise unfilled beds. As Thanet Council's then Chief Executive put it:

the realization that a regular and often enhanced rent could be gained because of a person's demand on the DHSS (Department of Health and Social Security) has resulted in some   resort proprietors even advertising in large cities to attract the unemployed to their area . . . there has been a considerable change of use of tourist accommodation and . . . the greater the number of unemployed, handicapped and elderly in an area, the less the likelihood for an innovative approach to lead the town forward into the current demands of tourism. (Gill, 1986: 4)

The 'likelihood' of problems engendered for tourism by these developments arguably has a demand-side and a supply-side dimension. On the demand-side, the
holidaymaker is the transient visitor, rather than the elderly resident or the DHSS
boarder. It is the tourist who will retreat from any conflict of interest. For example,
the model C2 family, the growth market for seaside tourism, would think carefully
before staying in an area inhabited, on the one hand, by the elderly and infirm,
and, on the other hand, by long-term young unemployed and associated lifestyles.
On the supply-side, economic interests in the new service economy inevitably feed
into the politics of the area. Although, in principle, conservative politics with both
a small and big 'c' respect entrepreneurship regardless of the field of business, it
must be supposed that this conflict of interest over the environment must be an
issue when, for example, planning applications for change of use of premises are to
be considered, or when the whole question of municipal intervention in support
of tourism is at stake.

Second, the role of what was has been termed the 'service-class discourse' needs
to be considered. Thrift (1989: 22) has argued that the influence of service-class
culture, in which the refined and tasteful are privileged over the supposedly vulgar,
has achieved hegemonic status, particularly in the south-east of England. This of
course is where the Isle of Thanet is located. In a revealing feature in the *Guardian*,
arguably the primary newspaper of the liberal intelligentsia, Broadstairs is described
as 'the perfect bayside experience', presumably because it has escaped Dionysian
development, such as amusement arcades, and thus accords with the service-class
tastes of that newspaper, its readership and journalists. Elsewhere, the journalist
encountered a contrasting attitude:

> Following my first taste of Broadstairs, a rather wearying pair of Canterbury snobs, in
> whose oast house I had the misfortune to be staying, poured cold water on my
> enthusiasm by constantly applying the term 'Thanet' to the area as a perjorative that
> was, I presume, supposed to sum up its sorry proletarian plight. So extreme was their
> dismissal of the place . . . (Thanet) . . . was just . . . a blighted outcrop in the estuary
> that was best forgotten. (Anthony, 1994)

As suggested earlier, 'good taste' needs 'vulgarity' in order to be seen as good taste.
A proper survey of the nature of the service-class discourse surrounding seaside
resorts would require a rigorous content analysis of coverage in key newspapers
over a period of years, and lies beyond the intended scope of the present paper.
Typically, however, comment is habitually dismissive, and, if complimentary, is
grudging:

> For children it's a treat, as my own three would testify . . . 'Crummy and
> cockneyfied?' Depends what you're looking for. In the name of fascinations both
> sincere and morbid, I shall make it back. The English can be weird like that. (Hill,
> 1993)

> Seaside towns are being urged to refurbish their heritage . . . Will the clean-up extend
> to tidying up the social casualties who flock to the coast, as well as to the municipal
> fixtures and fittings? . . . much of the criticism in a study called Turning the Tide by
> the English Tourist Board is directed at the Kent coast – Margate, Ramsgate and

Broadstairs in particular. It highlights garish advertising on buildings as a contributory factor in their demise. (Johnson, 1993)

Third, there follows an attempt to speculate on the way in which public discourse of this kind influences the self-perception of a community such as that of the Isle of Thanet.

A useful theoretical paradigm to apply at this point is the concept of 'interpellation' as advanced by Louis Althusser (1992). Very briefly, the idea is that ideologies, far from being solely definable as a structured set of beliefs promoted by a state or institution, are ubiquitous. So ubiquitous and so obvious are they, that they are invisible. The whole of life is subjected to and permeated with, in my own term used earlier, fundamental cultural precepts. According to Althusser, ideologies 'hail' or 'interpellate' us when we least expect it. We may consider ourselves free-thinking subjects, but without conscious reflection we can be interpellated and subjected by ideology at any time. Take, for example, the anecdote from the committee meeting related earlier. To favour a candidate because he is a 'small man' who would 'put his shirt on it' is an ideological statement. To respond with a murmur approval for this sentiment, or to remain silent instead of pointing out what is really at stake, is to be *subjected* by the ideology. In this way, the 'culture' of a community is established and circulated, invisibly, permeating discourse and debate everywhere: on the street, in the works canteen, and in the council chamber.

In the case of the Isle of Thanet, the 'entrepreneurialism' and the privileging of the small business ethic in the form of the uncredentialled 'small man' was the defining feature of the culture of the area. However, this culture was itself open to two wider influences: first, a national discourse, inspired by the national politics of the day, which at that time favoured economic individualism and entrepreneurship; and, second, another national discourse, that of the service-class values, in which cultural individualism, educational credentials and the achievement of distinction through demonstration of good taste were the markers of individualism. Of the two, the second was, according to Thrift (1989), hegemonic and hence dominant. The multidimensional paradox in the Isle of Thanet was a struggle between two service industries, tourism and residential care, both cited as successful examples of entrepreneurial behaviour, yet subsisting on state subvention: municipal intervention in the case of the former, DHSS funds in the latter. The entrepreneurial self-sufficiency of private sector businesses in both the tourism and residential care/DHSS accommodation sectors, and the ideological cornerstone of the culture of the Isle of Thanet, was in this sense an illusion.

Conclusion

In the face of these multidimensional contradictions, it is hardly surprising that political leadership in the Isle of Thanet was inconsistent. It was pulled in different directions by the paradox of an entrepreneurial economy dependent on public subvention, and a communal ideology opposed to it. This explains the lack of support in the field of tourist destination marketing. Faced with an occluded vision of what valid objectives were, and paradoxical ideologies as to what the appropriate municipal role should be, ambivalence is the inevitable outcome. The words of the council's chief executive, cited earlier, suggest that by the mid-1980s when the words were written, he had already come to that conclusion. The preoccupation with special events can be attributed to the opinionation associated with *petit bourgeois* culture, and the need for individual and communal self-actualization in the face of multiple pressures. Out of the content of this chapter, I summarize the following five points which act as markers in my analysis:

1. At national level, financial pressure from an authoritarian government created simultaneously a problem and a role model for the municipality of the Isle of Thanet and its entrepreneurial culture.
2. The problems of the tourism industry were occluded by misunderstanding/ignorance of the facts, misattribution of decline to climatic factors, and subjection to the ideology of 'good' taste which marginalized seaside tourism.
3. Entrepreneurial ideology was opposed to intervention, but small tourism businesses relied on intervention. 'Conservatives' faced a choice between enacting their ideology, and opposing the interests of small business.
4. Service-class discourse marginalized seaside tourism, but lower middle-class culture is aspirational. Subjected by service-class ideology, entrepreneurs lost confidence in their own product.
5. The new service economy, based on residential care and hostelry for special needs cases and the unemployed, competed with tourism for the common environment. The needs of these, and tourists, are mutually exclusive.

As Buck *et al.* (1989: 196) stated, somewhat pessimistically at the conclusion of their study of the Isle of Thanet:

> ... this (study) has suggested how the history of one such place leads to the build-up of political as well as economic impediments to restructuring: indeed, an economy based on small businesses, private services and disorganized labour seems to be incapable of restructuring itself.

To return to the purpose of this contribution, as set out in the introduction, the process of policy, planning and development of tourism in a mature destination such as the Isle of Thanet is not straightforward. Local lore in the Isle of Thanet was apt to regard their elected representatives in the time period covered by this case as lacking in capability; the idiosyncracies of the local politics of the area were blamed for apparent failure. As has been shown, those local politics were themselves the product of the interaction between a distinctive local social and economic culture, and two prevailing national cultures which were themselves, ideologically speaking, mutually antagonistic. Particular individuals and groupings, while displaying all the opinionation and aspiration associated with *petit bourgeois* culture, are revealed to be 'subjected' rather than 'subjects', leading to consequences which are tantamount to being deterministically predictable.

Epilogue

Although the purpose of this contribution has been to identify explanations for events which occurred during a set time period, it would perhaps be inappropriate to conclude without an update on progress in the Isle of Thanet. First, the effects of the various forms of inmigration, and disillusion with local Conservative leadership, finally manifested itself in the ballot box: of the c. 70 seats on Thanet Council, only three Conservatives were returned in the May 1995 local elections. The Labour Party acquired a substantial overall majority. Second, a new form of legitimacy appeared in the form of full recognition from the national government of the area's regeneration needs. Development area status was given to the area in 1994, making available financial incentives from national and European Union sources for businesses to locate in the area, and for other economic regeneration measures (Halsall, 1993). What is interesting, from the perspective taken in this paper, is the way the change was represented by an officer working on tourism development initiatives for a partnership body called the East Kent Initiative, whose purview included the Thanet area. Alluding to the problems of decline and the failure to address them, the officer stated that it was 'impossible to quantify the extent of the decline in Margate, due to a lack of local research ... There is renewed hope, however', and went on to pose the question as to whether the community of Thanet could embrace the opportunity offered by the new entitlement to state and European intervention (Curtis, 1997). The charge of lack of local research is, as evidenced in this paper, unsustainable. Whether it is altogether wise to dismiss the past and count the arrival of development area status as a 'year zero' is debatable, but the implication that the arrival of national and European intervention is the sole grounds for optimism is probably correct. Much rested, wrote the official, on the ability of the Thanet community to make use of the opportunities on offer. History has shown that European states associated with economic success in recent decades, such as Germany and France, have owed that success not to *laissez-faire* liberalism but to state apparatuses which are actively interventionist in identifying and supporting investment and growth in key sectors of the economy (Leys, 1985: 24). Whether the community of the Isle of Thanet can adjust its communal culture to the acceptance of this reality, and acknowledge the failure of the *petit bourgeois* individualist ideal, remains to be seen.

Acknowledgement

I would like to thank my colleague Mike Walton for his reading of the first draft of this chapter and for his useful suggestions.

References

Althusser, L. (1992) Ideology and ideological state apparatuses. In: Easthope, A. and McGowan, K. *A Critical and Cultural Theory Reader.* Open University Press, Buckingham, pp. 50–58.

Anthony, A. (1994) The last resort. *Observer Life,* 13 March, pp. 28–30.

Battersby, D. (1990) Lifting the barriers: employment and training in tourism and leisure. *Insights* 1, D7-1–D7-8. English Tourist Board, London.

Beioley, S. (1991) Short holidays. *Insights* 3, B-7, B-29–B-38. English Tourist Board, London.

Bishop Associates (1987) *Thanet Tourism: the Way Forward.* Bishop Associates, Canterbury.

Bourdieu, P. (1984) *Distinction: a Social Critique of the Judgement of Taste.* Routledge, London.

Britton, S. (1991) Tourism, capital, and place: towards a critical geography of tourism. *Environment and Planning* 9, 451–178.

Brown, P. (1995) Cultural capital and social exclusion: some observations on recent trends in education, employment and the labour market. *Work, Employment and Society* 9 (1), 29–51.

Buck, N., Gordon, I., Pickvance, C. and Taylor-Gooby, P. (1989) The Isle of Thanet: Restructuring and municipal conservatism. In: Cooke, P. (ed.) *Localities: the Changing Face of Urban Britain.* Unwin Hyman, London.

Burgess, T. (1980) Accountability makes councillors good accountants. *Guardian,* 14 July.

Butler, R. (1980) The concept of a tourist area cycle of evolution: implications for management of resources. *Canadian Geographer* XXIV (1), 5–12.

Butler, T. (1995) The debate over the middle classes. In: Butler, T. and Savage, M. (eds) *Social Change and the Middle Classes.* UCL Press, London, pp. 26–36.

CSO (Central Statistical Office) (1993) *Social Trends 23.* HMSO (Her Majesty's Stationery Office), London.

Curtis, S. (1997) Seaside resorts: Spanish progress and British malaise. *Insights* 9, C9–C18, September. English Tourist Board, London.

Eastbourne Borough Council (1991) *Eastbourne Tourism Study 1990.* Eastbourne BC, Eastbourne.

ETB (English Tourist Board) (1992) *Shorelines.* English Tourist Board, London.

Eurostat (1992) *Tourism in Europe: Trends 1989.* Eurostat, Brussels.

Evans, B. (1992) Bill Evans looks at the vibrant scene in . . . Margate, Ramsgate and Broadstairs. *The Stage and Television Today,* 20 August.

Featherstone, M. (1991) *Consumer Culture and Postmodernism.* Sage, London.

Frow, J. (1993) Knowledge and class. *Cultural Studies* 7 (2), 240–281.

Gill, I. (1986) Tourism and entertainment services in local government. *The Future Role and Organization of Local Government,* Functional study no. 4, Leisure Working Paper 4.6. Institute of Local Government Studies, Birmingham.

Greenstreet, R. (1994) The questionnaire: Ronnie Biggs. *Guardian Weekend,* 5 February.

Halsall, M. (1993) Once-rich South moves up the queue for aid hand-out. *Guardian,* 24 July, p. 8.

Henley Centre for Forecasting (1989) *Leisure Futures.* Henley Centre for Forecasting, London.

Hill, D. (1993) Mayday for May Bank Holiday. *Guardian,* 1 May.

Johnson, A. (1993) Victorian values washed up on the seashore. *Guardian,* 9 August, p. 16.

Leys, C. (1985) Thatcherism and British manufacturing: a question of hegemony. *New Left Review* 151, 5–25.

Lumley, R. (ed.) (1988) *The Museum Time-Machine*. Comedia/Routledge, London.

Marketing (1989) *Marketing Guide 3: Demographics*. 5 January.

Meethan, K. (1996) Place, image and power: Brighton as a resort. In: Selwyn, T. (ed.) *The Tourist Image: Myths and Myth-Making in Tourism*. John Wiley and Sons, London.

MEW Research (1992) Holiday destination choice survey 1991. *Insights* 4, A-17–A36, July. English Tourist Board, London.

Middleton, V. (1989) Seaside resorts. *Insights* 1, B5-1–B5-19. English Tourist Board, London.

Middleton, V. (1991) *The Future for England's Smaller Seaside Resorts: Summary Report*. English Tourist Board, London.

Middleton, V. (1995) The leaky bucket syndrome: is there a need to reassess policy priorities? *Insights* 7, A1–A8, July. English Tourist Board, London.

Nichols, G. (1995) Contract specification in leisure management. *Local Government Studies* 21 (2), 248–262.

Pickvance, C. (1990) Council economic intervention and political conflict in a declining resort: the Isle of Thanet. In: Harloe, C., Pickvance, C. and Urry, J. (eds) *Place, Policy and Politics: Do Localities Matter?* Unwin Hyman, London.

TDC (Thanet District Council) (1990) *Marketing Plan for Tourism Services: November 1990*. TDC, Margate.

TDC (Thanet District Council) (1991a) *Kent's Leisure Coast Holidaymaker Survey 1991*. TDC, Margate.

TDC (Thanet District Council) (1991b) *Kent's Leisure Coast Tourism: the Key Facts*, 1st edition, January TDC, Margate.

TDC (Thanet District Council) (1991c) *Draft Marketing Plan Update: November 1991*. TDC, Margate.

TDC (Thanet District Council) (1992) *Kent's Leisure Coast: the Holidaymaker's Guide to Margate, Broadstairs and Ramsgate*. TDC, Margate.

Thrift, N. (1989) Images of social change. In: Hamnett, C., McDowell, L. and Sarre, D. (eds) *The Changing Social Structure*. Sage, London.

Tourism Society/DoE (1992) *Joint Industry Committee for Tourism Statistics (JICTOURS) 1991/2: Report of the Working Group*. Tourism Society/DoE, London.

Travis, P. (1992) The seaside fights back. *Insights* 4, C-9–C-18. English Tourist Board, London.

Urry, J. (1988) Cultural change and contemporary holiday-making. *Theory, Culture and Society* 5, 35–55.

Urry, J. (1990) *The Tourist Gaze*. Sage, London.

Urry, J. (1996) Cultural change and the seaside resort. In: Williams, A. and Shaw, G. (eds) *The Rise and Fall of British Coastal Tourism*. Cassell, London.

Voase, R.N. (1992) The relaunch of the Kent's leisure coast resorts of Ramsgate, Broadstairs and Margate as a tourist destination. Dissertation produced for the Chartered Institute of Marketing.

Voase, R.N. (1995) *Tourism: the Human Perspective*. Hodder and Stoughton, London.

Walsh-Heron, J. (1988) Bradford: the myth-breakers? *Leisure Management*, February.

Wheen, F. (1999) Blood, sweat and carbuncles. *Guardian Weekend*, 10 October, pp. 10–18.

Re-planning for Tourism in a Mature Destination: a Note on Mallorca

4

Marco Antonio Robledo[1] and Julio Batle[2]

School of Tourism, University of the Balearic Islands, Palma, Mallorca

Introduction

The product life cycle concept (Butler, 1980) has been extensively applied by marketing practitioners to interpret product and market dynamics. This model suggests that a product follows a cycle akin to that of a living being: birth, growth, maturity and decline, finishing with the death of the product. The sales pattern of the product is projected to change over time, normally following an S-shaped curve, allowing different marketing strategies to be applied according to the stage in which the product is located. The model has been commonly applied to tourist destinations; the Balearic Islands are certainly in the mature stage of their development. The challenge for a mature destination such as the Balearics is to maintain its attractiveness for the tourist and thus to ensure its continued life and success.

The Balearics are a good example of prime raw material for tourism development, coupled with the negative consequences of such development. An archipelago blessed by sun and nature has been affected by overdevelopment in parts of its territory. Indeed, 'balearization' has come to mean coastlines of concrete, land speculation, 'theme parks for lager louts' and, to a lesser extent, the loss of indigenous culture and identity. Luckily, the more-affected areas are localized in very specific spots and some of them can be retrieved, though not without effort. A sustainable development strategy is necessary for the survival of such a mature destination. Such a strategy's typical components should combine sensible planning, care for the environment, and concern for the forthcoming generations. Sustainable tourism tries therefore to harmonize economic interests with ecological, social and cultural ones, as stated in the first article of the *Charter for Sustainable Tourism*, the result of the World Conference on Sustainable Tourism held in 1995 in Lanzarote:

> Tourism development shall be based on criteria of sustainability, which means that it
> must be ecologically bearable in the long term, economically viable, as well as
> ethically and socially equitable for the local communities. Sustainable development is
> a guided process which envisages global management of resources so as to ensure
> their viability, thus enabling our natural and cultural capital to be preserved.

The Balearics need a model of sustainable development, especially if we keep in mind that their long-term survival as a tourism destination will depend on how well preserved is their environment. Tourism's economic importance is substantial, accounting for more than 60% of GNP (Robledo, 1995: 42). Quoting again the *Charter for Sustainable Tourism*, in its 11th article we read: '. . . special treatment should be given to spaces that have been degraded by obsolete and high impact tourism models'. However, the success of any treatment will be the result of the commitment, participation, and cooperation of all the different actors involved: central government, local government, tourism companies and population; in a nutshell: everybody. Some initiatives have been taken and the results can already be seen. Probably the most ambitious one is the subject of this chapter.

The Need for Action

There is a high level of consensus on the need to carry out a reconstruction of the tourism sector in the Balearic Islands, and also on the diagnosis of the problems which make this necessary. The overdevelopment of the tourism supply-side, the deterioration of the environment and the in many cases obsolescent infrastructure of the hotel industry are problems patent and obvious to everyone. It is difficult to find any disagreement in the evaluation of these problems and their negative repercussions as far as the economic development of the islands is concerned. When we talk of the Balearics' tourism industry, we have to bear in mind that we are dealing with a mass-tourism model that, by general agreement, has outgrown its capacity and has reached its point of saturation. The consequences of this are the down-market positioning of the product, and the price wars that over-supply brings about. The well-known axiom that 'tourism poisons itself in small doses' comes to mind and appears to be very well founded when we glimpse at many tourism resorts throughout the Balearics, such as Magalluf, Cala Major, El Arenal, etc.

The term 'balearization' is, shamefully for us, used abroad when referring to chaotic and destructive tourism development. The economic and environmental imbalances, quite apart from the social and cultural ones, which are generated as a result of this anarchic pattern of development are so serious that perhaps it would be advisable to approach the question with a more comprehensive focus. To change or revise the development model for the Balearics becomes imperative. This is a historic challenge for the islands today. It is not a matter of ethics; it is a matter of business and marketing. The resources making up the Balearics' attractiveness are mainly natural, and stand in need of conservation if their power of attraction is not to diminish. In particular, it would be desirable to provide holistic and integrat-ive solutions that could secure the prosperity of the region through a process of rationalization or rearrangement in the industry, adopting a long-term strategic approach and aiming not only at economic goals such as revenues and job creation, but also at a series of parallel goals such as the sustainability of the tourism attractiveness. In other words, we are talking about public tourism planning that develops frameworks for sustainable tourism development. The following may be worthy objectives:

Protection:	Preservation and sustainable use of resources and physical environment.
Defence:	Development of territorial and environment policies and legislation.
Conservation:	Minimization and rationalization in the consumption of natural resources as well as in the generation of waste.
Rehabilitation:	Recuperation of areas affected by the negative and degrading effects of tourism.

These are interventions which not only can entail no negative interference in the market dynamics, but actually will bring about a better match between supply and demand in the long term. This is the intention behind the governmental action which was taken: to re-arrange and order the tourism supply-side. It is a process which calls for a series of joint actions:

1. Restrictive space planning policy.
2. Protection and conservation of landscapes, coastline and environment.
3. Fostering of the tourism products and agents capable of attracting a more up-market tourist demand.
4. Provision of infrastructure in accordance with the up-market tourist demand.

Pla de Ordenació de l'Oferta Turística ('POOT')

The *Pla de Ordenació de l'Oferta Turística* ('POOT'), translatable as 'Tourism Supply-side Regulation Plan' is a decree of the Tourism Ministry of the Balearics Island Government approved on 6 April 1995, aimed at regulating the tourist industry supply according to the decision taken by the Balearics Parliament in February 1989 (Llei General Turística, 1999). It is also encompassed in the recent General Tourism Law, an enactment aimed at regulating all the different elements of the tourism industry. It is an ongoing project of the Balearics Government whose approval has taken more than 6 years. It is regarded by most people involved in the tourism industry as an imperative for Mallorca that could not be the subject of further procrastination. The hoteliers' association has criticized the delay in approving this plan, arguing that since 1980 some kind of regulation over the tourism supply-side was necessary. During this period, *c.* 200,000 new bedspaces have appeared (Aguiló *et al.*, 1996: 36).

The essential goal of POOT is to regulate all the activities that may have an effect on the tourism supply-side. This regulation is based on the recognition of the need to preserve the environment and also on the desirability of developing an integral tourism planning in order to attain a better, upgraded and more quality-oriented tourist supply. At the moment, POOT only applies to Mallorca, but soon the other Balearic Islands will have their own plan. The fact that POOT is a very ambitious and complicated project has deferred its promulgation for a very long time. The long-awaited and repeatedly demanded POOT had its first legislative antecedent in June of 1984, when the Tourism Ministry of the Balearic Government approved a decree that was known as Cladera I after the Conseller's name. One year earlier, the Statute of Autonomy for the Balearic Islands had been proclaimed, by means of which tourism matters, including tourism planning and territorial and infrastructure planning, became competencies of the autonomous region.

This Cladera I decree was very brief. Its main feature was the requirement for 30 square metres of land for every new tourist bed. It also required the use of part of the land for leisure purposes. This regulation is a landmark in the history of the tourism industry in the Balearics and the first serious attempt to rationalize the industry. However, the tourism supply-side kept on growing considerably, to such an extent that in 1987 the Tourism Conselleria finally made the decision to enact another decree, Cladera II, which derogates Cladera I and increases the required land per tourist bed from 30 to 60 square metres. In addition, it decrees that new hotels should have either 4 or 5 stars (3 or more keys for tourism apartments). In the preface to this decree, it is declared that the tool to restructure the tourism industry should be POOT. This is the first formal recognition and commitment by the government of the need to develop some kind of integrative and comprehensive regulation.

The Cladera II Decree had a very important flaw: its contents were made public too early. Therefore, before its formal approval, there was an avalanche of applications for building permissions that did not suit the Cladera II requirements, but which had to be granted. Thus, the initial effect of Cladera II was to achieve just the opposite of what was intended. This led to some disappointing consequences in terms of the built environment.

The implementation of POOT has been lengthy and intricate, and many political barriers had to be overcome. The most important was, arguably, the lack of real political willingness by the conservative Government, in power in the Balearics since 1983, to enact POOT to its fullest extent. However, it was an established political promise and there was a lot of pressure from the industry, especially from the Hoteliers' Association, to implement it. Added to that, the minister for tourism, Jaume Cladera, was the main advocate of POOT. This led to conflict with some other colleagues in government. When, in summer 1994, Jaume Cladera was replaced by a new minister, Joan Flaquer, his departure was to a large extent due to disputes and disagreement with the president of the government, Cañellas, on the POOT issue. Many people thought that POOT was finally dead and would not proceed. However, the implementation process continued, and the analysis of the comments offered by different tourist and political agents, such as political parties, councils, and industry associations, made after the first public information stage of POOT in 1992, was completed. Some minor legal modifications were introduced.

So, in November 1993 the new, lighter blueprint of POOT was again put before the public for consultation, to give the tourist organizations a chance to make some more comments prior to its final enactment. Many comments, circa 90, were made, the tourism ministry analysed them, and changes in the legislation were made accordingly. The definitive text was presented and the Council of Mallorca rejected it. The Spanish Minister of Tourism declared his dissatisfaction with the new POOT, since he thought construction criteria dominated at the expense of tourism criteria. Despite all that, POOT received its assent on 6 April, 1995. A long process had ended, and another was about to begin.

POOT: the Details

POOT is intended to be the cornerstone of tourism planning, but around it there are several previous regulations that are complementary to and consistent with it:

- The Territorial Planning Law.
- The Natural Spaces Law.
- The Embellishment Law.
- The Hotel Modernization Law.
- The Complementary Supply Law.
- The Coasts Law.

According to POOT, and in order to develop a tourism development plan for Mallorca, the island was divided into 37 different areas. These are solely coastal areas which are zones of tourist visitation. The reason of the division is to assign different ratios, measures and actions for tourist resorts that are, in some cases, very different. Each of these areas has been analysed and, in accordance with the analysis, specific solutions have been suggested.

How is tourism planning implemented in this case? The measures comprised with POOT are as follows:

1. Optimum ratios

POOT defines the value of different ratios that the 37 areas should observe. These ratios refer to the provision or supply of:

- green, open areas and gardens;
- public services;
- beach areas;
- communications;
- drinking water;
- water disposal;

- other infrastructure and public services;
- parking areas;
- sports areas;
- sanitary services.

Some of these ratios have been calculated specifically for some of the areas, taking into account their particularities, whereas others have a general nature. Among the latter, we can highlight the following:

Population density:

- For areas with existing planning permissions for 100 inhabitants per hectare;
- for areas with no existing permissions, the ratio is only 60 inhabitants per hectare;
- a building capitation of 35 square metres per inhabitant;
- beach provision of 7.5 square metres per user.

One very controversial aspect is the definition of minimum surface for single-family and multiple-occupancy houses. That has been eliminated in the final draft for areas with planning permissions already approved. In other areas, new housing or residential developments will require 800 square metres for single-family houses and 1000 square metres for multiple-occupancy ones, with an intensity index of one house per 125 square metres. Also, there is a limit in terms of storeys: three for single-family houses, four for multiple-occupancy houses; for parking provision; and maximum volume: 2100 square metres for single-family, 8000 square metres for multiple-occupancy.

Altogether, these ratios define the degree of saturation that is allowed for each area and, on that account, also the opportunities for further development in each area, by comparing the existing circumstances and optimum ratios.

2. Discontinuity strip areas

In order to prevent neighbouring tourist resorts merging into one, discontinuity areas ('green belts') have been created. They will be lateral strips, located between the limits of different tourist areas, with special legislative protection. The intention is to prevent connections between resorts. In other words, it is intended to avoid the creation of macro-resorts. If this connection already has taken place, disqualification of properties/land and purchase of it by the government is decreed.

3. Hinterland protection areas

In order to prevent urban development expanding backwards and, in doing so, creating third, fourth, fifth or even more hotel lines, which would increasingly saturate the demand on beaches, equipment and infrastructure, a strip of at least

500 m is created, situated behind the tourist resort. This strip, like the discontinuity strip, will also enjoy legislative protection.

4. Provision reserve

In addition to the hinterland protection areas and located just behind them, another protection area is defined. Its extent will be dependent on the particular circumstances of each of the 37 zones. This strip of land will consist of public property, in particular council-owned property, and will be available for development in order to create the required sanitary services, park areas etc. In this sense, it will be a cushion area that can be very helpful in reducing the congestion of the existing resorts.

5. New establishments

Additionally, POOT defines the conditions which new tourism establishments have to fulfil in terms of:

- minimum total surface per bed (60 m^2);
- minimum surface for sporting activities per bed;
- parking per bed (3 m^2);
- green areas per bed;
- swimming pool cubic meterage per bed;
- maximum height (four storeys).

Each new establishment will have a minimum total land area of 12,000 m^2. In addition, no further establishments will be allowed to be built up within a 600 m coastal strip, in order to prevent additional congestion.

All these conditions can be even more restrictive in some areas, depending upon the existing degree of saturation in the tourism resorts.

Discussion

POOT will enjoy automatic validity for all the towns and villages within the designated areas. Town planning will have to be adapted to POOT, incorporating its ratios and other provisions. It means that the local councils lose, in part, their powers to regulate development; this, not surprisingly, is a very important topic of discussion. POOT in its first article asserts explicitly that, considering tourism is, and will be, the engine that drives the Balearic economy, its enhancement has to be a priority in any territorial planning which could exert some kind of influence on the tourism supply. This appears quite sensible, but regrettably is not wholly or entirely accepted by the different interest groups in the island. The old adage that 'the interests, not the ideas, act as the real barrier among people' is seen to be validated.

Actually, POOT is a very interesting case of struggle between different groups to defend their interests and positions: government, ecological groups, councils, hoteliers and the construction industry. The latter, which represents an extremely important lobby in the conservative Government, was initially regarded as very 'unenthusiastic' about POOT, since the building of new hotels would be severely limited. In the event, the government has been less demanding in terms of restrictions on new building. This is regarded by the hoteliers' association as a concession to the construction lobby.

For the local councils, POOT is also negative because they will have to adapt their territorial planning to it, losing power as well as potential revenues because of the planning permissions that in future they will not be able to grant, taking into account the new restrictions that POOT introduces. Probably for this reason, the new minister excluded the requirements and minimum ratios that in the first blueprint were contemplated for the residential constructions in areas with permissions already approved. It seems that some compromise was necessary to reach an agreement.

However, in December 1993, there were some declarations by the General Director of Tourism Planning of the Conselleria, Bartomeu Sbert, that are very significant and, in our opinion, very appropriate and based on good reason: the essence of POOT, or of any tourism planning, should not be the result of any political balance or accord. In the case of Mallorca, to remove the ambitious and important points from POOT would jeopardize the future of the industry, since its future is very much dependent on POOT. The opposition in parliament also criticized concessions to the pressure from the construction lobby, and the lack of deadlines for the demolition of obsolete accommodation buildings.

A very important aspect of this kind of regulation is that it risks being ineffective when publication and implementation are separated by a substantial time period. As mentioned earlier, the Cladera II decree was an example of this. Now with POOT there is political willingness to avoid this effect. In March 1993, Cladera still being the minister, a decree that anticipated the POOT density ratios was enacted, which required applications for new hotels to meet the anticipated POOT criteria. Applications accounting for more than 20,000 tourist beds were refused, since none fulfilled the POOT requirements. In line with this, a moratorium for new planning permissions was decreed in September 1993. The moratorium ceased once POOT was enacted.

The cost of the project has been estimated as 60 billion pesetas, which includes the cost of land reclassification, development of green areas and infrastructure (between 20 and 36 billion pesetas needed for infrastructure investment), renovations of hotels, etc. Indeed the source of funding for all these costs is one of the most controversial aspects of the project. No indication is included in POOT about sources of finance. A solution that has been suggested is the constitution of some kind of joint body, in which the local and regional governments and the tourist agents would cooperate in the management and financing of the project. Another option is the creation of a tax by the local government, in order to finance the forecasted expenses. In any case it would be a partial financing, since the total amount is quite high.

The solution through a tax is arguably especially suitable, since it would make possible a levy on those tourist organizations which, taking into account the features and the effects of their business activity, should be reasonably held accountable for the burden of the project. The idea is to tax tourism organizations operating hotels and apartments, for which the blueprint does not contemplate their compulsory reconversion, but which are contributors to the problem which POOT seeks to rectify. The assessment of these negative effects could be based on parameters such as proximity to the coastline, height of the buildings and area of green space per room.

Accordingly, the tax would act both as a corrective and as a financing tool. Needless to say, the final selection of the variables is open to any suggestion or refinement that could provide an adjustment between contribution to the problem and tax-paying. By way of illustration of these suggestions, the corrective-financing levy could tax not only hotels and apartments, but also second residences and other variables such as excess age or even aesthetic impact. The latter would certainly be very difficult to quantify. Similarly, there are other factors that could be weighed, such as funds reinvested into refurbishment, modernization or renovation of the tourism establishments, which could lower proportionally the tax burden as the reinvestment grows higher. According to the words of the minister, Joan Flaquer, it seems that governmental sources will cover 20 billion, and the private sector the remaining 40 million pesetas. That includes the elimination of *c.* 40,000 obsolescent bedrooms.

Another forseeable problem is that local councils still have planning jurisdiction. The application of POOT is to a considerable extent in their hands. It has been argued that the executive competence should have been transferred to a supramunicipal body, which would have a global vision of the island. The municipality of Alcudia has already expressed its will to follow strictly the principles of POOT, but there are grounds for concern that this will not be the standard for all municipalities. However, all the actors think that POOT is an important and necessary step ahead towards sustainability, but there is still a lot to be done in the rest of the island. POOT only affects 10% of the island's territory, and rural protection legislation covers 30%, therefore about 55% of the total territory is without regulation. The government had promised that legislation would be drafted no later than the year 2000. There is an urgent need for additional regulation; arguably it should have been included in POOT.

Legislation is also required for other long term strategies of the kind which integrate tourism development with cultural and environmental constraints, such as land use, water management, coastal zone management, and areas covered by rural protection legislation, if tourism development and environmental management are to be mutually reinforcing. It is essential if the maintenance of an activity of such an economic and social importance to the Balearic Islands is to be sustained, and is to deliver an auspicious legacy to future generations. 'Balearization' could become, conceivably enough, a new synonym for sustainable and successful re-planning and refurbishment in mature destinations.

References

Aguiló, E. *et al.* (1996) *Pla de Marqueting Turístic de Balears, 1996–1998.* IBATUR (Institut Balear de Promoción del Turismo), Conselleria de Turisme, Govern Balear.
Butler, R. (1980) The concept of a tourist area cycle of evolution: implications for management of resources. *Canadian Geographer* XXIV (1), 5–12.
Llei General turística de les Illes Balears (1999) *BOCAIB* núm. 41, 4 January.
Robledo, M.A. (1995) Orfeo y las Sirenas. *Hosteltur* 15, May, p. 26.

Part 2

The Economic Context

Introduction:
The Economic Context as Dominant

Richard Voase
University of Lincoln, Lincoln Campus, Lincoln, UK

The unifying context for the three case histories in this part is, arguably, that they are all located in peripheral regions. Hence, not surprisingly, the imperative is of an economic nature: the creation of wealth and employment by means of tourism as an instrument.

Lewis' contribution discusses the way in which farming in Wales had undergone something of a transformation, from what, deploying the terminology applied to tourism in this volume, might be termed an 'old' farming to a 'new' farming. Traditional agricultural practices, which respected traditional boundaries and used traditional built structures, had been replaced by moves toward large-scale cereal and livestock production in which traditional practices, traditional landscapes and traditional wildlife habitats had been the casualties. This shift from 'old' to 'new' farming had been encouraged by European Union subvention schemes, which led to overproduction and over-grazing. Simultaneously, the growth of a new rural economy based on visits to the countryside, created new demands on the rural landscape and a new set of environmental threats. The schemes which are the object of discussion in Lewis' contribution are the means by which farmers are encouraged, by means of new subvention systems, to assume the role of environmental manager and take measures to harmonize production, consumption and sustainability issues.

The Finnish case history by Lindroth and Soisalon-Soininen and the Swedish contribution from Böhn and Elbe are both written in the Scandinavian narrative style and contain much detail about how named individuals saw their roles and developed their economic activity. It is unusual and refreshing to see the essentials of a process enumerated in this way. The two regions, while similar to the Welsh example in being 'peripheral' regions in European terms, are qualitatively different. Böhn and Elbe's location is an inland rural region in central Sweden; the central issue of the case is the entrepreneurial abilities of a particular individual, the establishment of an inbound tour operation based on niche products and the generation of business by means of interpersonal contact. The Finnish location is coastal and, in terms of the economic imperative, a post-industrial economy which needs to create new employment opportunities. Unlike the Swedish case, European funding is involved, but like the Swedish case, much emphasis is placed on the entrepreneurial role of individuals.

© CAB *International* 2002. *Tourism in Western Europe: a Collection of Case Histories* (ed. Richard Voase)

In reading these case histories, it may be useful to bear in mind three factors which appear in common:

1. *The role of the individual entrepreneur in developing the product.* This could not be more explicit in the Scandinavian cases, but it is also true for Lewis' contribution. The point of the subvention schemes made available to farmers in Wales was that uptake was discretionary, and involved a devolution of responsibility to the individual farmer. When discussing the role of European Union support for the development of tourism in peripheral regions, it is easy to get the impression that these are grand designs, grandly executed. This is not so. For example, in the Yorkshire region of the United Kingdom, well over 90% of tourism businesses employ fewer than ten people. The tourism 'industry', inasmuch as it can be defined as a single industry, is not only disparate, but highly dependent upon the action of individual entrepreneurs and businesses. That is why the personal detail in the two Scandinavian histories in this part of the volume is so important: it is the real essence of tourism development.

2. The development of tourism in each of these locations involves *the deployment and consumption of the natural environment.* In rural Wales, where the acceleration of intensive farming was already causing environmental problems, coupled with accelerating demand from the populations of the cities of England and Wales for countryside recreation, the need for a sustainable approach was immediate. This is less evident in the two Scandinavian contributions, since levels of demand do not on the face of it pose, at present, an environmental threat. Nevertheless, there is the question as to the point at which the environment, like any resource, becomes over-consumed and a problem, rather than an asset. Robledo and Batle's chapter on Mallorca, which features in part 1, is a classic example of this.

3. *Each of these cases can be seen as a response to the discourse of the 'new' tourism.* Lindroth and Soisalon-Soininen refer to the growth of interest in cultural and heritage tourism as a rationale for the developments which they discuss. Significantly, they suggest that museum authorities in Finland had become convinced, albeit with a hint of reluctance, that 'the past' could be harnessed for economic development purposes of the kind planned for Loviisa. Böhn and Elbe's primary purpose is to discuss the development of tourism to Älvdalen in terms of the application of relationship marketing techniques *avant la lettre*, but it is interesting to compare their exposition with that of Lohmann and Mundt in part 3. Much is made of the success of the efforts of Böhn and Elbe's 'tourism manager' in forging successful inbound tourism relationships with German tour operators. Lohmann and Mundt look in detail at some of the qualitative changes in the German out-bound market to which these successes may be linked. Finally, the characteristics of the subvention schemes for rural Wales are referred to in interesting discursive terms. Tir Gofal aims to encourage the 'quiet enjoyment of the countryside', as opposed, presumably, to 'noisy' enjoyment involving off-road vehicles and the like. It also aims for the maintenance of an 'appropriate' landscape: 'appropriate' being a subjective term, depending on whether one's interests are, for example, birdwatching or, for example, using off-road vehicles. Controversially, we can suggest this to be a partisan view of the countryside, which, in terms of the exposition in Chapter 1, can be associated with the values of the credentialled middle class, emanating perhaps from the desire to see the countryside in binary opposition to the city: a theme park of the pre-modern where culture takes an orderly second place to nature.

Tir Cymen and Tir Gofal: Agri-environmental Schemes and Recreational Access in Rural Wales

5

Alison Lewis
University of Lincoln, Lincoln Campus, Lincoln, UK

Background

1999 marked a significant shift in official attitudes to public access in the country-side in Britain. The new Countryside Agency for England and Wales was launched with *The State of the Countryside 1999* and *Tomorrow's Countryside: 2020 Vision*. Detailed study of these documents reveals substantial implications for rural areas, not least in the role of destinations for recreational tourism. This contribution focuses on specific schemes in the principality of Wales and their implications for the creation of an experience of rural tourism.

In England and Wales, the Secretary of State for the Environment pledged new legislation to give walkers new rights of access in rural areas. In Wales, Tir Gofal, the new All Wales Agri-environment Scheme (AWAES) will promote new access opportunities for people to enjoy the Welsh countryside, in conjunction with payment for whole-farm conservation of landscapes and habitats. The Countryside Commission produced a range of proposals to secure England's Public Rights of Way (PRoW) and the Countryside Agency, its successor from April 1999, is central to the development and implementation of the government commitment to improved access. In Scotland, the Land Policy Reform group achieved extensive agreement on the principle to give all people a right of access to all countryside, with land only taken out of access for exceptional reasons.

The convergence, at this time, of these responses to long-standing demands for access to the countryside may be coincidence. It is also one expression of the upheavals in rural areas and agricultural economies in England, Wales, Scotland, throughout Europe, and internationally. Access to rural areas for recreation is inex-tricably linked to larger issues in rural areas, not least of which is farming. 'Farming does not shape the countryside, farming is the countryside' (Harvey, 1997).

© CAB *International* 2002. *Tourism in Western Europe: a Collection of Case Histories*
(ed. Richard Voase)

Nowhere is this more evident than in Wales, a nation of 28,000 farm holdings, 78% of the total land area in agriculture and a landscape quality and diversity to warrant three National Parks, which cover one fifth of the total land area (CSO, 1998: 35).

This chapter will focus on two agri-environment schemes in Wales, piloted first as Tir Cymen (pronounced: teer *cum* men) and then introduced in March 1999 as Tir Gofal (pronounced: teer *gov* al). It will outline the convergence of policy requirements for recreational access, rural economies and environmental enhancement. The schemes are not unique in Europe, but are innovative in Britain. In the long term, the whole-farm, all-Wales approach to rural areas, recreational access and the environment may offer an alternative to the single-issue approach to rural development found elsewhere

Changes in Agricultural Practices

The relationship between rural communities and the rural economy has changed in character and intensity since the 1940s at an increasing rate, so that agriculture and forestry now contribute only 2.4% of the GDP of Wales in contrast to the 7.5% earned by tourism (CSO, 1999). Generations of farmers have modified the various Welsh landscapes in order to survive and to make a living in open moorland, steep valleys and lowlands. As farming has changed so has the use of land, traditional farm boundaries, buildings and trackways. Most recently, much of the wide variety of semi-natural habitats maintained by traditional practices has been lost, either replaced by high-intensity agriculture or absorbed into non-agricultural use (Jones, 1998). These changes have been driven by social and economic pressures in response to shifts in national and European Union (EU) policies, to market forces and to technological change. The introduction of large-scale forestry and specialist cereal and livestock production in response to changing tax and subsidy regimes has externalised the control of large tracts of land in Wales, away from resident farmers to commercial enterprises. In the current depressed economy of farming, it is anticipated that the next 10 years will see a continued decline in the number of farmers throughout Wales.

The changing fabric of the agricultural landscape in Wales has parallels throughout Europe, the common factor being the Common Agricultural Policy (CAP). As this has been modified since its inception, so have the farming communities across Europe adjusted to its regimes. Landscapes and communities have taken the impacts. The early 1960s was a period of increased productivity, stable markets and technical change when financial incentives were readily available. Initially, no environmental controls on water, air and soil were included in the CAP. The priorities were, for example, to maximize production and to ensure a fair standard of living for the agricultural community (Barnes and Barnes, 1999).

By the late 1960s, agricultural surpluses had appeared, there was a decline in the contribution by agriculture to national economies and a significant reduction in agricultural employment. These coincided with a concern about the disproportionate amount of the EU budget allocated to the CAP (60%), and a growing awareness of the environmental damage arising from cultivation practices of monoculture and intensification. For example, the quotas and head-age payments for livestock and the grants for afforestation and land improvement represented a significant proportion of farmers' income, albeit modest, in many cases in rural Wales. However, in order to maintain an income, the response to such payments has often been to overstock, resulting in damage to grassland, moorland and water courses.

Enlargement of the European Community (EC) in the 1980s brought different demands for agricultural support, particularly from the Mediterranean areas, as did the development of regional and structural funds, all with new expectations from the EC budget. Increased levels of agricultural production, high environmental costs and liberalization of world trade agreements affected CAP payments to farmers which, although adjusted to fit policy frameworks of member states, have changed in type and quantity throughout this period. Therefore, an individual farmer may be at the mercy of decisions made in the international arena, yet still have to create a livelihood locally. For many farmers, the mobility and flexibility assumed in commercial farming are not an option. Constrained by local conditions and social characteristics, the CAP created both a dependency on European funds and an environmental threat.

Effects of Farming Practices on the Environment

Concern for environment and landscape deterioration and for agricultural decline converged in England and Wales in 1977, when it was suggested that those in LFAs were 'so dependent on grant aid that the Ministry could in practice force them to follow any guidelines laid down' (Sheail, 1995). At that time, it was also recognized that farmers were in an ideal situation to make a contribution to the environmental quality of 'the rural estate'. This latter proposal may equally have been an attempt to shift the cost of environmental compensation and improvement from the agricultural budget to conservation organizations, despite the evidence that countries with the highest levels of agricultural support in the EU were also those with the most intensively farmed land.

The reluctance of the agriculture industry to accept some responsibility for environmental deterioration persists, despite the 1981 Wildlife and Countryside Act, which was a move towards linking and funding the reparations between agri-culture and the environment in the UK. The introduction of Environmentally Sensitive Areas (ESA) in 1985, where 'the maintenance or adoption of particular agricultural methods is likely to facilitate conservation, enhancement or protection', offered farmers the stability of 10-year agreements, with annual hectarage payments. It was taken up to the extent that by 1994 there were 5600 agreements in England and Wales, embracing 400,000 ha of land (Potter, 1998: 93).

If farming *is* the countryside and if the countryside is valued per se, then it becomes a priority to maintain it in the best possible state. Concern in the

EU for environmental deterioration, generally and as a result of specific agricultural and industrial policies, resulted in a range of measures to reduce and ameliorate damage to European environments. Environmental health was to be integral to every other EU programme and legislative development. Individual member states and the EU undertook to redress practice which would further damage the environment, thereby responding to changes in international consensus on the environment.

In this context, the various EU rural development schemes have reinforced the environmental criteria and aim to underpin the social and economic component of sustainable rural communities. To this end, emphasis is put on rehabilitation and enhancement of rural environments and the livelihoods of those who will manage them. This is not seen as a process of fossilizing traditional communities but as an opportunity for flexibility, which is as an important part of survival as are the resources on which the economy is based. In further discussion, there will be consideration of the viability of long-term rural areas if the political and economic components of rural systems are not supported adequately, independent of their non-commodity function.

EU programmes to fund, facilitate and encourage rural development have increased since the late 1990s. For example LEADER I (1992–94) and LEADER II (1995–99) asserted the importance of all aspects of the rural economy, not just agriculture, and showed a recognition that 'economic prospects for rural areas are seen to depend increasingly on non-agricultural activities' (Storey, 1999: 308). Tir Gofal, like its predecessor, is another such rural programme whose priority is the restoration and enhancement of the environments in which Welsh agriculture operates. Payments for environmental improvement indirectly benefit the farm economies, yet carry an obligation to increase public access across farmland onto unenclosed uplands for 'quiet enjoyment of the countryside'.

Deterioration of landscapes and habitats has been identified and explained by changing land use and farm practices, by increased recreational pressure on landscapes and by the expansion of commercial forestry. On any one farm the impact on the landscape may be small but cumulatively there is widespread change, affecting the character and detail of any area. Afforestation with conifers creates a monoculture woodland and obliterates heathland, wet grassland and other habitats in the interests of long term economic gain. Increasing sheep densities, partly in response to more attractive grant regimes, cause overgrazing of grass and heathland, thus changing the habitat for ground-nesting birds such as black grouse, curlews and lapwings. Farm mechanization is a partial response to changing technology and social and economic practices, yet it may have the effect of compacting soils, contaminating water courses and requiring modern buildings such as large barns and silos. The economic necessity of many such changes is not contended here. Tir Cymen is part of an ongoing experiment of programmes in Europe to link environmental improvement with cost-effective farm practices, to minimize the negative impacts on landscapes and habitats.

The physical boundaries between urban and rural are increasingly blurred in practice and in concept (Cloke et al., 1994), and Pierce (1996) suggests that there is a close and inseparable link between rural and urban ecosystem health. Rural communities now include urban commuters and homeworkers, dependent on PCs but linked to urban employment. The technology to improve mobility and electronic networking may increase opportunities for urban incomes, but marginalize rural residents whose livelihoods are dependent on particular locations. Within agricultural communities there may be appointed farm managers who are business agents with few local loyalties. New mobile occupants of urban outliers and peri-urban residents experience rural areas differently, as spaces for recreation and residence, for 'consumption' rather than production. They may have an idealized perception of the 'rural' and create their own local loyalties which differ from those of long-term residents among the rural 'producers'. These new social constructions of rurality mean that rural has become a 'symbolic reality' rather than a material location of production (Pierce, 1996). Rural areas are becoming part of the non-commodity resource for general consumption, idealized and marginalized in a predominantly urban and technical society. Their productive capacity or commodity function is declining in an era of agricultural over-production and increased demand for recreation and space to live (Marsden *et al.*, 1993).

There is not necessarily a significant geographical distance between the commodity and non-commodity use of rural areas. The restricted space of the relatively small land mass of Britain, and the proximity of urban and rural areas, put pressures on the land, create potential conflict, and are highly dynamic. Hence, the divergent demands for rural 'goods' and services may be in conflict with the need to protect both natural and human resources. The anomaly of this confrontation of consumption and production, urban and rural, is that demands for the protection of environmental resources and for recreational access in rural areas have been most outspoken from urban users. That which they wish to consume, i.e. the rural environment, is perceived as threatened, yet the demands from a predominantly urban and industrial society intensify the threats to that same rural landscape. For example, wind turbines on prominent uplands supply energy mainly to urban consumers and 4×4 cross-country tracks offer excitement in response to excursionist demand. Increased recreational access is part of this anomaly.

There are further contradictions. The landscape and environments so desired in rural areas by the new consumers are increasingly subject to regulations and management regimes which are dependent on *external* markets, national, European and international. These are generated by values and perceptions alien to the actual locations themselves. The outcomes are the EU agricultural policies, which have worked inadvertently for four decades to create rural uniformity over swathes of European landscapes, and to eliminate local diversity, both social and environmental. Yet the new rural 'consumers' desire distinctive and contrasted rural experiences. There is emerging a recognition of 'the interaction of people and the environment (which) has produced regions of distinctive cultural, ecological and aesthetic value' (Pierce, 1996: 216).

Not only are local characteristics now seen as an asset, but the economy and society which maintains them is increasingly seen as central to their survival. Once the source of knowledge and skill is lost, the distinctive local characteristics will change. Such paradoxes underpin the significance of heritage resources, both in the built environment and in landscapes, as a means of identifying distinctiveness. For Tir Gofal, the incentive to re-establish and enhance traditional landscapes may, indirectly, aim to maintain the Welsh heritage resource in rural areas, but it is explicitly intended to strengthen the semi-natural habitats and diverse ecosystems so distinctive to Welsh landscapes. These schemes combine the inherent attractions of distinctive Welsh rural areas with ecological enhancement, both of which add to their recreational value and contribute to rural economies and community life.

The Countryside: Access Issues

The focus of this chapter is the emerging link between public access to open land for quiet enjoyment and agri-environment schemes, in Wales. It is apparent thus far that amenity land, and access to it, has to be understood in the context of the whole changing rural economy and, in this case, Welsh landscapes and communities. Whether rural residents see this access provision as an opportunity or merely as a necessity, it has become a key option within the AWAES.

The expectation is that rural areas will continue to provide for recreation and tourism (Welsh Tourist Board, 1999). The United Kingdom Tourism survey of 1997 found that of the 57 million holidays of 4 or more nights, 20% had physical activity as their purpose, hill walking, rambling and orienteering being the most frequent (CSO, 1999). By 1997, walking represented 41% of recreational activities, followed by swimming and yoga/keep fit at 17% each. Walking epitomizes the recreational use of the countryside in that its popularity depends in the long term on the inherent quality of the landscape. Thus the health of the landscape reflects the management priorities and affects the demand for the access.

Calls for increased access to open countryside have a century-long history in England and Wales. Key events in the process of extending rights of access for the 'physical and spiritual refreshment of being able to enter and enjoy the countryside and coast' (McIntosh cited in Sheail, 1995) are documented elsewhere (Shoard, 1989; Harrison, 1991; Glyptis, 1991). The National Trust, founded in 1907, and the Society for the Promotion of Nature Reserves (1912) were early developments, both of which included demands for the right of access for the public, but were constrained by the Government consistently refusing national funds to underwrite the promotion of outdoor recreation. The *National Parks and Access to the Country-side Act* of 1949 provided the means for local authorities to negotiate, define and record PRoW as well as to inaugurate the National Parks of England and Wales, but by 2000 the PRoW will still not have been completely recorded and mapped.

Priority for food and forestry production persisted until 1978, when pressure was increased to promote conservation and amenity alongside economic farming (Sheail, 1995: 84). Even then, opposition persisted from entrenched attitudes among landowners, culminating in 1996 in a massive public demonstration organised by the Country Landowners Association (CLA). A persuasive voice was added by Shoard (1980) who documented the extent of losses of access and habitat and identified the conflicts in rural areas between sectoral interests of government departments, planning regulations, obligations to European commitments and public-interest groups. Organizations such as the Ramblers Association and the Open Spaces Society have maintained that the countryside is a common heritage, that access is of right, and that historic practices need to be renegotiated for the future. The ebb and flow of interests and influence between agricultural reformers, public-access pressure groups and wildlife conservationists have continued with a range of positions, both extreme and consensual. What has eventually emerged is a recognition that, despite the time of uncertainty, landowners and farmers are expected to permit access and become environmental managers.

The resolution of the polarized positions over countryside access proposed by the Environment Committee of the House of Commons in 1995 seems modest. This committee offered the model of the Peak District National Park, where, for negotiated limited access, farmers receive payment (House of Commons, 1995). The detailed negotiations between landowner and access officers to facilitate new routes may be central to the effectiveness of improved rural access, regardless of the clarity of any legislation. The Countryside Stewardship Scheme in England offered payment to farmers for improved access, but the implementation is considered to be of limited value as sites and linear routes are not well signposted and are not part of environmental improvement, despite the fact that 13,517 ha and 3970 km of footpaths have been opened (House of Commons, 1995: xxxiii). These programmes are direct payments for temporary access, but they neither prevent more intensive framing elsewhere in order to maintain output, nor resolve the local problems associated with increased access.

The ingredients for increasing access routes include commitment at national and local levels, a legal framework, adequate finance, negotiation, mediation and goodwill. Once the routes are in place, those who use them will have an obligation to act responsibly and perhaps to understand them in the context of the local community. At a national level, the Labour party was elected in 1997 on a manifesto that included a commitment to introduce a bill for Access to Open Countryside in England and Wales. Threatened by a private member's bill and unable to rescind this commitment, a White Paper was produced in 1998, and at the time of writing was under consideration, which proposes free and permanent access to open countryside by the public for quiet enjoyment. Access to open land will be by PRoW, all of which should be open and recorded by 2000, and by negotiated routes. The threat to withdraw 'all farming subsidies and government grants from landowners who obstruct footpaths or refuse to sign a declaration providing public right of access' in the private member's bill has highlighted the interdependence between access and agricultural and access funding (Brown, 1999). This, compounded by complex and deep-seated attitudes to property rights, makes access a significant national issue.

The CLA proposes voluntary access agreements, negotiated with owners and occupiers, on the basis that a statutory right of access would be 'a recipe for conflict with economic land use and environmental objectives, and because it would not deliver more access where it is needed most.' It states that open access and footpaths have increased by about 5% per year since 1991/92 in England and Wales. There is no mention of costs – statutory access would be free to the public (Salmon, 1998). Not only does opposition come from private landowners, but also from others such as the Ministry of Defence and the Crown Estates of 'public land', where de facto use may exist and some land is open by agreement. Marion Shoard maintains that the proposal to increase public access to 'open' land is a retrogressive step, in that there should be a right of access to the whole countryside (Shoard, 1998). Such a development is proposed for Scotland. In England and Wales, the combination of permanent and voluntary arrangements would be a compromise to accommodate the different management needs of a working environment and, supported by effective and available public maps and a new Country Code, might offer flexible arrangements yet increase public access to open land.

A central problem emerging from these approaches to access for England and Wales is the definition and delineation of 'open' land. Not only do landowners change land use, natural processes change, often in response to the ambient environment, so any designations of 'open' by habitat type would be difficult to identify and problematic to map with any certainty. The boundaries between legitimate access and trespass threaten to make these access proposals a legal quagmire. For example, open countryside, defined as mountain, heath and cliffs, in Wales is estimated as between 40% and 50%, including Common Land, but this may be an underestimate as in Wales there is also additional extensive rough grazing. It is evident that the problems in the official definition of 'open' land are considerable, and will affect legitimacy of access for walkers and delay attempts to increase rights of access to the countryside.

Wales as a Rural Landscape

The landscapes of Wales are varied, as in any rural region worldwide. The distinctive features of the Welsh landscapes are influenced by the particular geology and landforms, and by centuries of human residence and use. Of the 1.5 million hectares of land in agricultural holdings in Wales, 81.8% are under grass and rough grazing and 14% are arable, the rest are mainly Set Aside land or woodlands. 74.6% of the farm holdings are predominantly for livestock, including 46.4% in Less Favoured Areas (LFA). Farming in Wales has created characteristic landscapes which are now valued more widely for their own sakes. If these same landscapes are an amalgam of the habitats, historic features and farming practices then, it is argued, payment to maintain each component must offer a benefit to both the farmer and the public. This reciprocity is offered in the form of increased public access for quiet enjoyment of the countryside.

However, farming businesses cannot be fossilized in a historic landscape which subscribes to obsolete and uneconomic practices and a relic industry. Any rural reform must attempt to achieve business modernization and flexibility on each farm, acceptable to the farmer, and combine these with appropriate standards of landscape and habitat management. Tir Cymen recognized the central role of Welsh farms in maintaining both rural landscapes and habitat diversity within them. It aimed to halt further deterioration of landscape, to protect and enhance the existing sites and to increase the number and range of habitats in keeping with local characteristics. Typical of many upland areas in Europe, the seven Welsh Unitary Authorities, which also include extensive LFAs, have higher populations of pensionable age and lower population densities, e.g. Powys 24 persons per km^2 and Gwynedd 46 persons per km^2 compared with the Welsh average of 141 persons per km^2 (CSO, 1998). They also make up 75% of the total area of Wales which underlines the significance of rural reform.

Tir Cymen is ambitious in that it plans to accommodate environmental gains by a whole-farm environmental plan, requiring that the characteristics of the locality are maintained sympathetically and that the whole contributes to overall landscape enhancement. Individual farms have their own particular combination of habitats which may or may not be representative of the larger district, and which add to local diversity. The approach is ambitious, but it is increasingly endorsed by Welsh, UK and European Union requirements.

The Countryside Council for Wales, a government organization, had a central role in the development of Tir Cymen and in recording and managing the PRoW in Wales. For example, in the National Nature Reserves in Wales (NNR), for which it has responsibility, the CCW is committed to keep open all PRoW shown on the definitive maps and to encourage owners and managers to do likewise on other NNR. This provides approximately 160 km of PRoW and permissive paths in Wales. Also, the CCW provided £1.2 million grant aid in 1997/98 to help national parks and new unitary authorities to open up their PRoW. One thousand kilometres were opened in 1997, and a report was completed of the state of 7500 km of PRoW in Wales. It is evident that long-term planning for public access for various purposes in Wales is required.

The Wales Access Forum offers the necessary cooperation with the overall objective of improving opportunity for public enjoyment of the countryside. CCW's participation in this forum, and its extensive experience in Wales, led it to recommend to a government consultation 'that a mixture of statutory and voluntary arrangements is desirable to help realise its objective of a substantial increase in public rights of access to open countryside on a permanent basis.' (CCW, 1998a). It proposed a new law granting legal and permanent right of access on foot to mountain, moor, heath and common land but recommending voluntary access agreements on to more intensively managed land, such as in the Tir Cymen agreements.

Permissive access, as developed in Tir Cymen and introduced in Tir Gofal, may offer both the flexibility desired by politicians and landowners in Wales, and develop the conditions required for EU agricultural reform. The following studies outline the integration between recreational access, environment and farming business, but might not address a more-fundamental contradiction in England and Wales of rights of access to land.

Tir Cymen – an Experimental Scheme

Tir Cymen is an experimental scheme to provide for countryside conservation in Wales. It was introduced in 1992 by the Secretary of State for Wales as a 5 year whole-farm project, and extended into the sixth year. All agreements last for 10 years and so will end in 2008/9 when the last group of 143 farms will complete. It is under the management of the Countryside Commission for Wales (CCW). Farmers in three former Welsh administrative districts were given the opportunity to undertake Tir Cymen agreements in the pilot scheme, prior to its availability, in modified form, as an All-Wales Agri-environment Scheme. The CCW is directly responsible for the management of the pilot districts of Dinefwr and Swansea, but responsibility is delegated to the Snowdonia National Park officers for the Meirion-ydd district (Fig. 5.1). It offers 'farmers annual payments in return for the positive management of their land for the benefit of wildlife, landscape, archeology and geology, and for providing new opportunities for quiet enjoyment of the country-side' (CCW, 1992).

Funding for the scheme comes from the budget of the Secretary of State for Wales, and it also qualified for part-funding from the European Union under EC Regulation 2078/92 within the European Agricultural Guidance and Guarantee Fund. It is administered and managed by the CCW from Bangor, Aberystwyth, Llanidloes and Swansea under a remit endorsed by its powers within the *Countryside Act* of 1968 (Section 4), the *Wildlife and Countryside Act* 1981 (Section 40) and *Environment Protection Act* 1990 (Section 130).

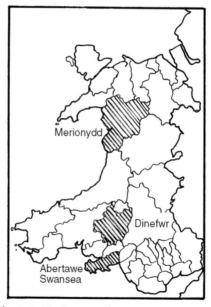

Fig. 5.1. Tir Cymen pilot areas, 1992–1998.

Tir Cymen, best translated as 'well-crafted landscape', aims to 'combine, on a whole-farm basis, good farming practice with the conservation of existing semi-natural habitats and where possible, habitat improvement and expansion, landscape conservation and the protection of archeological features while promoting opportunities for the public to enjoy the countryside and coast' (Evans, 1997).

In order to achieve these objectives, farmers who undertake a Tir Cymen agreement receive grants to assist in the implementation of each part of the programme. In exchange they undertake environmental improvements on the farm, planned for the 10-year programme, and modify their farming practices both to enhance the environment and to improve access for the public to unenclosed uplands. This is not just a 'hand out' for farmers to improve both environmental quality and public access. It is an attempt to demonstrate that environmental 'goods' can be created and marketed in cost-effective ways. Landscape quality and environmental health are thereby identified as marketable 'goods', and assistance in maintaining them is balanced by extended public access in a manner which will not damage farm economies. The pilot projects were monitored to assess the long-term and all-Wales application of the scheme (ADAS, 1996; CEI, 1997; Entec, 1998).

Tir Cymen agreements were available only to farmers and involvement was voluntary. In 1992, information packs were made available in the pilot districts. Each included bilingual management guidelines, a farmers' handbook and guidelines for standard capital payments, as well as sample maps to assist in the completion of the application forms. These outlined the ways in which farmers were expected to manage their land in return for annual payments, gave a 'question and answer' introduction to implementing the scheme, and encouraged farmers to contact the Tir Cymen officers at the district offices. Throughout the process there was close cooperation between the field officers and farmers, this being one of the identified strengths of the scheme (Entec, 1998: 81). As the whole farm is included in the agreement, it was surveyed and details of habitat, stock, crops and features were recorded. Agreement was reached on the proposed plan, which was designed to meet the requirements of the scheme and the business requirements of the farm. Maps were produced with detailed individual farm characteristics, but using a key common to the whole scheme. These were deposited at the Tir Cymen offices and at other key centres such as Tourist Information Offices and main libraries in each District.

It was planned that Tir Cymen would cover 50% of the eligible area after 5 years of the pilot schemes. By 1997, only Meirionydd had reached this level with 55,510 ha (50.1%). Dinefwr stood at 32.6% and Swansea at 36.6%, giving an average of 43.5%. (CCW, 1997). By the end of 1998, 47% of the total eligible area was included in Tir Cymen, representing 89,304 ha (CCW, 1998a). New agreements have ended, but the project continues until all farms have completed their 10-year commitments.

Uptake of Tir Cymen whole-farm agreements during the trial (1992–98) totaled 1023 farms. Year 1 included 197 farms, the highest uptake, and 1996 the lowest uptake with 174, but the pattern in each pilot district differed. Uptake in

Meirionydd was 84 farms in 1992, falling to 53 farms in 1997, whereas in Dinefwr the number of participants increased from 85 to 107 farms during the period. In Swansea, uptake varied between a 37 high in 1994 to 20 farms in 1996 and 1997 (CCW, 1998b). Explanations for these variations are suggested by the different agricultural characteristics of the three districts and the way in which the wider agricultural economy impacted on them. For example, Meirionydd was affected differently by the decline in grants per head for ewes and calves, than was Dinefwr with its preponderance of dairy farms.

Variations in uptake between the three project districts also reflect the different levels of unimproved land in each district, the average size of holdings and the dominant characteristics of boundaries. Hedges are typical of Dinefwr, whereas stone and earthbank walls are prevalent in Meirionydd. Farm sizes vary considerably, the largest being in Meirionydd and the majority of small ones in Swansea. Similarly, the availability of funding and of Tir Cymen officers in the districts differed and may have affected the uptake of the scheme. Numerous smaller farms in Dinefwr would each require similar *input* from the Tir Cymen officers as any individual larger farm in Meirionydd. In particular, there is less unimproved land in both Dinefwr and Swansea so the incentives to use Tir Cymen to enhance remaining habitats was less attractive. Not only are there variations between the three pilot districts but there are also differences within each district.

The objectives of the so-called Tir Cymen Code were to maintain traditional rural landscapes through viable farm economies, to implement sound environmental standards for habitat conservation and landscape quality, to enhance environmental features and to maintain farmers' commitments to the programme. All farmers in the scheme who received whole-farm grants agreed to the code. Its precise wording is as follows:

- 'Existing walls, hedges and earth banks and slate fences should not be removed or "quarried" and should be maintained.
- Safeguard scheduled and unscheduled archeological and historic features from damage by stock, farming or other operations, including tree planting.
- Traditional farm buildings which are weatherproof should be maintained in a weatherproof condition using traditional materials. Other traditional stone features (e.g. sheep folds, sheep pounds) should be similarly maintained.
- Geological features and land forms should be protected from damage. There should be no extraction of rock, sand, gravel, shingle, clay or peat, other than on a small scale for farm use.
- The farm should be kept free from rubbish, litter, derelict machinery and equipment; fences should be kept in good repair using locally appropriate fencing materials.
- Water features are important on the farm: wells, springs, open drains and ditches, streams and canals, swamps, fens, bogs, reed beds, ponds and lakes. These should be managed in a way that will safeguard them from damage and make the most of their potential as wildlife habitats. In particular keep the water clean and of good quality and keep the water table high throughout the year (as far as this is within your control).

- Look after trees and small groups of trees on the farm and replace them where appropriate.
- If you propose to make noticeable alterations to the farm then you should first consult your Tir Cymen officer in writing.
- Manage the land in a way which does not cause environmental damage such as pollution or damage to the soil structure.'

(CCW, 1992)

This Tir Cymen code identified the standards required in return for the whole farm grant of £20 per hectare per annum, to a minimum of £500 and a maximum of £3000 per annum depending on size. Public access on unenclosed moorland and upland was required for no additional payment, but linear access to these areas is assisted. In addition, capital payments were available for items such as the erection of gates and stiles, controlling bracken and installing nesting boxes. Farmers also needed to undertake specific programmes of habitat management, landscape improvement and permissive access creation, for which additional special project grants were available. The clearing and maintaining of Public Rights of Way are required by law and do not attract additional funds. The special projects for which grants were available were for environmental and access projects. They included the creation of permissive footpaths, bridleways and paths suitable for people with disabilities, small car parks and picnic areas. Grants were available to improve existing habitats and to create new ones.

During the first 5 years of Tir Cymen, 38% of payments were granted to whole-farm agreements and 62% to habitat-specific management, out of a budget of £3.2 million (Entec, 1998: 15). Of the total capital expenditure, most (41%) was allocated to boundaries for environmental management and an additional 41% for traditional walls and hedges. By the end of the pilot project, 1600 km of boundaries are scheduled for completion. (Entec, 1998: 20). They are a dominant landscape feature in many agricultural areas and a crucial element in farm management. The emphasis on funding them is not unexpected, while recognizing that ongoing maintenance will be required beyond the pilot project. Grants were also available for tree planting, for certain habitats and for moorland management. Tir Cymen offered an alternative approach, more in keeping with the long-term and overall sustainability of the landscape and those whose livelihoods depend on it.

A 'whole-farm' approach was central to Tir Cymen. It recognized that each farm is unique, but also that any agri-environmental scheme must be sufficiently adaptable to the local circumstances. By encouraging the scheme in a neighbourhood, it was possible to integrate increased public access to open countryside and to support larger-scale habitat management. This was not easy in the rugged upland areas over large distances, but it was one of the few ways in which farmers could obtain supplementary grants for wall and building maintenance. It is a two-way process. By identifying a code of practice, criteria for habitat management and a 10-year agreement with farmers conditional upon continuing commitment, Tir Cymen is demonstrating an over-riding commitment to maintaining the characteristic landscape, supporting rural farm economies and increasing public access to the countryside. Its goal is a 'well-crafted landscape'.

The boundaries of farms do not necessarily coincide with the boundaries of landscape features, and farms may include more than one landscape feature. These might be river valleys, limestone uplands or sand dunes. It is the objective of the Tir Cymen officers to record landscape character areas on each farm plan and, in the management programme, to incorporate the environmental enhancement on a farm into the wider landscape. In this way, individual farms contribute to maintaining and improving the landscape characteristics of the area. It is therefore to the advantage of Tir Cymen if adjacent farms participate in the scheme, thus maximizing the benefits of individual farm participation for the wider benefit of the landscape.

Landscape quality is not only considered on a 'macro' scale. Sites and features in the landscape contribute to its value and attraction. Archaeological sites, such as hill forts, settlement remains and routeways, are part of the heritage of the Welsh landscape. Similarly, historic features contribute distinctive elements; abandoned or neglected boundary lines, ancient trackways and isolated sheep folds and barns are integral parts of the landscape. Farmers are bound by a Tir Cymen agreement to prevent damage to such sites, to repair them if appropriate and to maintain their quality. Tir Cymen grants enable farmers to manage and enhance such features as part of the whole-farm plan, thereby retaining 'micro' components which contribute to the characteristic landscape.

It is expected that the grants and the 10-year agreements will enable farmers to achieve the results required for landscape management and to overcome the initial problems in adjusting to the Tir Cymen requirements. The payback for society is improved access for quiet enjoyment in a healthy countryside sustained by a viable economy.

A range of Tir Cymen habitat objectives apply to the main habitat types: moorland and heathland, unimproved grassland of many types, coastal land above mean High Water Mark, broadleaved woodland and trees, arable field margins, traditional boundaries such as hedges, drystone walls, earth banks and slate fences. The principles for each type were to safeguard existing habitats, to restore the quality of damaged ones, to manage each for long-term improvement and to create new sites. Additional grants were available for such individual farm habitats and a programme was agreed for the duration of the 10-year agreement. Examples of such work include fencing off a woodland to prevent stock from grazing and thereby to encourage natural regeneration of the woodland and to increase flora diversity. Ponds or streams had to be cleared, derelict farm machinery removed and drains cleared to exclude contamination of water and marshland. A significant length of hedge planting and laying took place, especially in Dinefwr, which enhanced that particular habitat and the characteristic landscape, improved stock management and was grant-aided. In some cases, the opportunity to increase part-time skilled and traditional jobs in the locality was also improved (Entec, 1998).

Survey examples showed that after 5 years in the Tir Cymen scheme, 47% of moorland, 35% of grassland, 75% of coastal lands and 10% of woodland were maintained at high value in the surveyed habitat 'parcels' on farms. There was also an increase in desirable species in 36% of moorland, 6% of grassland, 16% of woodland, 50% of arable field margins and 100% of orchards. This meant that in some habitat parcels there was little or no improvement and scope for improvement remained. However, the intervals between evaluations were short, and some habitats required longer than others to adjust. Some sites were to be restored later in the Tir Cymen farm agreement or were dependent on a sequence of planned improvements and available finance and labour. Significantly, the original management scheme might not have been the most appropriate, and modification was required and work was not implemented to a high standard. Overall 'the quality of work carried out by most farmers was considered by the surveyors to be good or acceptable' (Entec, 1998: 51).

One outcome of the scheme was that more farmers were aware of environmental issues and were conservation-minded as a result of participation in Tir Cymen. Entec suggested that, overall, 23% of them indicated such a change of attitude (Entec, 1998: 78). Direct benefits to farmers were identified mainly as better stock control, as a result of improved boundaries, and an improved appearance of farms and landscape. Other benefits accrued to wildlife, local employment, better-quality stock and farm finances. It was difficult to demonstrate whether these environmental improvements were a direct result of the Tir Cymen scheme or whether they might have occurred regardless. After only 5 years of the scheme, it was suggested that the environmental benefits were greater than they would have been without the scheme (Entec, 1998: 79).

The third objective of Tir Cymen was to increase opportunities for public access into the open countryside while maintaining valuable landscapes and wildlife habitats. This was in line with the responsibility of the CCW and the Government White Paper *Access to the Open Countryside* (1998). The Tir Cymen objectives for access were detailed as follows:

- 'New paths will improve opportunities for people to enjoy the landscape and its wildlife, without disrupting farming activities
- new paths will provide safe, convenient ways of reaching existing access areas such as those on the open hill or coast;
- new paths will complete or create circular routes or otherwise form part of a sensible network
- modifications to existing paths would provide improved access without closing the existing rights of way
- to provide by agreement, small scale areas and access for picnicking, car parking and viewing
- to keep existing rights of way on the farm free from obstruction'.
  (CCW, 1992: 32)

Tir Cymen requires farmers to maintain existing PRoW free from obstruction. These may be footpaths and bridleways and are protected by law. In addition, it provides opportunities to create new, permissive and concessionary access

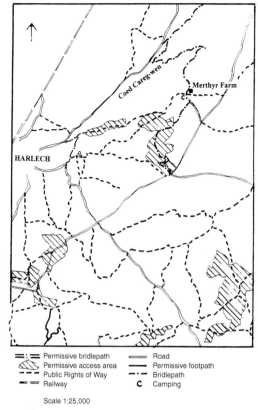

Fig. 5.2. Recreational access east of Harlech (Merionydd), including the Tir Cymen permissive routes.

available to the public at no charge for the duration of the agreement. It does not create new rights of way. Access will be only for quiet enjoyment, not for use by bicycles or motorized vehicles, or for sports or camping, with a few exceptions relating to farm use only. Where Tir Cymen management guidelines apply on open moorland, heathland and unimproved upland grassland, the farmer is obliged to permit walking and quiet enjoyment, at no charge. The farmer may exclude dogs or require their control. Access routes through the farm to this open countryside may be funded through the scheme. It is in the interests of Tir Cymen to create viable access routes for walkers including new routes and circular walks (Fig. 5.2).

The provision of access was optional for farmers on land which was included in other categories of the Tir Cymen agreements, such as broad leaved woodlands, coastal land and arable field margins. In an individual farm agreement under Tir Cymen, access may have been introduced and improved by the provision of footpaths, bridlepaths and paths for people with disabilities. For each, specifications were set and grants were made available. Capital works included the provision of seats, bridges, stiles and gates, new surfaces for footpaths, signs and information boards. During the 10-year pilot project, payments are £100 per kilometre per annum for footpaths and £200 per kilometre per annum both for permissive paths for people with disabilities and for bridleways.

This approach to PRoW and negotiated footpath provision was in response to public interest in access to countryside and open space. It also recognizes that if farmers are paid for landscape and habitat maintenance and farm improvements, then the 'public goods' should be available for public use. The conditions have to be negotiated carefully to maintain reasonable access and at the same time not to interfere with environmental quality and farm economic activities. The role of the Tir Cymen Officer is central as a negotiator, for the success of any agreement may depend on the skills of the individuals concerned.

Access may be improved, but unless the public is aware of the routes they will not be used. Information about Tir Cymen access is available on maps at local Tourist Information Centres and libraries, but cannot be distributed more widely because of copyright restrictions. One aim is to include all access routes on official tourist maps of each area, but as long as access is short-term this will not be possible (CEI, 1997: 38). Additional information is available on signs on the permissive paths.

By 1998, 61 km of new permissive paths had been established, most of which were footpaths. This had increased from 55 km in 1997, but few bridleways and paths for people with disabilities had been created. In addition, 700 km of PRoW were under special maintenance by 1997 and the public had access, under the Tir Cymen agreement, to over 35,000 ha of open moorland (CEI, 1997). Public use of the new access routes has not been well documented. Informal use of open countryside is not easy to record even in more-controlled environments. Paucity of information for the public and inadequate records mean that numbers are unobtainable. Farmers have not endorsed the access scheme with much enthusiasm. The increase in permissive routes is limited. There may be no significant change until national legislation is in place which may supercede parts of the AWAES.

Access to the open countryside, as identified in Tir Cymen, is clearly part of this innovative approach to rural development. Central to the agreement is the need to enhance habitats and to maintain landscape quality, each with their different contribution to a 'well crafted landscape'. In order to achieve these outcomes the financial support to farms as functioning, economic units is inherent in the whole-farm approach. The interdependence between sustainable farm economies, viable and diverse habitats and landscape quality is recognized in Tir Cymen. With these objectives, the 'public good' was made available as improved access for quiet enjoyment. Tir Gofal is the successor to Tir Cymen. It is broadly similar in content and approach but appears to have shifted emphases.

Tir Gofal: the All-Wales Agri-Environmental Scheme from 1999

Tir Gofal was launched in March 1999 by the Secretary of State for Wales. It is the All-Wales Agri-Environmental Scheme (AWAES) that has been developed from Tir Cymen, but it also replaces six other agri-environmental schemes in Wales, including Environmentally Sensitive Areas (ESA), the Hedgerow Renovation Scheme, the Habitat Scheme and the Moorland Schemes. Of these, Tir Cymen was the only whole-farm scheme, the others were limited in scope and were restricted to geographical areas. The development group was chaired by the Welsh Office Agricultural Department with members from the CCW, from the Forestry Authority, the Farming and Rural Conservation Agency (FRCA), CADW and Farming Unions, and representations from the Snowdonia National Park Authority and the Environment Agency.

Those who have 'a controlling interest in the land for the duration of the agreement' and have land which is managed in agricultural production are eligible to apply for a Tir Gofal agreement, so Tir Gofal will become available to most of the 28,000 holdings in Wales, except those under 3 ha. Potentially, it could cover a total agricultural area of 1,509,000 ha (CSO, 1998) and include the whole range of agricultural holdings and habitat diversity within Wales. Those currently with a Tir Cymen agreement will become eligible when their agreement expires. If a farm has current agreements under ESA or a Woodland Grant Scheme, for example, then Tir Gofal and the other scheme can co-exist as long as there is not double funding. Unlike other agri-environmental schemes, the whole farm is included in an agreement, even if the holdings are scattered. Common Land can be entered into a Tir Gofal agreement on the understanding that all who have common rights on that land are signatories.

Participation in Tir Gofal is voluntary. Applications will be made annually, at a time determined by the CCW and starting in May 1999. Unlike the Tir Cymen scheme, the process is competitive and discretionary, restricted to an estimated 600 agreements per annum for the first 3 years. The applications will be assessed and subsequent visits by trained field officers will identify farms for which agreements will be offered. A whole-farm plan will be made for the 10-year agreement and, once agreed, will be the basis of Tir Gofal for that land.

Farm applications 'will be selected according to the degree of environmental benefit they offer', based on a standardized scoring system which will take account of existing environmental features and optional additional benefits, such as improved access. The first applications have not yet been processed, so there can be no assessment of the procedure, and the criteria against which applications will be assessed are not available. The applications forms require specific information about the management arrangements for the farm and about landscape features and habitat types on the farm. These include details of traditional boundaries, landscape and historic features and habitats in seventeen categories. Cumulatively, they could provide a new record of landscape, habitat quality and diversity and details of informal access routes.

Tir Gofal is a scheme with limited funds. Although it has received part-funding from the EU, the amounts committed by March 1999 of £1.4 million for 1999/2000, £4 million for 2000/01 and £7 million in 2001/02 are apparently small. Not only is the potential number of holdings over 21,000, Tir Gofal will replace existing schemes although future funds available for Tir Gofal may be restricted relative to those for Tir Cymen and ESA combined. Additional budgets of £12 million will be made available for the completion of the existing projects.

As with Tir Cymen, there will be annual payments for the obligatory whole-farm component of the agreement, and annual payments and some capital payments for the voluntary component. The whole-farm element requires Management Prescriptions for each of the habitats submitted under the agreement and a wide range of whole-farm issues. These latter are summarized below and include:

- all existing traditional boundaries and features to be retained, hedges to be managed and buffer strips on field edges to be managed without cultivation
- archeological and historic features and buildings to be maintained
- individual trees, alive and dead to be retained
- no non-native species to be introduced without agreement
- safeguard rock features and geological sites and protect all water sites and courses
- rubbish to be disposed of and non-farm waste used on the farm only by agreement
- stocking rates to be held at 1998 levels unless otherwise agreed
- public access on foot to be permitted on to unenclosed moorland, heathland and grassland via existing rights of way or by new permissive footpaths
- 'Legal public rights of way on agreement land must be complied with.'
- other legal requirements must be complied with for the functioning of the farm
- manage the land in following the Codes of Good Agricultural Practice for Air, Soil and Water
- consult the Project Officer before significant changes are made to the buildings, farm economy or excavations occur.

(CCW, 1998)

The Management Prescriptions for each of the habitats are specific, detailed and demanding and the Project Officer designated to each agreement is the arbiter in less-precise matters such as the burning of heathland, peat cutting and treatment of notifiable weeds. As with Tir Cymen, the role of the Project Officers is central to the management and monitoring of the scheme, but the range of specialist skills they also require is considerable.

The additional voluntary options in the agreements, such as improvement of landscape and historic features and habitat creation, are to be funded. These might be significant factors in the approval of an application in areas where intensive farming predominates, but subject to the approval of the Project Officer. Capital payments are available for traditional field boundaries, protective fencing for environmental management, habitat management, restoration and creation, new permissive public access and 'special' projects. Details are available and accessible for all applicants in the Farmers' Handbook for Tir Gofal and throughout Wales seminars were held to inform and advise prior to submission of the applications.

Of significance for this discussion is the provision for access via enclosed land to unenclosed moorland, heathland and grassland in the Tir Gofal agreements. The proposals are similar to those of Tir Cymen in that farms in agreements will make available unenclosed moorland, heathland and grassland. The new permissive linear routes such as bridleways, cycleways and access routes for the disabled should be available, free of charge, for quiet enjoyment by the public. In Tir Gofal, cycleways are mentioned specifically, newly included in the scheme, but there is no mention of the right of cycles onto unenclosed land; presumably they are excluded, even though the new technology of cycles now makes such places an attraction. Capital payments for waymarkers, stiles, footbridges and gates are available as in Tir Cymen (Fig. 5.3). New permissive access *areas* are also included in Tir Gofal to provide spaces for picnicking and parking. Tir Gofal continues the approach of negotiated access via permissive routes for the duration of the agreement of ten years. These, combined with the PRoW, are to be advertised more widely for the benefit of local users. Lack of readily available local information was a criticism of Tir Cymen

Fig. 5.3. Merthyr Farm, Harlech. Public Rights of Way signpost from the road to Moel Goedog. New Stile over the repaired wall.

access routes, which may be resolved with Tir Gofal. Under Tir Cymen, only 61 km of negotiated paths were achieved up to 1998.

Under Tir Gofal, a third and additional new access development will be funded on farms. Access for educational purposes is to be encouraged. Details of specific 'educational' farms will be circulated to schools and colleges throughout Wales. A minimum of six visits per annum to the farm, adequate records of all visits, free visits and public liability cover will be the minimum requirements for the additional grant. For such educational activities, additional funds will be required to provide facilities under health and safety regulations, such as hot and cold water and toilets. Suitable indoor space, allocated for visitors, perhaps with chairs and a projector, in case of inclement weather may be required if the educational activities become frequent. The transition from an occasional educational farm visit to a developed rural attraction may be slow, but the focus for Tir Gofal is on education rather than as an educational business.

The potential for such a scheme is exemplified by a farm which has developed, with the support of the Snowdonia National Park, its educational role and has subsequently featured on the internet as an educational resource (www.nfu.org.uk/education). On open days at Merthyr Farm there may be 100 visitors, mostly holiday makers from nearby resorts such as Harlech and Barmouth, and up to 90 groups visit the farm each year, ranging in size from 10 to 70 people. The interest in farm visits such as this can ameliorate the concern of many farmers that increased public access onto open land will create excessive and expensive damage to their farms and livestock. This educational access provision contributes to a better understanding by the public of Welsh upland farming and of the hazards of uncontrolled access, and to an appreciation of the qualities of the Welsh landscape.

The Royal Welsh Agricultural Society and the Countryside Council for Wales have initiated an annual award for farmers who undertake work which benefits the environment. This is to encourage and reward farmers for the 'vital role they play as custodians of our landscape and wildlife'. Such an educational project of quality would be eligible for this Agri-environment Award and, under Tir Gofal, farmers are to be encouraged and funded and the farm visits advertised. Schemes such as Tir Gofal may not, by themselves, achieve their maximum effect. As part of other rural initiatives which reflect local and national interests, the AWAES is more likely to be accepted.

Discussion

This chapter has introduced Tir Cymen and Tir Gofal as schemes which promote increased public access to the Welsh countryside for quiet enjoyment. It has made reference to other factors such as reforms of the CAP, changing relationships between rural and urban and new demands for rural access, all of which now reflect the interdependence of environmental health, local social and economic needs and access to land for recreation. The Welsh AWAES are small-scale and not yet well-established but they are innovative, designed for a particular and distinctive European region and offer public 'goods' in return for local benefits. This discussion will reflect particularly on issues arising from the schemes which indicate the difficulties of implementing reform, especially to recreational access, at a time of rural contraction.

Tir Cymen was deliberately small-scale with a restricted timescale. There was transparency in the application and selection process and support for the farmers. The intention was to create an All Wales Agri-environment scheme based on the experience and evaluation of the pilot projects and evaluation reports, and in consultation with a variety of agencies. Tir Gofal is competitive and discretionary, but the criteria against which the applications are to be measured are not public. Environmental gain is the dominant requirement for Tir Gofal. Wales has great diversity in its agriculture, landscapes and rural traditions, and a large number of eligible holdings so how can a mere 600 schemes per annum be perceived to be allocated equitably across such a nation? The constraints are mainly financial, based on an average grant per agreement of £5000. Should the environmental gain of one application be considered worthy of a larger grant, then others will be smaller. The potential increment from improved access, landscape enhancement and economic benefits are second to the environmental gains. On this premise, access appears to have less prominence in Tir Gofal than in Tir Cymen.

The total funds available long-term for Wales' agri-environmental schemes may not be adequate to achieve the optimum outcome for the environment, for farm economies, for rural communities and for increased access, yet this scheme was launched with 'the potential for putting Wales at the forefront of environmentally friendly farming throughout Europe' (CCW, 1999).

An upland farm with a relatively traditional farm management system may be as vulnerable to deterioration as more intensively managed farms in lowland areas. The deterioration, possibly as a result of declining farm incomes, will be evident in many ways, economic, social and environmental. If the main criteria for approving the Tir Gofal agreements are environmental, the means of achieving 'environmental benefits' are those stated in the Handbook, but the specific long-term objectives are not identified. The priority given to environmental benefits may meet the requirements of Agenda 2000 and EU funding regimes but, in Wales as elsewhere, the characteristics and qualities of the rural landscapes and communities are not enhanced only by nature conservation. Williams (1999: 2) argues that the central issue is to help farmers to stay in business and to safeguard the rural economy and way of life. The continued decline in agricultural subsidies and payments, particularly in upland Wales, will increase the relative significance of funds from agri-environmental schemes. For some it might mean the difference between economic survival or death.

Farmers may have been reluctant to commit themselves to Tir Cymen at a time of upheaval in agriculture in Wales. Dramatic changes in markets for traditional livestock and arable products, declining prices and cuts in agricultural subsidies, especially for hill farmers, has made them reluctant to engage in yet another economic and social adjustment. Compensation for reduced stock levels, for changing practices of cultivation and for loss of grazing has to be seen to be adequate. Any scheme of this sort only works if the economics are feasible; £5000 on one farm may be a considerably more significant sum than on another.

The ADAS evaluation in 1996 reported that in the absence of Tir Cymen, the average income per farm would have fallen over the survey period. Additional loss resulted from Tir Cymen restrictions, such as livestock reductions. However, the Tir Cymen payments offset these losses. If a similar pattern pertains in 1999, then farmers will not undertake the even more stringent Tir Gofal Management Prescriptions and survive the reduced headage payments for stock unless there is confidence in adequate Tir Gofal payments. These payments are not 'money for nothing', but an investment in 'environmental capital', increasingly sought by politicians and public. (DTER, 1999). The ADAS evaluation also records the effect of Tir Cymen on the local economy. It identifies the increased employment opportunities arising from Tir Cymen after only 3 years, 'The study has confirmed that at least 123% of the value of Tir Cymen capital payments finds its way directly into the local economy as increased spending on both labour and materials' (ADAS, 1996: 5). The survival of economically viable farms will benefit rural communities and economies directly and indirectly.

Farmers may search for alternative sources of income generation if the agri-environmental schemes are inadequate. Some options may be acceptable; others may not be, and may even be counterproductive if environmental health is the long-term objective for Wales. A level of financial support to recognize the partnership with landowners, the custodians of the landscape, may be essential if Tir Gofal is to be effective in the long term and make a significant contribution to enhancing the environmental capital of Wales. There is a responsibility for the funding process of Tir Gofal to ensure that the payments to landowners are retained in Wales to enhance the Welsh landscape and economy. In an economic environment where agriculture is trans-national, small-scale projects such as the AWAES may not have the resources for such scrutiny.

Quiet enjoyment of preferred landscapes is an aim which hides a number of difficulties for this wide-ranging scheme. The assumptions on which the schemes are based are subject to scrutiny as are the means of achieving them. For example, the traditional Welsh landscapes themselves are assumed to be an attraction for visitors. This underpins much of the tourist advertising for Wales. Coastlines, uplands and industrial landscapes feature in the marketing and reflect images of beauty, nostalgia, excitement and mystery. Landscape quality and landscape diversity are central to tourist advertising, yet the tourist industry 'consumes' the resources created and maintained by others. Tir Cymen and Tir Gofal are relevant to tourism in that they not only include opportunities for increased access to open countryside, but will also affect the landscapes on which tourism depends. In such a way landscape and access become commodities through the tourist industry.

However, the integration of new habitats into the overall landscape is not straightforward. In the original Tir Cymen plans habitat features were marked on the individual farm maps. These in themselves did not record the quality of a particular habitat, but gave only indications of habitat diversity to be included in individual farm plans. Much more detailed analysis was required than was possible by either farmers or Tir Cymen officers, despite their local knowledge. This approach required a wide range of skills from the officers: landscape evaluation, ecological competence and patient negotiating and management competencies. Tir Gofal has greater emphasis on habitat quality. This may increase the responsibility of the field officer to have both an overview of the locality and a detailed knowledge of sites. As the number of farms in the scheme increases year on year, the demands on a limited number of officers will be considerable, particularly given their central role in the allocation and management of agreements and therefore funds.

At an administrative level there are also related considerations. The formal evaluations required for Tir Cymen followed only shortly after the introduction of the scheme, a necessary process for the design of its successor. Evaluations of Tir Gofal are also likely to be required in the short term in order to demonstrate 'value for money', but landscapes may improve only slowly. Even during the landscape and wildlife evaluation a series of visits to farms to compare photographs taken in 1992 and 1997 did not give adequate detail of species enrichment (Entec, 1998). The long-term environmental objectives may be worthy but vulnerable to short-term political expediency, accountability to the EU funding agencies, fashions in public taste for rural recreation and landscapes and lack of accurate information on environmental value.

Measuring public preference for landscapes is not uncontroversial and results may be ambivalent. Macnaghten (1995) suggests that people do not have set and stable needs and attitudes towards countryside leisure and that these are affected by wider cultural controversies. This challenges assumptions in UK policy documents that leisure participants have 'unitary and stable needs and views which reflect internally consistent "attitudes"'. In the AWAES and 'Access to the Open Countryside' proposals (DTER, 1998) the standard for access is 'quiet enjoyment', but Tir Gofal now includes cycling within the definition, having consulted with various groups which represent rural leisure interests. Although the participation level in walking has remained consistent (41%), changes have occurred in the types of activities in which people engage in rural areas. As the public becomes better informed, more concerned with health and fitness, spends more on fashion sports clothing and takes more short-break holidays, so its use and expectations of rural areas change. Different expectations will affect values of and preferences for landscapes, will increase the range of attitudes and, potentially, will polarize conflicts among rural residents and visitors. Similarly, few can have missed the UK public debates during the past 10 years on rural issues such as declining farm incomes, deer and fox hunting, BSE and national water resources, all of which will have revived images of rural areas. They may also have changed attitudes to and expectations of them. These exemplify the contention that people have different and varying needs and attitudes towards countryside leisure and the countryside, which will affect the ways in which landscapes are perceived and valued.

Tir Gofal's main, but not exclusive, objective is environmental enhancement, but it is not yet evident which future environments are planned for and, in anticipation of landscapes valued for leisure, which are the preferred landscapes. 'Quiet enjoyment' of the countryside may not be compatible with the habitats preferred by environmental protagonists. Time is also a factor in that the transition from one habitat, such as intensive sheep grazing on semi-improved grassland, to another 'preferred' one, such as heather moorland, may produce temporary landscapes which are neither useful nor attractive (Bullock, 1995). A widespread reaction to the Set Aside scheme in England and Wales reflected the antagonism created by these new rural wastelands. Significant environmental improvement is a long-term process yet leisure and tourism are fickle industries, affected by short-term events as well as by wider cultural controversies. Users of improved access routes will expect to enjoy enhanced landscapes without necessarily appreciating the time required for significant change. There are unexplored questions arising from assumptions in Tir Gofal which connect access, via the visitor, to environmental change and landscape values. The contribution of the farmers and their communities to discussion of the underlying issues in Tir Gofal would enhance their participation in a scheme which has potential for profound impacts on the Welsh landscape.

This chapter has surveyed neither all aspects of rural access in Wales nor all organizations involved in access and rural issues. In itself that would be a considerable task. It has included the relationships between the various participants in the AWAES, partly to identify the changing relationship between public and private sectors in rural affairs.

The European Union, through its agricultural support schemes, part-funds Tir Gofal and Tir Cymen. Hitherto the funding has been negotiated through the Welsh Office, with some grants used to reimburse central government (CCW, 1998b). From May 1999, the Welsh Assembly's Department of Agriculture and Rural Affairs will manage projects such as Tir Gofal through the FRCA, the CCW and the Snowdonia National Park. The Tir Cymen field officers, as representatives of public organizations, have had a pivotal role in the success of the scheme and similar responsibilities have been given to the Tir Gofal officers. Of increasing importance in the wider agri-environmental changes are the conservation, amenity and recreation trusts (CARTs). These are non-profit or charitable organizations and their key aims are environmental conservation, the provision of amenity and recreational opportunity and the conservation of landscape heritage for their members and the general public (Dwyer and Hodge, 1996). In the evolution of Tir Gofal, CARTs were represented in the planning process and will continue to be influential by virtue of the land they own and manage and their membership. They lobby at all levels of the process, in Brussels, London and now Cardiff. The private sector, both through businesses and individuals, also has opportunities for both direct and indirect influence, particularly as farmers' and landowners' views are sought in the AWAES.

In this context, farmers and rural residents are those with the ultimate responsibility for achieving the desired outcomes – enhanced landscapes, environmental health and increased recreational access – in return for financial support. There are expected 'public goods' in the form of increased access and a 'well crafted landscape'. If such responsibility is given to farmers then they need to be confident that the financial support will be adequate for the duration of their agreements, so that as local environments improve the local economy does not deteriorate to the point where it jeopardizes the whole AWAES. A variety of such schemes exists across Europe, and Tir Cymen and Tir Gofal were heralded as pioneers in the whole-farm approach. On a European scale, even Tir Gofal, a nation-wide scheme, is small, yet it is a microcosm of the problems that beset the redirection of agricultural support.

References

ADAS (Agricultural Development Advisory Service) (1996) *Tir Cymen Socio-Economic Assessment.* Countryside Council of Wales, Bangor.

Barnes, P. and Barnes, I. (1999) *The European Union's Environmental Policy.* Edward Elgar, London.

Brown, P. (1999) Private bill forces ministers to act on right to roam. *Guardian*, 13 January.

Bullock, C. (1995) Measuring the public benefits of landscape and environmental change: a case of upland grazing extensification. In: Thompson, D., Hester, A. and Usher, M. *Heaths and Moorland: Cultural Landscapes.* HMSO, Edinburgh.

CEI (Centre for Environmental Interpretation (1997) *An Evaluation of the Access Provisions of the Tir Cymen Scheme.* Countryside Council of Wales, Bangor.

Cloke, P., Doel, M., Matless, D., Phillips, M. and Thrift, N. (1994) *Writing the Rural: Five Cultural Geographies.* Chapman, London.

CCW (Countryside Council for Wales) (1992) *Tir Cymen.* CCW, Bangor.

CCW (Countryside Council for Wales) (1997) *Tir Cymen: the First Five Years.* CCW, Bangor.

CCW (Countryside Council for Wales) (1999) (*Tir Cymen*), www.ccw.gov.uk

CCW (Countryside Council for Wales) (1998a) Legislation needed to secure permanent access to open country. Press Release issued 10 June.

CCW (Countryside Council for Wales) (1998b) *Annual Report 1997–98.* CCW, Bangor.

CSO (Central Statistical Office) (1998) *Regional Trends 33.* HMSO, London.

CSO (Central Statistical Office) (1999) *Social Trends 34.* HMSO, London.

DTER (Department of Trade, Environment and the Regions) (1998) *Access to the Open Countryside: Consultation Papers.* HMSO, London.

Dwyer, J. and Hodge, I. (1996) *Countryside in Trust: Land Management by Conservation, Recreation and Amenity Organizations.* John Wiley and Sons, Chichester.

Entec Consultancy (1998) *Tir Cymen Monitoring and Evaluation.* Countryside Council for Wales, Bangor.

Evans, M. (1997) Farming the Walker. *Countryside Recreation* 5 (4), 15–17.

Glyptis, S. (1991) *Leisure and the Environment.* Belhaven, London.

Griffith M. (1999) Press Release 5/3/99. Countryside Commission for Wales, p. 24.

Harrison, C. (1991) *Countryside Recreation in Society.* TMS, London.

Harvey, G. (1997) *The Killing of the Countryside.* Jonathan Cape, London.

House of Commons Environment Committee (1995) *The Environmental Impact of Leisure Activities.* HMSO, London.

Ilbery, B. (1998) *The Geography of Rural Change.* Addison Wesley Longman, London.

Jones, G. (1998) Welsh Landscape: the future? *Rural Wales*, Autumn, pp. 10–12.

Macnaghten, P. (1995) Public attitudes to countryside leisure: a case study on ambivalence, *Journal of Rural Studies* 11 (2) 135–147.

Marsden, T., Murdoch, J., Lowe, P., Munton, R. and Flynn, A. (1993) *Constructing the Countryside*. UCL Press, London.

Pierce, J. (1996) The conservation challenge in sustaining rural environments. *Journal of Rural Studies* 12 (3), 215–229.

Potter, C. (1998) Conserving nature: agri-environmental policy development and change. In: Ilbery , B. *The Geography of Rural Change*. Addison Wesley Longman, London.

Potter, C. and Goodwin, P. (1998) Agricultural liberalization in the EU: an analysis of the implications for nature conservation. *Journal of Rural Studies* 14 (3), 287–298.

Salmon, J. (1998) Voluntary access – the best way forward. *Adain y Draig*, Issue 22, p. 6.

Sheail, J. (1995) Nature protection, ecologists and the farming context: the U.K. historical context. *Journal of Rural Studies* 11 (1), 79–88.

Shoard, M. (1980) *Theft of the Countryside*. Temple Smith, Aldershot.

Shoard, M. (1989) *This Land is Our Land*. Grafton, London.

Shoard, M. (1998) *A Right to Roam*. Oxford University Press, Oxford.

Storey, D. (1999) Issues of integration, participation and empowerment in rural development: the case of LEADER in the Republic of Ireland. *Journal of Rural Studies* 15 (3), 307–315.

Welsh Tourist Board (1999) *A New Tourism Strategy for Wales*. WTB, Cardiff.

Williams, M. (1999) Gofal Tir – A Phobl? *Cymru Wledig/Rural Wales*, Spring, pp. 2–3.

Developing a Historic Tourist Product: the Case of Loviisa, Finland

6

Kaija Lindroth and Tuovi Soisalon-Soininen
Helsinki Business Polytechnic, Finland

Rationale

This paper concerns the development of a relatively small settlement on the coast of Finland as a tourist destination. The material for the paper was researched through detailed interviews with nine leading figures in the local tourism industry who, together, have made a major contribution to the current and ongoing progress of the project. This is therefore a 'case history' in the true sense of the word and is presented to the reader as a narrative. We believe this informal approach – that of the storyteller – will enable the reader to gain an insight into the human, political, social and economic dimensions of preparing a place for emergence as a tourist destination.

Introduction

On 22 September 1997, Ms Tuula Jäppinen, the municipal tourist secretary responsible for developing tourism in Loviisa, was reviewing the action plan for the historical tourist project in Loviisa that she had been working on together with the project leader, Ms Sari Glad. Their aim was to develop a set of products to establish Loviisa as a historic all-season destination. The historic period of focus was 1750–1850, because Loviisa had played an important role in the history of Finland during that era. The project was made possible through funding from the European Union, which enabled training and advice for the local tourism entrepreneurs in order to develop their products.

© CAB *International* 2002. *Tourism in Western Europe: a Collection of Case Histories* (ed. Richard Voase)

In preparation for the October meeting with the steering committee for the project, Ms Jäppinen wanted to develop her own ideas on how to make all the existing products into an easily accessible and saleable package for visitors.

Background: a Brief History of Finland and the Baltic Sea Region

The Baltic Sea has always been of great importance for communication and trade. Since AD 800, Viking expeditions had made their way not only westwards from Scandinavia but also to the East, going through the Gulf of Finland to Lake Ladoga and then southwards along the waterways of Russia as far as Constantinople. The trading association known as the Hanseatic League dominated the trade in the Baltic Sea from the 13th to the 16th centuries, connecting communities of northern Germany with areas on the south coast of Finland, and Estonia (Klinge, 1992: 9, 17).

In the middle of the 16th century, tension started to grow around the Baltic Sea as Russia, Sweden, Denmark and Poland all showed interest in the territory of the Baltic countries today known as Estonia, Latvia and Lithuania. The ingredients of the conflict were the following: Russia needed easier access to Europe through the Baltic Sea, whereas Sweden and Poland were prepared to do their utmost to prevent that. Denmark had ruled over Estonia before and was interested in regaining the control of the area.

These conflicting interests led to a series of wars between these parties about the control of the Baltic Sea (*Findlands Historia* 2, 1996: 41–43). For Sweden, this was the beginning of a 100-year-long struggle to become a major power in Europe and to dominate the Baltic Sea area. Finland had become subject to Sweden in the 12th century when the Catholic bishop Henry in England had told the Swedes to introduce Christianity to Finland. The Swedish era in Finland lasted until 1809. Therefore, the Finns were always affected by the politics of the Swedes. Sweden's position as a major power was not favourable for Finland as it shifted the focus of attention westwards, toward today's Denmark, whereas the poorer eastern parts of the realm, e.g. Finland, were left unattended (Klinge, 1992: 41–43).

At the beginning of the 18th century, the position of Sweden started to weaken. The shift of power in Sweden was made use of by Czar Peter the Great of Russia and by the Danes, who wanted to regain control of the territory they had formerly lost to Sweden. As a result of the Great Northern War, Sweden lost control of the Baltic Sea to Russia through the peace treaty of Uusikaupunki in 1721. For Finland this meant insecurity, brought about by the fact that Sweden had to cede parts of its territory in eastern Finland to Russia. Also, the new Russian capital, St Petersburg, was situated dangerously near the eastern border of Finland.

The hostilities between Sweden and Russia did not come to an end here. A couple of decades later, Russia conquered even more of the Finnish soil. This forced Sweden to pay more attention to Finland's defence in order to retain control of the northern coast of the Gulf of Finland, as it already had lost large areas in the southern parts of its territory. New fortifications had to be built in Finland to reinforce the defence of the eastern border and the coastline. The area of today's Loviisa was in the vicinity of this border, which made it an alternative when considering the location of the possible new fortresses.

In 1806–1807, Napoleon Bonaparte was at the peak of his power, allied at that time with Russia. His only enemy was England, the most important trade partner of Sweden. Therefore, the Swedish king considered it necessary to be on friendly terms with England. On top of this, he did not approve of the French revolution and, as a result of this, the relations between Sweden and France were tense. Following the Finnish war (1808–1809), fought against the background of the European power politics of the Napoleonic era, Finland was annexed by Russia as an autonomous state. The Russian Czar Alexander I needed Finland as a buffer state to safeguard his capital, St Petersburg. This marked the end of the long Swedish era in Finland. To enhance the gratitude of the Finnish people, the Czar annexed to the Grand Dutchy of Finland the easternmost part of Finland, Karelia, earlier occupied by Russia (*Finlands Historia* 1996, 3: 11–13).

The Russian era in Finland lasted from 1809 to 1917. On the whole, this period provided rather favourable conditions for Finland to develop into a state of its own, due to the very extensive autonomy granted to Finland by Alexander I (Klinge, 1992: 53). The Finns were allowed to keep their own language, religion, privileges and laws among other things. Towards the end of the Russian era, attempts were made in Russia to bring Finland more closely into its sphere of influence. This development was caused both by economic and political reasons, mainly pan-slavism in Russia. This caused a lot of opposition in Finland and it became evident that a crisis was at hand.

The solution was found in 1917 when Finland made use of the revolution in Russia and declared independence on 6 December. On 31 December 1917, Lenin's government announced its recognition of the new state, after which other countries followed (Klinge, 1992: 97–98). Finland, however, continued to be important to the Soviet Union because of its strategic geographical location.

The First World War hardly touched Finland, but in the 1930s the growing political tensions in Europe and especially in Germany drew Finland into the political game. The Russians were afraid of Germany attacking the Soviet Union through Finland, and therefore they demanded negotiations on this issue in 1938–1939. Finland refused, pleading neutrality. The Soviet Union's attack on Finland in 1939 was a surprise. During the Second World War, Finland fought its separate war against the Soviet Union, assisted by German troops after Hitler's attack on the Soviet Union in 1941. The final peace treaty was concluded in 1944 with heavy losses for Finland: Karelia was lost again and 400,000 people had to be resettled in other parts of the country. Finland also had to pay extensive war reparations and accept certain restrictions concerning the size of its army etc. This forced the country to restructure and modernize its industry and to develop exports (Klinge, 1992: 110–116).

During the Cold War period, Finland was not only engaged in developing its economy, but also in stabilizing its position between East and West. Extensive economic cooperation with the Soviet Union was also initiated, leading to the dominance of the Soviet Union in Finnish foreign trade. As a result of that, the collapse of the Soviet Union in 1990 caused great problems for the Finnish export industry, forcing companies to look for new markets. In the 1990s, again, with the market economy gaining ground in Russia, new opportunities were offered for Finnish companies as well. All parties, especially companies in eastern Finland, including Loviisa, were eager to utilize the proximity of the growing Russian market. On the other hand, membership of the European Union since 1 January 1995 facilitated business activity in other parts of Europe.

Loviisa: Background

Loviisa, situated in the eastern part of the province Uusimaa, 90 kilometres east of Helsinki, has an area of 93 km^2, of which 44 km^2 is land and 49 km^2 sea. The population in 1996 was 7700, of which 58.2% were Finnish-speaking, while 40.6% had Swedish as their mother tongue. In 1995, the majority of the inhabitants were employed in service jobs (60.1%), whereas industrial activities employed 35.3% of the population.

Loviisa was known as a boundary and fortification town, having been founded in 1745 after a peace treaty between Sweden and Russia. As a result of that treaty, Sweden had to cede the most eastern part of its territory in Finland to Russia. All the fortified towns of eastern Finland were on the Russian side of the border. A new border fortification was built at Degerby, which from 1752 was renamed Loviisa after the Queen of Sweden.

As Finland had no navy of its own, and the Swedish navy was located too far away to defend the Finnish territory, a new plan for the defence of Finland was based on fortifications instead (*Finlands Historia* 2, 1996: 345). It included the land fortifications of Loviisa, the maritime fortress of Svartholma outside Loviisa, Suomenlinna, a naval base outside Helsinki, and the double land fortifications in Helsinki. Artillery officer Augustin Ehrensvärd was responsible for the planning and construction of the three fortresses. The fortification plan of Loviisa consisted of a central fortification with six bastions, and two bastions outside the town, all surrounded by earthen ramparts. The construction of the land fortresses was never finished, and the whole fortress was never completed, as the funding ceased in 1775 and the importance of the place diminished.

On its foundation, Loviisa was granted rights for foreign trade, and by the end of the century it had grown to be the sixth largest town in Finland, with a thriving export activity. When Finland became part of the Russian empire, Loviisa lost its importance as a fortification town. The 19th and the beginning of the 20th centuries were Loviisa's health spa era, when as many as 1000 visitors per year were attracted by the healthy waters found in the town. Unfortunately, the spa buildings were burnt down in 1936 (Hirn and Markkanen, 1987: 251). Seafaring also played an important role in the development of the town, as Loviisa was the home of one of the biggest merchant fleets in Finland at the beginning of the 19th century. Steam engines, however, replaced sail boats, and Loviisa could not afford to modernize its fleet. Moreover, a railway track from Helsinki to St Petersburg was built north of Loviisa, leaving the town outside the most important trading route, thus accelerating the decline of its business life (Finlandia, 1986: 152).

In the 1990s, Loviisa still carries marks of its past as a fortification town, trading place and a once popular spa resort. The town centre was planned in the mid-1800s, following a town fire. Publicly, the present-day town is known for its nuclear power plants and the freight harbour, Valko. Loviisa was always a less well-developed part of the province Uusimaa, where the recession of the early 1990s affected the sources of livelihood very seriously. Unemployment was 17.9% in August 1997 (the average in Finland as well as in Uusimaa province being 12.5%). Because of this difficult economic situation, the town administration was forced to look for new opportunities to stimulate the economy of the town and to put a stop to the decline in the number of inhabitants. When Finland joined the EU on 1 January 1995, Loviisa area was classified as a declining industrial area, which offered possibilities to apply for European funding to improve the infrastructure. (See Appendix 6.1 for EU funding in Finland.)

These possibilities were also considered by the tourism authorities of the town. Already in the 1980s, a full-time municipal tourist secretary had been employed to develop tourism in Loviisa. The tourist information office operated in the centre of the town and was responsible directly to the town council. In 1997, the tourist information office employed two regular workers and one trainee. The office was shared with the local tourism association, with one employee and one trainee. For the summer season, six extra helpers were hired.

The tourism budget for Loviisa in 1997 was €155,800. Approximately €55,500 was used for marketing targeted on the capital, Helsinki, as well as the nearby towns of Lahti, Porvoo and Kotka. The main target groups were families with small children, boating tourists, middle-aged people interested in history, and history students. The competitors were the very places which generated the bulk of the visitors to Loviisa. Helsinki and Porvoo offered the same kind of historical and cultural products, and the attraction of these places was based on the same values (interview with Tuula Jäppinen 23.5.97).

Loviisa attracted approximately 60,000–80,000 people yearly with domestic visitors dominating. In 1997, Russian tourists were the fastest growing group of foreign tourists, whereas in 1996 the biggest groups were Scandinavians and Germans. The most important tourist sights in Loviisa were the following:

• the church	20,000 visitors
• the nuclear power plant	10,000 visitors
• the fortress island of Svartholma with regular guided cruises	8000–10,000 visitors
• the museum	3000–5000 visitors
• the home of composer Jean Sibelius	500–3000 visitors
• the old town with picturesque alleys and houses	uncounted

- the fortress ruins of Ungern and Rosen in the
eastern part of the town   uncounted

The estimated 80,000 visitors were expected to spend some €3.5 million in 1996. Tourism employed *c.* 140 persons. They worked in 30 cafés and restaurants, seven accommodation establishments, six museums and exhibitions and nine attractions of various types. Most of the tourism companies were small, employing one to three people. Only three companies employed more than ten people (interview with Tuula Jäppinen, 23 May 1997).

Fig. 6.1. Loviisa old town during an historical event.

An important aspect of tourism in Loviisa was boating. The guest harbour, i.e. the marina, had received investment during the previous 10 years. The town had spent €8500 per year to improve the facilities for boating tourists and €5900 per year to market the harbour services. The marina had very good facilities and in 1997 it was awarded the national prize for the marina of the year. This award encouraged further development and the yearly visitor numbers (*c.* 1200) were expected to increase.

As a result of the positive development of the boating harbour, the membership of two international organizations of guest harbours became possible. A Finnish-based chain, Sun Marina Guest Harbours, welcomed Loviisa guest harbour as a member. The chain has been operating since 1992 and had 27 members in Finland, Sweden, Estonia and Denmark in 1997. One of the functions of the chain was to market its member harbours in Europe, and for this purpose it obtained European funding through the Interreg II programme. The second membership was that of the Blue Flag Campaign. The Blue Flag has become a well-known and appreciated symbol of a healthy and tidy environment throughout Europe. The total number of marinas with the Blue Flag in Finland was 42 in 1997 (interview with Tuula Jäppinen, 10 September 1997).

When the different alternatives for suitable EU projects were considered in Loviisa, tourism emerged as one of the options. The town had a past as a spa resort and the general attitude among the municipal decision-makers was favourable to tourism. The vast archipelago and the cultural background were seen as the strengths of the town. The old sea fortress of Svartholma only provided ruins, but both tourism and archaeology experts could see the possibilities for turning it into a heritage product.

Cultural and heritage tourism had experienced an upswing during the past years. Even the museum authorities responsible for the conservation of valuable historical spots had gradually started to accept the idea of using history as a central ingredient in creating new tourism products. Since the European Union had also recognized tourism and the importance of the cultural heritage for its socio-economic dimension, it seemed like a feasible project to start developing something around this theme. An application for 1995 EU funding was made in order to start renovation work on the fortress, while in 1997, the application included the historical project of product development. Both applications were received favourably in Brussels and the corresponding national funding was also arranged (see Appendix 6.1).

The Fortress Island of Svartholma as a Tourist Destination Development

The fortress island of Svartholma, situated 10 kilometres off the south coast of Loviisa, had a fortress measuring 120 × 120 metres. The construction work commenced in 1748 and was completed in the 1780s. In its design, Svartholma was a regular bastion fortification. The Swedish fortification period ended in 1808, when the troops in Svartholma surrendered to the Russians with practically no resistance. From the 1830s, Finnish convicts were sent to the island and the fortress became a prison for Russian political prisoners and it served this purpose until the fortification was emptied in 1853. In 1855, during the Crimean War, a British naval detachment blew up the fortification on the island. After this, the fortress was left to fall into ruin (Finlandia, 1986: 150–151).

The National Board of Antiquities and Historical Monuments started to restore the ruins in the 1960s. During the 1980s and 1990s, the island became a popular venue for the town people as well as for tourists. In 1996 it was visited by 8,000–10,000 people. The services included a harbour for small boats, with access to fresh water, a kiosk with a café, toilets, and guided tours of the fortress. There was a regular boat service operating from the town centre.

In Finland, the National Board of Antiquities (NBA) was responsible for the preservation of the country's cultural heritage. To be able to develop tourist services at Svartholma, the tourism authorities in Loviisa needed the agreement of the NBA.

They also needed to convince the NBA of the meaningfulness of investing in Svartholma. The island already had a series of summer products under the 'pirate' theme that was aimed at families with small children. Since the launching of that product, visitor numbers to Svartholma had improved considerably. Using this as their main argument, the tourism authorities managed to prove to the NBA that, with a better level of services and a wider product range, the fortress island could be made into a popular attraction. Its location in the most densely populated province of Uusimaa, which included Helsinki, and its proximity to other major centres, spoke for itself.

In 1995, the NBA decided to invest €600,000 in a 2-year programme of renovation and excavation work at the fortress, while another €700,000 was provided by the EU. Loviisa town and the Ministry of Labour were responsible for upgrading the infrastructure of the island, including docks, toilets, historical displays, a café, foot paths, service facilities and a park for children. At the NBA there was a keen interest for the project, because the aims of the project comprised elements focusing very much on high quality and educational purposes, rather than on purely commercial values. The planned new products had to fulfil the expectations of the most demanding people acquainted with the historical background of the island. According to the NBA, this heritage product was among the most interesting new enterprises (interview with Minna Karvonen, 7 July 1997).

'Pirate' cruises had been launched in 1991 as a result of product development, in order to find new activities for families with children. The cruises were planned as a joint project of the municipal tourist information office and local entrepreneurs. In 1997, the product comprised the following: a cruise to the fortress island Svartholma, a pirate play at bastion Ungern on the outskirts of the town, a meal at any of the town's pirate restaurants, a shop of pirate products as well as economical family packages at the local hotel and camping site. During the cruise, the children met Svarttis, the pirate, with the help of whom they became familiar with the secrets of pirate life at sea. On the fortress island, the children went treasure hunting and eventually found the treasure. The information office employed three students to act as Svarttis and to develop the character. The adventures of Svarttis were also published as stories written by a famous Finnish historical writer for children, Maijaliisa Dieckmann (interview with Tuula Jäppinen, 10 September 1997).

During the first 2 years, the cruises were sold as charter cruises. In 1997, the guided 3.5 h pirate cruises operated on a regular basis seven days a week. In 1996, some 5500 visitors experienced the adventure and the number was expected to reach 8000 in summer 1997. Over the years, Svarttis developed into a brand, appearing in carefully selected products only. The figure of Svarttis was created by the artist Marjaliisa Pitkäranta, who was also responsible for the appearance of the official Father Christmas of Finland.

The majority of the children came from the nearby municipalities, which meant that there was a need to renew the product in order to keep up the interest of this target group. The original purpose was to make Svartholma a pirate island, a kind of theme park. The historical values of the island, however, weighed too heavily to allow the cultural possibilities of the island to be omitted totally. Among the general public there was a growing interest in history and culture, and many people visiting the island came there to experience the former military scene. Moreover, the purpose was to attract new target groups to visit the island during its 250th anniversary. Also, the NBA wanted to encourage products better suited to their purposes (interview with Tuula Jäppinen, 10 September 1997).

The 'Historic Loviisa' Project

Although local tourism entrepreneurs were satisfied with the large EU investment in improving Svartholma, they questioned the meaningfulness of investing so much money in a destination that is firstly not very easily accessible, and secondly operational only during the 4 summer months. The tourism authorities in Loviisa shared the concern of the entrepreneurs, as they had also been thinking of creating new attractive tourist products to celebrate the forthcoming 250th anniversary of the fortress Svartholma in 1998. The tourism authorities had come to a conclusion that the town did not offer enough for tourists during the off-season. However, they thought that the growing segment of families with children was best catered for in summer, i.e. the world of pirates, as well as customized pirate packages. As families with children seemed to be keen on adventures, the idea of a new product, based on the history of Svartholma and staged there, started taking shape in 1997. The problem of the winter season still remained.

A new project, called 'historic Loviisa', was launched in January 1997 to focus on the fortification era of the town (1750–1850). It aimed at creating new packages focusing on culture and history, in order to attract a wider range of tourists to Loviisa throughout the year. The funding was obtained through the European Social Foundation, the Ministry of Education and the Eastern Uusimaa Regional Council, and totalled €121,700 for the period 1997/98 (interview with Tuula Jäppinen, 23 May 1997). In May 1997, Ms Sari Glad was employed as a project leader on a consulting basis with overall responsibility for planning, implementation and reporting as well as marketing. She was a tourism and marketing expert with experience from several similar projects, e.g. marketing Vuokatti Ski Centre for Russians, and Arctic Wonderland and Santa Claus in northern Finland. The latter was a good example of a tourist product with Finnish heritage in a new form. The NBA joined the project by supplying a part time consultant, Ms Marja Tuomisto, responsible for the correctness of the historical data of the products. Tuula Jäppinen acted as the representative of Loviisa town.

The project comprised two main parts: training of entrepreneurs and product development. Altogether 33 people from 17 different local tourism companies participated in the 8-week training. The entrepreneurs represented, among others, restaurants, accommodation and programme services. Marja Tuomisto, the consultant, facilitated a series of training sessions including the history and culture of the 18th and 19th centuries. Training sessions also dealt with customer service and familiarization with fortresses in Loviisa in particular and in Finland in general. A visit to an 18th century style restaurant finalized the training in April 1997. After the training, 21 people from 12 companies and organizations were chosen to participate in the second phase of the project, which entails developing historical products in a business incubator led by the project leader. Business incubators are normally used to establish new business ideas and new companies. In this case, however, the goal was to widen the product range of existing companies and to guarantee employment in these small tourism companies (interview with Sari Glad, 10 June 1997).

In the interviews of the entrepreneurs conducted after the training, the participants had a chance to express their ideas and opinions about the project as well

Table 6.1. Development of historical products by small businesses.

Type of business	Products	Number of personnel
Cafés and restaurants		
Konditoria Café Vaherkylä Ek Ky	Café products in historical style	
C and D Fastfood Skeppsbron	Café and restaurant products in historical style	4–5
	Pirate products	6
Café Saltbodan	Historical menus and interieurs	6–9
Accommodation and restaurant		
Degerby Hotel Restaurant Ltd Oy	Accommodation	
	Meetings in historical milieus	35
	Catering in Svartholma	
Sepän-Sällin korpihotelli	Café in Svartholma	
	Historical menus outdoors	
	Programme services	1
Souvenirs		
Kukka Esplanad Blommor	Reproduction of 18th and 19th century porcelain	1
Nyländsk Hemslöjd rf.	Handicrafts in historical style	1
Bengt Göran Sirén	Pewter products in historical style	3
Tornitalo	Art Gallery in historical milieu	1
Others		
Loviisa Tourist Office	Ehrensvärd cruise, Historical adventures for children	2
Itä-Uudenmaan oppaat r.y. Östra Nylands guider r.f.	Guided tours	17 guides
Estas	Marketing in the Baltic countries and in Russia Product development	1

as their willingness to work for the project. Most of the ideas of the entrepreneurs were concerned with improving their existing services. The training had, however, inspired some of them to create totally new products. The business incubator was to help the entrepreneurs in the planning of the new products so that these could be promoted already in the autumn of 1997. Thus, the entrepreneurs committed themselves to the joint historical framework.

Ms Marja Tuomisto had supplied them with folders of historical material to be used in developing the products. Ms Sari Glad had already started preparing the action plan for the project: she insisted on a tight working schedule so that the individual products would be ready for marketing in early autumn 1997. Moreover, she thought that the new packages should be planned taking into account international marketing as well.

The products involved in the project have been summarized briefly above. What now follows is a closer look at the activity of three different organizations who concurrently developed their own products. The descriptions are based on interviews with company representatives.

1. Konditoria Café Vaherkylä Ek Ky

Mrs Pirjo Vaherkylä-Ek owned a baker's business together with her husband. They took over an old family company in 1986. They started to develop the traditional bakery into a versatile cake shop and café. In 1997, they had a turnover of €250,000 and employed four people in winter and six in summer. The business idea was to manufacture high-quality bakery products with cakes and pastries as the main line followed by bread and pasties. The main target group was individual local clients, but during the summer season tourists played an important role. They also had some companies as regular customers. The company, situated in the centre of Loviisa, had an image of offering products which were not the cheapest, but always of reliable quality.

The field was very competitive. Three other local bakeries operated in Loviisa. However, the biggest competitors were big national bakeries which dominated in the retail shops. Most retailers in Finland belonged to national chains which signed centralized agreements about their ranges. This made it very difficult for shopkeepers to have local products in their product range. Therefore, Pirjo and Håkan Ek considered it necessary to invest actively in product development in order to enhance their business in other ways. They decided to concentrate on cakes and pastries, opened a café and also started a catering business. In this way, they succeeded in diversifying their clientele, which had previously consisted mostly of elderly people.

The products were marketed by occasional advertisements in local papers, but the most important way of promoting the products was by word of mouth. The company had also participated in the pirate campaign together with other local entrepreneurs and the tourist information office.

Pirjo and Håkan Ek saw the historical Loviisa project as offering a possibility to carry on with the development process of the company. Their café was situated in an old building with a historical atmosphere, so a new product linked with the history of Loviisa was a welcome addition expected to generate extra revenue. During the summer of 1997, a new cake was developed. The hope was to launch this cake as the Loviisa cake, which would be served with coffee at official receptions as well as being a dessert on the historical menus planned by local restaurants. In addition to this, Pirjo and Håkan expected their historical café to be visited by a growing number of tourists on guided historical tours.

The problem in developing the café for tourists was the fact that it only seated 15 people, which made it impossible to welcome tourist groups coming by bus. On top of that, the location of the café was not the best possible as it was located in a less busy area of the town.

In spite of this, the Eks eagerly participated in the historical project, which gave them a chance to improve cooperation with other entrepreneurs. They were also inspired by the training and by the new ideas brought up during the training sessions, even if the project required a lot of their time.

2. Ehrensvärd cruise product

During the latter half of the 18th century, artillery officer Augustin Ehrensvärd spent 22 years in charge of the entire work of constructing the fortress of Suomenlinna outside Helsinki and that of Svartholma outside Loviisa. He was also the founder of the 'archipelago fleet', expressly created for Finland's archipelago and unique in that it was commanded by army officers. The Ehrensvärd cruise product aimed to commemorate his work.

In 1997, Tuula Jäppinen, the tourist secretary of Loviisa, cooperated with the Governing Body of Suomenlinna and with Helsinki City Tourist Office to plan the 250th anniversary of the fortresses Suomenlinna and Svartholma in 1998. In a meeting with Mr Pekka Timonen of Suomenlinna, the two came up with the idea of reviving the voyage Mr Ehrensvärd had made in 1747 in order to explore the Finnish coastline east of Helsinki for defence purposes. All three parties decided to cooperate on this venture. The cruise was organized by Classic Tours, a tour operator based in Helsinki offering event programmes for companies. They specialized in taking their customers to the archipelago or to the sea for the events. The vessel they chose to use for the Ehrensvärd cruise was s/v Tradewind, the most genuine sailing ship available in Helsinki, which had also submitted the best bid. The pilot cruise took place on 15 August. The test group consisted of the representatives of the National Tourist Board of Finland, the national airline Finnair, Classic Tours as well as members of the organizing bodies. The guests boarded the cruise ship s/v Tradewind early in the morning in Helsinki to sail first to Suomenlinna. There they visited the Ehrensvärd museum to familiarize themselves with the historical theme. An hour later, s/v Tradewind started the voyage towards Svartholma. On board the ship, which was registered for 40 people, the test group heard about the experiences of Mr Ehrensvärd and participated in various tasks undertaken on sailing ships. A buffet table with suitable beverages was enjoyed during the voyage.

Fig. 6.2. s/v Tradewind.

The group arrived at Svartholma in the evening to experience a historical event as guests of the commander-in-chief of Svartholma towards the end of the 18th century, Mr von Schantz. The programme continued in the fortress with military exercises, ballads and speeches. The historical dinner served in the open air by Degerby Hotel Restaurant Ltd Oy rounded off the evening. Around midnight the party sailed to Loviisa.

Ms Jaana Laine of the tourist information office of Loviisa was responsible for the programme in the fortress. She was pleased to see that the idea of the Ehrensvärd cruise worked well and would add nicely to the tourist facilities in Loviisa. However, in her opinion, the product would not be an easy one to realize, as it engaged a great number of people and involved many special arrangements. In future, the tourist information office would like to see one of the local entrepreneurs become the organizer of these events.

The programme of the test cruise was as follows:

8.30	Departure by s/v Tradewind
9.00	Suomenlinna
10.00	Departure for Svartholma
13.00	Lunch

Fig. 6.3. Dinner at Svartholma.

20.00	Svartholma
20.30	Dinner
23.00	Departure for Loviisa
24.00	Loviisa

3. Degerby Hotel Restaurant Ltd Oy

In 1992 Containerships Finance Ltd Oy, a family business based in Helsinki, decided to expand into the hotel and restaurant business. Their main activity, however, was still in container ships and transportation. In 1997, the company operated the following premises: the Degerby, a modern business hotel with two restaurants; the Scandinavia, a city hotel with a bar and take-away service; the Degerby Gille, a theme restaurant; the Kappeli, a summer restaurant and an architectural evocation of the spa era; the Pilasterit, a meetings and conference venue and the former home of the owners; the Villa Veltheim, a venue for small-scale meetings and training sessions; and Reimarvik, a venue located in the archipelago, offering facilities for small-scale meetings and also services relating to enjoyment of the natural environment. Except for the last two, the premises were all situated in the city centre. Degerby Gille, the oldest house in the town, and Pilasterit were officially listed as historically valuable buildings.

The business idea of Degerby Hotel Restaurant Ltd Oy was to offer accommodation and restaurant services of high quality. In 1997, the company employed 35 people during the winter season and 45 during the summer. Of the total turnover of €2 million, restaurant services accounted for 65% and accommodation for

35%. The restaurant services offered a wide variety and mostly catered to the local population. People coming for meetings and various courses comprised the majority of the accommodation clientele. Individual tourists were of minor importance. With respect to accommodation and meeting facilities, the closest competitors were in the nearby towns of Kotka and Porvoo, while a couple of local entrepreneurs competed in the restaurant business.

Clients for meetings and accommodation were reached mainly through direct marketing to companies and through frequent-use programmes. To promote the restaurants, the company advertised in local papers and sent marketing mail to the inhabitants of Loviisa. In marketing to tourists, they cooperated with the city tourist office and the regional tourism promotion organization based in Loviisa. The company had been developing new products for tourists: wedding services and an indoor variant of the Svartholma experience. The Svartholma-inspired interior of the newly renovated restaurant Scan, connected with the hotel Scan (former Scandinavia), was to be opened in October 1997.

Ms Iina Pälväjärvi, General Manager of Degerby Hotel Restaurant Ltd Oy, participated in the historical tourism project in Loviisa. She saw it as a good opportunity to develop the attractions of Loviisa and to find new target groups through joint marketing. She also believed that the company would be able to expand their cooperation network, especially in the field of event programmes. Moreover, the historical elements involved in the project were already represented in some of their products.

The company wanted to continue the historical theme when planning their new product in the business incubator. The purpose was to put together a meeting product with historical features in Pilasterit, which dated back to the 18th century. The place offered a perfect setting for customers who demanded something more than a conventional meeting venue. Ms Pälväjärvi was satisfied with the help and contacts she got during the training and the business incubator activity. The sessions took a lot of time, especially during the high season, but were worth the trouble because they managed to establish new networks and the product development progressed. Her only worry was the future of the product development after the end of the project in 1998. Ms Pälväjärvi left the company in August 1997, but her successor, Mr Jon Wedde, took over the work.

Marketing the New Products

The year 1998 was a great challenge for Ms Tuula Jäppinen and Ms Sari Glad who were responsible for the marketing of the 250th anniversary of Svartholma in that year. Some of the anniversary events were to be shared with Suomenlinna and would also celebrate Mr Ehrensvärd's achievements. The most important joint event was the Ehrensvärd cruise, but several of the Loviisa incubator products were also ready for marketing.

The marketing for 1998 comprised the historical products and special events taking place that year and also the regular marketing measures conducted each year by the tourist information office. Therefore, the funding was also twofold: some of the money came from the historical project funding while Loviisa town provided the remainder. The former concentrated on promoting the products brought about in the business incubator and the latter aimed at boosting the various events taking place in Loviisa during that year.

Another challenge was the year 2000, with Helsinki as one of the 'cultural capitals' of Europe. That same year, Suomenlinna was to be the venue for the Tall Ships Race, an annual event for old sailing ships in the Baltic Sea countries. The visitors coming to these two events were thought to be excellent target groups for the new historical products of Loviisa. By that time, the product development was sure to be well under way to implement the plans for 'historic Loviisa' in 2008, which marked the end of the 10-year planning period (interview with Sari Glad, 18 September 1997).

Ms Jäppinen and Ms Glad were, however, of the opinion that it was equally important to awaken the interest of the local people for the historical project. They understood that a handful of people would not be able to create the right atmosphere for the product. During a study tour of similar events, they had experienced the enthusiasm generated by locals eagerly participating in the arrangements and adding something extra to the experience of the visitors.

Engaging people outside the tourism companies was necessary because a lot of people were needed to stage the historical events and to organize different programme services. Because the tourism companies only employed a few people, they were unable to invest in the practical arrangements since their employees were needed to run the business. Furthermore, enhanced participation was sure to create a more favourable attitude towards tourism in Loviisa. This had already been proved in connection with the Ehrensvärd cruise.

Partners were also needed outside Loviisa. Luckily, Loviisa was situated along the so-called King's Road, once the most important route connecting Norway, Sweden, Finland and Russia. This medieval road was at the time marketed as a joint Nordic product for tourists interested in history and culture, the main market being North America. The national tourist boards of Norway, Sweden and Finland had given this product priority in their marketing efforts abroad. Not only had they published brochures about the road, they had also invited American journalists on familiarization tours. A historic road was not enough as such; it was necessary to offer the travellers different attractions along the route. The Nordic countries had been involved in developing this route for years, trying to add suitable products into the King's Road packages. According to the tourist secretary and the project leader, the historical products of Loviisa were well suited for this purpose.

The historical project in Loviisa did not only aim at developing new products, but also had cooperation with other sea fortresses from the same era as one of its targets. The fortress cooperation was twofold. In Finland it comprised the fortresses of Suomenlinna, Bomarsund, Hanko, Kotka and Hamina with which work had already begun. The Baltic Sea cooperation, due to start in 1998, involved Narva, Rakvere and Kuresaari in Estonia, Kronstadt in Russia, and Karlskrona, Kalmar and Waxholm in Sweden (interview with Tuula Jäppinen, 10 September 1997).

These 18th- and 19th-century sea fortresses set the following goals for their cooperation:

- historical programme services;
- joint publications;
- historical souvenirs;
- marketing quality products.

Boat owners were identified as the primary target group. Accordingly, the first joint promotions took place at various boating fairs in Finland and Sweden where the first products were to be launched. For future needs, other target groups were also considered.

The frame of the project started taking shape. Tuula Jäppinen was now aware of the ideas of the enthusiastic entrepreneurs involved in the project. She was convinced that the framework for the action plan for the historical project would be agreed at the meeting in October. With the help of all the committed parties, the individual products within the framework could be launched in 1998, setting the scene for the 250th anniversary and leading the way to future development. In preparation for the meeting, she wanted to identify the measures to be taken in order to implement the historical image of the town and make both Finns and foreign visitors aware of its attractions.

Conclusion

This case history has summarized the initial stages of a tourist product development process. The aim of the product development project was to create an image for Loviisa as a historic tourist destination and to create new tourist products in line with this theme. The Loviisa example shows that with innovative thinking product development does not necessarily require new investments, but can be based on existing infrastructure and local culture and tradition.

There were several factors that enabled progress to be made within this project. First, the National Board of Antiquities, the Loviisa Tourist Office and the entrepreneurs all had faith in the chosen theme. Second, EU funding made training and expert help possible. Third, the fortress island Svartholma was an established venue for day trippers. Last, professional and inspiring project leaders played an important role in the shaping of the project.

One of the problems in this joint process was to motivate the small businesses to invest their time in training, and to believe that this investment would turn profitable in the long run. On top of that, the fact that the training sessions coincided with the busiest season also presented a clear problem. A project like this involving many different interest groups and entrepreneurs also required good cooperation to succeed.

Loviisa as a declining industrial area was in need of regeneration. The ultimate aim of this project was to bring more visitors to the town, to create new jobs and thus generate badly needed extra income. Involving local people in the project was a prerequisite in the creation of historic products. Furthermore, participating in joint events might also work as a tool to enhance the local people's faith in the future.

Acknowledgements

The authors are grateful for the information provided for this case history by the following interviewees:

Ek, Pirjo, Entrepreneur of Konditoria Café Vaherkylä Ek Ky, 18 August 1997

Jäppinen, Tuula, Municipal Tourist Secretary of Loviisa, 23 May 1997 and 10 September 1997

Glad, Sari, Project Leader for Loviisa Historical Project, 10 June 1997 and 18 September 1997

Karvonen, Minna, Planner of the National Board of Antiquities, 7 July 1997

Laine, Jaana, Clerk at Loviisa Tourist Information Office, 28 August 1997

Mutka, Kari, Managing Director of Classic Tours, 29 August 1997

Pälväjärvi, Iina, Hotel Manager of Degerby Hotel Restaurant Ltd Oy, 2 September 1997

Tuomisto, Marja, Consultant of the National Board of Antiquities, 4 June 1997

Wedde, Jan, Hotel Manager of Degerby Hotel Restaurant Ltd Oy, 26 September 1997

References

Anttonen, M., Eriksson, S., Eromäki, S. and Heiskanen, M. (1997) *EU-rahoitusta Vuosina 1995–96 Saaneet Matkailuhankkeet*, Sisäasianinministeriön aluekehitysosaston julkaisu 6/1997.

Department for Regional Development (1997) *Regional Development in Finland.* F.G.Lönnberg Oy, Helsinki.

Finlandia, Otavan iso maamme kirja (1986) Otava, Keuruu.

Finlands historia 2–3 (1996) Schildts Förlags Ab, Ekenäs.

Hirn, S. and Markkanen, E. (1987) *Tuhansien Järvien Maa, Suomen Matkailun Historia.* Gummerus Oy, Jyväskylä.

Karvonen, M. (1997) *Kulttuuri- ja kulttuuriperintöalan rakennerahastohankkeet vuosina 1995–1996*, muistio, Museovirasto (NBA).

Karvonen, M. (1997) *Euroopan unionin tuki kulttuurimatkailuhankkeille Suomessa*, muistio 17.4.1997, Museovirasto (NBA).

Klinge, M. (1992) *A Brief History of Finland.* Otava, Keuruu.

Brochures

Brochures of Loviisa

Brochures provided by the National Board of Antiquities and the Ministry of Trade and Industry

Appendix 6.1: Project Funding

In 1995, Finland and Sweden joined the EU, but they differ greatly from most of the other member states due to their geography and climate. The countries were characterized by sparse population, long distances, and great seasonal changes.

In Finland, the EU regional and structural policy was aimed at through the following programmes:

- Objective 6 area status for very sparsely settled and least developed regions, covering the northern parts of the country. This programme applied to Finland and Sweden only.
- Objective 2 area status for regions suffering from industrial recession. This programme was applicable to the Loviisa area.
- Objective 5b area status for promoting the adjustment of the enterprises to the open internal market.

In 1997, as much as 53.6% of the total population of the country lived in these three areas. During the period 1995–1999, Finland was allocated 1.7 billion ECUs from the EU structural funds (Department for Regional Development, 1997: 15).

The development strategy of the objective 2 areas in Finland in 1997–1999 included increasing job opportunities, restructuring industries, enhancing competitiveness, improving know-how of the employees, as well as increasing international cooperation. The goal of the initiative was to help especially small- and medium-sized enterprises (SME).

Loviisa was classified as an objective 2 area. This gave the town new opportunities for restructuring and stimulating its declining industry and commerce. The archipelago and the cultural environment of the area also enabled the development of the tourism industry on top of the conventional metal and wood processing industries. The location of Loviisa along the E18 highway to St Petersburg, as well as a well functioning goods harbour, furthered the possibilities for development (Department for Regional Development, 1997: 24–25).

Tourism projects in Finland were funded from various structural funds involving several ministries: the Ministry of the Interior, the Ministry of Trade and Industry, the Ministry of Education, the Ministry of Agriculture and Forestry, the Ministry of Transport and Communications, the Ministry of Labour and the Ministry of the Environment. According to a survey by the Ministry of Interior in 1995–1996,[1] a total of 520 projects involving tourism were partly community-funded with a total budget of €39.9 million. The EU covered 33% and the state 46%, while the share of the municipalities was 15% and that of the private sector 13%. The rest of the funding was generated through various project activities. In eastern Uusimaa, 20 different tourism projects were funded in 1997.

Within cultural tourism, central EU programmes and actions were the Objective programmes and Community initiatives, both realized through structural funds.

[1] EU-rahoitusta vuosina 1995–1996 saaneet matkailuhankkeet 6/1997

On top of these, the Raphaël programme and the Philoxenia programme also aimed to support cultural tourism.

In Finland, the NBA made a survey on the funding of the regional cultural projects in 1995–1996 (Karvonen, 1997). The survey showed that 91 projects were funded with a total of €5.2 million (community funding €3.1 million and national funding €2.2 million). On top of this, the Ministry of Education funded cultural projects with a total of €2.96 million (EU €1.6 million and national €1.36 million) in the same years.

In 1995–1996, the community funding for the objective 2 programme in Finland totalled €6.7 million. Of this sum, €15.6 million were transferred to the next period 1997–1999 when the corresponding figure was €130.8 million.

The objective 2 programme included several cultural tourism projects, e.g. the following:

- Svartholma fortification project;
- Promotion of Karelian culture, tourism and business life by Lappeenranta City Theatre;
- Ahvenkoski–Ruukki international nature and cultural tourism project;
- Historical tourism in Rauma region;
- Toivonen domestic animal zoo and farming museum in Kälviä;
- Joint marketing project of cultural events and tourism in central Finland. (Karvonen, 1997: 2–3)

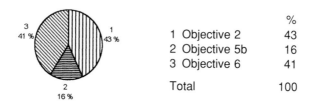

		%
1	Objective 2	43
2	Objective 5b	16
3	Objective 6	41
	Total	100

Fig. 6.4. European Community funding in 1995–1996 in Finland by programme. Regional cultural programme objectives 2, 5b and 6.

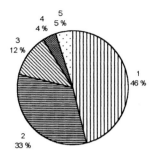

	%
1 Architectural heritage, industrial heritage	46
2 Cultural environment, development of regions and villages, construction and planning	33
3 Cultural tourism and marketing	12
4 Museums and exhibitions	4
5 Others	5
	100

Fig. 6.5. European Community funding in 1995–1996 in Finland by theme. Regional cultural programme objectives 2, 5b and 6.

The Älvdalen Story: Marketing an Inland Destination in Rural Sweden

7

Solveig Böhn and Jörgen Elbe
Dalarna University, Sweden

Introduction

This chapter takes the form of a narrative, because its subject matter, the development of tourism in a rural area in central Sweden, is inseparable from the entrepreneurial activity of one individual. The story is about how one man, over a period of 25 years, worked to develop tourism in Älvdalen, a small and relatively unknown area of Sweden. It begins in the 1960s and finishes when the supply-side of Älvdalen's tourism industry was restructured at the end of the 1980s. The research undertaken to produce the chapter includes the use of written records that the man left behind after his death in the early 1990s, articles in newspapers, and interviews with people who worked closely with him, and also with other associates, one of whom is the author of this chapter.

Background

The municipality of Älvdalen is situated in the province of Dalarna, an established tourist region in Sweden. By the beginning of the 19th century, the province was one of the most visited in Sweden. The province has been called 'the heart of Sweden', because of its typically 'Swedish' character and old traditions, such as costumes and dialects, which have survived with only slight influence from outside. This is especially the case around the Lake Siljan area (Tynderfeldt, 1991: 7). The image of the area owes much to artists and writers, who observed the landscape and its people and painted and described it. The most famous of these are Carl von Linné, the Danish writer Hans Christian Andersen, and the Swedish artists Carl Larsson and Anders Zorn. Substantial help also came from Artur Hazelius, the creator of the world's first open-air museum, Skansen in Stockholm. This museum was built around structures and objects originating from Dalarna.

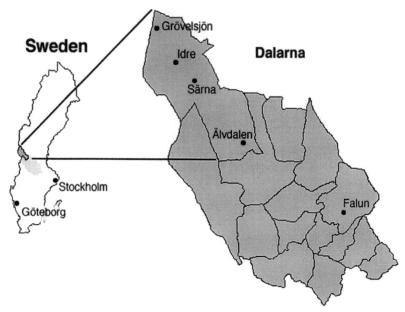

Fig. 7.1. Dalarna province: location.

The province of Dalarna has also been known for its industry. Most notable was Falu Koppargruva (Falu Copper Mine) in Falun. This dates from the Middle Ages, and during its heyday in the 17th century was responsible for two-thirds of Europe's copper production (Tynderfeldt, 1991: 58). The mine was economically important for Dalarna and Sweden over a long period and is believed to have been fundamental to Sweden's industrial development.

Following the Second World War, a winter tourist trade was established, and the northern part of the province became Sweden's most popular region for skiing, both cross-country and downhill. Apart from the natural prerequisites for this sport, other contributing factors are a well developed infrastructure and closeness to the population centres. The area is a 4–5 h car journey from Stockholm, a distance that, in this part of Sweden, is considered to be acceptable for a weekend visit.

The province of Dalarna is still today the most visited province in Sweden. Just as it was 100 years ago, the province is associated with what is called 'the heart of Sweden'. The visitors are attracted by the natural environment, the folklore and the traditions, as well as for winter activities. Approximately 85% of the visitors to the area are Swedes.

Tourism in the Älvdalen Municipality

Älvdalen is the northernmost municipality in the province, with an area of 6914 km² and with 8200 inhabitants. It is sparsely populated, with 1.2 inhabitants/km².

Sweden as a whole has 22 inhabitants/km^2 (Lundström and Sundgren, 1997: 22). The municipality consists of three parishes: Älvdalen, Särna and Idre. Between the northernmost centre of the parish of Idre and the centre of Älvdalen, which is the municipality's administrative and service centre, is a distance of 110 km. This means about 1.5 h drive by car. Unemployment in Älvdalen municipality is among the highest in Sweden: 18.5% of the available workforce (Lundström and Sundgren, 1997: 94). The restructuring and rationalization of agriculture, and especially forestry, has contributed to this high figure.

Tourism has a long history in Älvdalen. During the Middle Ages, pilgrims passed through Älvdalen on their journey to the great cathedral in Nidaros (Trondheim, Norway). The first 'modern' tourists arrived in the 19th century to study porphyry work dating from 1788. Porphyry is a hard volcanic rock which was worked into art objects by local craftsmen (Tynderfeldt, 1991: 81). Anglers from England visited the northern part of the municipality during the same century (Bauer, 1996: 83). In the first half of the 20th century there was a tourist industry in the municipality of Älvdalen, but of a limited scope.

In the north of the municipality, to the north of Idre, is Grövelsjön, a small mountain lake. It is surrounded by typical Scandinavian mountain terrain (fjäll) close to the Norwegian border. Here the road ends. Tourists came to this area for hiking, hunting and fishing. Mountain farmers started to let rooms to the tourists and later started building boarding houses. In 1937, a mountain hotel was opened. Then, as now, it was owned by STF (Swedish Tourist Federation) which is a non-profit organization, owned by its members and founded in 1885, which now deals largely with youth hostels and guest houses. Other accommodation in the municipality was available in the form of small boarding houses, and cabins or cottages with few, if any, amenities, as well as a small hotel in the town of Älvdalen. The main activities of visitors to the area were skiing in the winter, hiking and fishing in the summer. Idre is also home to Sweden's southernmost Lapp village.

Since the 1960s, the municipality has witnessed an explosion in tourism development, though not evenly distributed over the municipality. Today, there are a total of 25,000 bedspaces, which together generate over 1.3 million guest nights. The turnover is more than SEK 500 million (Resurs, 1997). Approximately 16% of the available workforce is employed in industries depending on tourism (Lundström and Sundgren, 1997: 82). Those who visit the area are almost exclusively leisure travellers, though in Idre there is some conference industry, and the town of Älvdalen is naturally visited by business travellers. However, the extent of this is so slight that when we continue to talk about tourism it will only be in relation to leisure travellers.

Overall, progress of the kind that happened in Älvdalen is due to entrepreneurial activity and sociocultural conditions in the form of the political environment, economic state, social trends, human values and lifestyles (Gunn, 1997: 21–42). All these together shaped the conditions for development. The story which follows tracks the role of one contributor to this process, a man who worked to develop tourism in the area. He is of interest because he worked using methods which were sometimes perceived as ineffective and unmodern. However, to market a little-

SKANLAND

Fig. 7.2. Darlana province: hiking, hunting and fishing.

known area without large economic resources demanded new methods, which
would later show themselves to have been ahead of their time.

Development of the Älvdalen Municipality as a Destination

In Sweden, until the 1950s and 1960s, it was common to find non-profit-making
local tourist associations in places that had visitors who came for leisure and recreation. In Älvdalen, as in many other places, the local tourist association took
responsibility for providing accommodation and arranging activities and events for
the visitors. Many of these visitors came to the area by public transport and, as a
result, were dependent upon local arrangements. The majority of visitors to northern Dalarna were Swedes.

The expansion of motoring after the Second World War resulted in new travel
patterns and destinations, as well as expectations of, and demands on, the reception
services. This in turn caused many of the local tourist associations in Sweden to
make their presence more noticeable, as was the case in Älvdalen. This development
in Älvdalen was closely connected to one person, a 29-year-old former commerce
teacher who came to Älvdalen in the middle of the 1950s to work in the municipality's schools. After his arrival, he soon came into contact with the local tourist
association and thus began more than 30 years of work in the tourism industry.
Supervising pupils in a classroom soon became of secondary importance in his life.

Instead, he felt his mission was to educate people from near and far about the mountainous wilderness of northern Dalarna and teach them the geographical location of Älvdalen.

As a new arrival in an area, one wants to learn about the surroundings, and so it was with this new teacher. He found Älvdalen so beautiful that he realized more people should have the opportunity to see and experience the area, not just Swedes. As he had studied in Heidelberg, Germany, his first thought was of the Germans. During his stay in Heidelberg he had arranged study trips for other students, so, with this experience and his interest in promoting northern Dalarna, he soon became the driving force of the local tourist association.

What the tourist association had to offer is not especially unique: a combination of beautiful landscapes and a traditional culture. It was the agent for accommodation, including boarding houses, privately owned cabins, cottages and rooms with basic amenities, and a hotel in the centre of the parish of Älvdalen. The means for marketing the association's services were very limited. Up until this point, it had been word of mouth that brought people to the area, as well as locally displayed posters on noticeboards and in shops. The activities and events that the tourist association arranged for visitors were just expected to break even in financial terms. Though the municipality may sometimes have funded the association with public money, this was not a regular source of income, and all the association's services were offered as non-profit-making enterprises.

When the local tourist association wanted to expand, it had to face many different issues. Establishing a tourist bureau and a new hotel, among other things, did not just require financial contributions but also great enthusiasm and commitment from the community. More privately owned cabins and rooms to let were needed and local events and activities needed development and a coordinator. Last, but not least, it needed to launch the product on the market.

By the beginning of the 1960s, the municipality had started to feel the structural changes that were taking place in Sweden's economy. More and more people were leaving agricultural work and rationalization had begun in the forestry industry. Big companies and the Swedish government were large owners in the municipality, and the inhabitants began to realize that they could no longer rely on the traditional industries of forestry and farming to support them. Consequently, interest grew in the opportunities that tourism had to offer.

In 1964, the aim of developing tourism in the municipality was made official with the opening of a tourist bureau. Support for its opening had been established in a public debate. It was located in a small building next to the railway station. The chief of this enterprise was the local tourist association's driving force, the teacher who had moved into the town. To help him run Älvdalen's tourist bureau, he recruited two women from the tourist association. Neither of them had any specialized education, though the first employee had gone to secondary school and so had some knowledge of German. The second went to the tourist bureau one day to see her friend who was working there, when the tourism manager asked, 'Can you take care of a bus with a group of tourists going to Sälen (a neighbouring town).' 'Well, I know the route quite well so why not', was the answer she gave, and that was the start of 23 years of full-time work for Älvdalen's tourist bureau. Later, other tourist bureaux were opened in both Särna and Idre.

There were no special tasks or specific duties in the tourist bureau and working hours could be very irregular. The work was split up according to the different people's qualifications or according to demand. However, one of the employees was given the responsibility of maintaining the network of people in Älvdalen who had offered their cabins or rooms for hire. The reason that she was specifically chosen to do this was that she could speak 'Älvdalska', a dialect only spoken in Älvdalen. That she was able to do this offered some kind of reassurance to those inhabitants who were a little unsure about letting out their property to tourists.

The tourism manager was responsible for an equally important area, that of external contacts. The contact network was based upon the ideal of, as he put it, 'further extending the development of a tourism economy' as stated in a local newspaper.[1] This network was built upon the support of contacts in travel agencies, tourist bureaux, associations and carriers, both in Sweden and abroad, and also partly with tourist organizations and manufacturers of tourist products within Sweden. The tourism manager started this by using the contacts he had made during his time in Heidelberg, which resulted in more and more Germans discovering northern Dalarna.

In order to learn how to run the tourist bureau as an agency, he travelled around in Sweden visiting tourist bureaux and talking to tourism managers. In a tourist bureau on the Swedish west coast he found a very useful contract form. He took it back home and copied it. Some time later, a friend of the tourism manager on the west coast said he was going to Älvdalen and showed him the contract for a stay in a cottage. The tourism manager recognized the form, got angry, called the tourism manager in Älvdalen and told him he could not take a form designed by another bureau, copy it and use it. 'Excuse me, but why don't you take your family and come up and visit us in Älvdalen' was the answer the man received. So he did, and a long period of friendship and cooperation began.

By travelling around in Sweden visiting people, the tourism manager became involved in tourist organizations and quickly secured positions on their boards. In organizations such as 'Föreningen Sveriges Turistchefer' (Swedish Association of Tourism Managers) and 'Svenska Turisttrafikförbundet', an organization that in 1978 was replaced by the Swedish Tourist Board. Living in Älvdalen, close to Norway, he also visited the neighbouring municipalities on the Norwegian side. Borders were, for him, not a problem: 'We have to be large, therefore we must be boundless', as he pointed out many times.

In these organizations and companies, the tourism manager found people who shared his ideas about the development of tourism, about personal contact with the guests and about close cooperation with distributors and tour operators. Joint products developed out of referring tourists to other organizations and bureaux. An example of this is Team Skandinavia, which was to become known as Skanland,

---

[1] *Mora Tidning*, 3 August 1987.

an informal cooperative organization made up of six tourist and recreation areas in Sweden and Norway. They developed and produced package tours and car and bus tours for tour operators. The tourist bureaux within Team Skandinavia's areas together had good service and reception facilities. They guaranteed that the customer would get good service and that the customer's visit would be an enjoyable 'boundless' summer experience. As Team Skandinavia stated, 'Through ties with the area's tourist organizations it is guaranteed that you will be well looked after'. In Älvdalen, for example, this meant that guests were many times spontaneously invited for coffee.

Cooperation was built upon trust and knowledge, through personal contact and a joint belief in personal commitment. Travel suggestions for tour operators and agents were not presented in brochures, but rather as personally composed material with detailed descriptions mixed with postcards and leaflets from different areas. This may be thought to be amateurish, but when resources were limited, as in Team Skandinavia's case, factual content was given a higher priority than aesthetic appearance and layout. They established contacts between different people and maintained them through personal involvement.

Because Team Skandinavia offered products tailored to the customers' demands, they had to have a flexible organization. The network for a product was built up of people who were able to take responsibility for that product being produced at the best price and with personal service. For example, sometimes it could be that the staff at an establishment needed to be able to speak German, as a holiday village may suddenly receive a whole new group of Germans as guests. Everything was continually checked so that the producer was always able to live up to the motto 'the best care for the customer' and this checking was done using personal knowledge. Every guest who had made a booking through the tourist bureau in Älvdalen was greeted personally on arrival, and this was to be the case everywhere a guest was booked in. When, however, Älvdalen did not have the desired product, there was no hesitation in booking the guest into an establishment elsewhere in Sweden. The conditions were simply that the establishment or cabin warden could offer the guest good personal attention. These other places or establishments, 'second partners', were, however, not dealt with unless the tourism manager himself or a partner bureau's manager had personally spoken with the people responsible for the products and services.

The establishment of a network to reach the market and to get customers to come to Älvdalen was just as important as building and maintaining the network of 'second partners' or the production network. Products were always developed through a dialogue with 'the market', or, to be more correct, with the representatives of the market. Confident of having tourist products for the European market, he started to travel around Europe in the same way he had been travelling in Sweden, visiting tour operators and agencies. First in Germany, then in the Netherlands, Denmark and England, many times with his friend from the west coast, who was now a tourism manager in a Swedish municipality, Sunne, in the neighbourging province of Värmland. An example of a new contact was a manager of an automobile touring club in Germany, whom he had met on one of his tours.

Through him he got new contacts. He became a member of FICT, an international federation of tourism managers, and new doors were opened for him. All the people he met he invited to Älvdalen, and when they came he gave them a great deal of personal care and attention, many times inviting them to his own home. Regular trips to Europe were then made to maintain established contacts.

As an agency, Älvdalen tourist bureau worked both as an intermediary, for example booking accommodation on a commission basis, and as a broker, offering package products or being a partner in a network such as Team Skandinavia, where each partner was responsible for the tourists' stay in the different areas. The tour operators or agents communicated with the tourist bureau by telephone, telex or later by fax. This way of working was accepted by his partners in Germany, the Netherlands and Denmark, but in England they insisted on having a formal incoming tour operator as an intermediary. To overcome this problem, they had to establish an incoming tour operator, and thus the Inter Holiday company was born. This company was started as a division of Gothenburg's tourist bureau, but developed into one of the most significant companies of the 1970s and beginning of the 1980s in bringing tourists into Sweden. The two tourism managers from Älvdalen and Sunne were from the start the only owners. As managers they appointed a friend, a former tourism manager, and the man from Älvdalen became the chairman of the board. Stocks were then sold to a number of regional and local tourist bureaux and ferry lines.

Inter Holiday wanted to satisfy the demand for an effective booking system for the hire of cabins and cottages at a reasonable price. Swedish holiday homes were cheap to hire and demand was rising, but the problems were bookings and the accessibility of information. Through Inter Holiday they appealed to the market in a more traditional way, as the products were featured in various catalogues. Inter Holiday annually distributed catalogues of holiday cabins and cottages that were written in English and German. In 1972, 60,000 catalogues in English and German, containing details of package tours, were distributed. They contained, among other things, 'Autoholiday', a complete car tour package in which Älvdalen was one of the stops. A camping package was also available, where guests bringing their own cars were sold ferry transport and a packet of camping vouchers. These vouchers enabled the customer to pitch a tent or caravan on a number of different camping sites throughout Sweden. In Sweden, this type of camping package was an innovation. It is possible that 1972 was the first time that this was done anywhere in the world, though this has not been confirmed. These new concepts were sellable due to an original presentation and construction. The driving forces were the man from Älvdalen and his friends in Team Skandinavia. One year, they even developed and sold fly-and-drive packages to the northern part of Scandinavia and North Cape.

Inter Holiday opened new markets for Älvdalen through its distribution network, and offered new services, such as booking systems to make products more accessible, but it was still necessary to maintain the foreign contacts. An annual visit to the agencies concerned in Europe was one of the goals of the tourism manager, and, as always, a set of slides was brought along to be shown to those who were interested. Alternatively, these visits could focus on trade fairs. Every year, the tourism manager travelled to the tourism trade fair, ITB, in Berlin. On March 7, 1988, the newspaper *Berlin Today* announced 'Ove (his first name) ist wieder in Berlin' (Ove is back in Berlin). According to the article, the motive for visiting ITB and Berlin was that '15 years ago 10,000 Germans annually visited Älvdalen, now it is 25,000'.

Public relations activity was constantly used as a cheap way of promoting the area. There are many clippings from foreign newspapers, mostly German, that describe Älvdalen and its tourism manager. Journalists were invited to Älvdalen and greeted by the tourism manager, also they were often invited to visit him at his home. However, it sometimes happened that a little more than was possible to fulfil was promised. One famous story is about a film crew which was promised the opportunity to film a bear. There were certainly bears in the area, but not always at a suitable time and place. The solution was for the tourism manager to go out into the woods dressed in a bear-suit and to hide behind a tree. At a later date, the film was shown on TV in Berlin, Germany. A professor, an expert on wildlife, saw the film and noticed something that looked like a shoe beneath the foot of the supposed bear. A news programme and television debate followed. After that the tourism manager was named 'the bear from Älvdalen' by his friends in Berlin.

Another technique used to attract visitors to Älvdalen was the creation of twin-town links. Evidence of this can be seen today outside Älvdalen's tourist bureau, where there is a stone on which is written, among other things: 1122 km to Schönberg, a gift from Schönberg to Älvdalen. In 1975, at a music festival in Schönberg, northern Germany, the tourism manager had met a local musician. This was the beginning of a long relationship, not only between the two men, but also between their municipalities. Many trips have since been arranged between the two towns.

There are many other stories about the tourism manager in Älvdalen and how he worked to develop tourism in Älvdalen. We have only mentioned a few. Though it sometimes looked very amateurish, everything he undertook had a specific purpose. One of the fundamentals in developing tourism to a destination is, as he has written:

> ' . . . to tell that we exist. No one else will do it for us. The marketing wheel must be spinning, new contacts must be made, old contacts cultivated. We must find and test new distribution channels at the same time as the product development process is going on, in a boundless cooperation between different companies and institutions within our municipality. Our views must be in all directions so that we, in the future, can appear as a part of a greater whole, as a very attractive recreational area full of activities to experience.' (freely translated)

In 1960, the small tourist association handled bookings for 2500 guest-nights; in 1976, for more than 100,000. Many of these guests came from Germany. During one period, Älvdalen had more German tourists than any other inland municipality in Sweden. The story ends in 1990 when it was decided that the tourist bureau should move into a newly built hotel. One of the former employees at the tourist bureau put it like this, 'It will be a little more difficult to get anglers with fish-hooks in their hats to step into a hotel'. Already in 1986, however, Särna, Idre and Grövelsjön had started up their own tourist organization and were running tourist bureaux. As the tourism manager said: 'The people up in the northern part of the municipality have always been longing for their "freedom"'. At the same time one resort, Idre Fjäll in the north, had successfully been expanding and had its own ideas in developing and marketing tourism. As a result of the closure of the tourist bureau and the transfer of the service into the hotel, the tourism manager was released from his duties.

Tourism in the Älvdalen Municipality Today

Älvdalen as a recognized destination had begun with an enthusiast who had dedicated his life to a tourism organization. Municipal aid had helped to open a tourist bureau in a modest building next to the railway station. In the winter of its first year, one cabin a week was all that was hired out. Now in the Älvdalen municipality, they speak of 1.3 million guest-nights generated by various companies and intermediaries. In the northern part of the municipality there are many hotels, high class holiday villages, an airport with daily flights to Stockholm and even a golf course; a development for which the tourism manager laid the foundation. There are plans for further development in ski-lifts and accommodation. In the parish of Älvdalen, however, development has stagnated. Altogether around 50,000 guest-nights are distributed across a single hotel, a youth hostel, two small holiday villages and individual cabins and cottages. Some individuals are working in tourism development, but no one has been able to act as a catalyst in the same way as the former tourism manager.

What remains from the 1970s and beginning of the 1980s? Are the Germans still there? Unfortunately we cannot tell from available statistics. There is a residual number, including those who, on the tourism manager's advice, bought holiday homes and so became faithful to Älvdalen, but the numbers of German caravaners have considerably decreased, as have also the numbers of those who come on bus tours to stay at the hotel. The contacts with Schönberg have however once again intensified and the Danish ferry lines are still sending tourists to Älvdalen, but the Inter Holiday company has closed its office. Team Skandinavia exists no longer, but there is one thing that has survived from the days of the tourism manager, and that is Skanland – the cooperation between municipalities on the border between Sweden and Norway. In this case, the municipal authorities involved have decided to promote tourism and Interreg II aid has been applied for, and received, from the EU. However, this is no guarantee for success in the future. The place in the woods, where many guests in Älvdalen were invited for coffee, is now a summer-café.

Germans are still attracted to the area, though the 'new' Germans come because the wilderness is enticing. The tourist bureaux are still intermediaries, but now there is a new actor working, a German, who came to the area to work as a teacher, but has 'stayed on' and opened an incoming bureau in Idre. He is a representative for some of the 'old' German tour organizers, but also the owner of a travel agency that sells 'De Skandinaviska Fjällen' (The Scandinavian Mountains) in Germany. He cooperates with companies in the area that took care of the German guests during the 1970s and 1980s. This incoming bureau has, however, also built up its own contact network to produce products in demand now in the 1990s. With knowledge of the market and with its own travel agency, the prerequisites of being able to increase the number of Germans visiting the whole Älvdalen municipality are again good. However, sadly, the personal reception and service that made the place so famous among the Swedes, and even among the Germans, Danes and Dutch, is no longer there and will probably not return.

Discussion

A case history like this one is often told from a certain perspective; this is the way that the case study tells us something and becomes meaningful. The perspective is chosen according to what the author of the case study wants to point out. In this instance, the case study is of the development of tourism in Älvdalen over a 30-year period. If we regard the process of marketing as one through which people 'obtain what they need and want through creating, offering, and exchanging products of value with others' (Kotler, 1994: 6) we could say that the case is told from a marketing perspective.

Of course, it is possible to maintain that the tourism manager and his colleagues did not shape the tourist products in Älvdalen, because they did not have control over all the incoming production resources. Instead, we can establish that they put together different and necessary components to create attractive products and made them accessible to a market. A consequence of them not possessing all the resources for the product they offered, and therefore, we can maintain, a major concern for the tourism manager and his colleagues was marketing.

What is it that makes this case interesting from a marketing perspective? The case contains many fascinating aspects, but in our interpretation we have chosen to highlight two things that we feel are important. The first reflection that was made, when we started to investigate the case, was to wonder how a destination that was, in principle, unknown to the market, could develop to such an extent despite an almost total lack of economic resources. This is the aspect with which we will principally concern ourselves. We will attempt to set the working methods of the tourism manager and his colleagues into a theoretical context. The second aspect on which it is useful to reflect is why the municipality wished to restructure its tourism industry after 30 successful years. We end our discussion with some thoughts on this, but these are, we admit, maybe more speculation than analysis.

If we begin with the first aspect, that of the working methods of the tourism manager and his colleagues, we were struck by the fact that the interest and engagement they had for their tasks was, in principle, self-defined. They worked in a spirit of optimism and were encouraged by the freedom they had to structure their own work. Even if we can establish that they were enthusiastic and probably the right people for their jobs, this is not the whole secret of their success. The case history also shows that the tourism manager persistently worked with a long-term strategy, namely to create, develop and maintain relationships.

Relationships were developed with a long line of different people and organizations: travel agencies, organizers, transporters, local destinations with complete products, suppliers of cabins and different activities within Älvdalen itself. Accordingly, we can establish that the tourism manager gradually built up a network of relationships with producers and distributors. This network became the tourism manager's, and therefore the destination's, most valuable asset. The attentive reader will of course have noticed that the tourism manager and his colleagues spent a lot of time strengthening relationships with the destination's guests. These customer relations will be returned to later, but first we shall discuss the relationships between the tourism manager and the different producers and distributors.

To understand better what we mean when we talk about relationships, we shall pause for a while and think about what this concept means. One definition could be that 'a relationship is mutually oriented interaction between two reciprocally committed parties' (Håkansson and Snehota, 1995: 25). How does one reach the point where interaction between the parties is characterized by reciprocality and commitment? One way to try to understand this is to study the history of the relationship.

A relationship can be seen to be built out of the different episodes of interaction that take place between the parties. These episodes can take the form of exchanges of information, business deals, or simply some form of social interaction. In the long run, these episodes can lead to the parties getting to know each other better and taking defined roles, i.e. one ascribes to the other an identity based upon the understanding he has of what the other party can and cannot do (Håkansson, 1982).

A partner who is familiar can by experience be trusted. Therefore, the relationship comes to be characterized by mutual trust. The parties accordingly reduce some of the feeling of uncertainty that is a stumbling block when doing business. They already know each other and know what to expect from each other. Over time, the parties may become dependent on each other as their resources become connected and their activities are linked together (Håkansson, 1982). The planning for the next season, for example, happens as a reciprocal exchange. The relationship is shaped according to each party's resources and joint activities develop. We can therefore say that relationships create mutual dependency at the same time as they are a way of managing a dependent relationship.

In this case, a production network was created that consisted of deliverers of different services (for example people with rooms for hire) and deliverers of activities within, and sometimes outside, the destination. With regard to the people who hired out rooms, we can see the significance of one of the workers being local and being able to understand and speak the local dialect. This probably contributes to trust being quickly established. Contact with parties outside the destination was with people that the tourism manager knew and trusted, so they dared to rely on each other's judgement and could therefore move guests between each other. Naturally, the tourism manager was dependent on his producers and, at the same time the producers became dependent on his business.

The development of relationships with the distributors of tourism products grew out of the tourism manager's own social network. The contacts he had in Germany were of importance. This is a natural first step. The parties knew each other from previous social episodes and were therefore quick to create trusting bonds. One contact led to another. The relationships were built up on successive episodes that each contributed to the establishment of trust. In this way, the different parties in, for example, Germany came to ascribe to Älvdalen a certain identity. This identity was probably not so much about the place itself, but rather that the parties knew that their customers would be cared for. They knew what expectations they could have of the reception services in Älvdalen and, through earlier experiences, could feel relatively sure that their expectations would be fulfilled. Through their relationship with the tourism manager and his organization in Älvdalen, they could reduce some of the uncertainty associated with sending customers to a destination in a foreign country. At the same time, as the uncertainty was reduced, the different parties' dependency on the tourism manager and his destination increased.

With time, the tourism manager also became part of more formal networks, for example, the Swedish Tourist Board, Team Skandinavia and Inter Holiday. That he was able to have great influence within these organizations depended of course upon the business he had built up and the confidence he inspired (the identity others ascribed to him, his organization and the destination). So, over time, many people came to be dependent on his business.

In a formal sense, his organization consisted of just him, two assistants, a small tourist bureau and a modest municipal subsidy, but, in practice, they had an influence on many other organizations' resources, as well as coordinating activities with these other organizations. Therefore, we can say that Älvdalen's tourist business was adapted to a number of external parties, who also adapted themselves to Älvdalen. A variety of reciprocal cooperative and dependent relationships had developed, and this contributed to a well-established tourist industry without the use of more traditional marketing methods, like the marketing mix model. In reality, the organization had access to considerably more resources than a formal description of it would imply.

It was not only the relationships with the producers and distributors that were maintained; the guests themselves were also a focus. One can justifiably assert that the business was customer oriented. For example, the staff at the tourist bureau in Älvdalen did not hesitate to book a guest into a place outside of their own destination if they could not fulfil the guest's wishes themselves. They also had an ambition to personally welcome every guest they had booked in, which was an almost unbelievable achievement.

To be able to understand how the tourism manager and his colleagues worked with the guests, we need to discuss how we can evaluate quality, i.e. what it is that creates a satisfied customer or guest. We will start the discussion from more general reasoning about the idea of quality in service production. A service can be considered to be a process where one only has one chance to do something right, so therefore it is important to offer quality that meets the guest's expectations. Because it is the guest's expectations that control the experience of quality, it is valid for the producer to try to create the right expectations in the customer, i.e. those that can be fulfilled (Grönroos, 1983). The tourism manager and his colleagues did that partly through the direct contact that they had with the guests, noticing what the guests' expectations were, and partly through holding a constant dialogue with the travel agencies and arrangers about the products' contents.

When we talk about the notion of service quality, we can divide it into two aspects (Grönroos, 1983). We can talk about the service's technical quality and about its functional quality. The technical quality concerns what the customer receives, i.e. that the parts of the product hang together and are of reasonable quality. For example, the hotel room is cleaned, the booking process works, etc. This aspect of quality can be measured and is often taken for granted. We first become negative in our outlook when something of this technical nature does not work. Functional quality concerns how the service is delivered and so is connected to the interaction between the customer and the staff. Accordingly, it is about treatment, readiness of service, flexibility, etc. This aspect is harder to measure but is often the one that can raise the quality of the experience.

The tourism manager and his colleagues did not, as highlighted earlier, have checks over production resources, and therefore could not directly control the quality of work among the interested parties. A result of this was that they had close cooperation with the different producers who were dependent on the municipality's tourist business, and in this way they probably had some influence over the quality of the products. Technical quality could plausibly be affected by the contacts they had with the different producers, while they could more directly affect the functional quality through meeting the guests themselves.

The personal care and attention that the tourism manager and his colleagues offered can also be seen as a way of strengthening relationships with the guests and so creating customers that are loyal and return year after year, as indeed they did in this case. Naturally, a service company's most important investment is that which goes into developing satisfied regular customers. In this way, a customer base can be developed that is relatively cheap to maintain. At the same time, satisfied customers can act as marketers through telling others about services with which they are pleased. Thus, the personal contact that the tourism manager and his colleagues had with their customers can be seen as a way in which they were able to control quality and as a way in which they could learn more about the customers' preferences.

It is clear that not only were the relationships important that developed with the producers, distributors and customers, but also those with the news media. The methods used were not always conventional, but they produced the desired result. Despite the fact that Älvdalen cannot generally be described as a well-known destination, it received a significant amount of space in the press. The press was an important channel for communicating offers to the market and, besides, it was not especially costly. Also, offers published in the press are generally, rightly or wrongly, apportioned high credibility.

'Relationship Marketing': a New Name for an Old Game

The working methods that the tourism manager and his colleagues developed through their careers in Älvdalen did not have a working title, at least at that time. Today we would probably call their methods 'relationship marketing'. A definition of this term is: 'Relationship marketing is marketing seen as relationships, networks and interaction' (Gummesson, 1995: 245). This definition may not be especially precise, but it does show that relationship marketing focuses on something other than that with which the traditional view of marketing has been concerned.

Traditional marketing has, to a great extent, been concerned with how companies are able to obtain a market for their products and services, i.e. how they shall prosper through transactions with their customers. A result of this is that traditional marketing has a short time perspective and its dominant function has been the marketing mix, where the variables of price, product, promotion and place are adjusted to bring about an effective offer. This type of marketing, which is sometimes called 'transaction marketing', and can therefore be contrasted with 'relationship marketing', is maybe most suitable for a product where the price and the technical quality are the main criteria.

Relationship marketing companies therefore aim to build long-term relationships, through which many transactions can take place. Consequently, this perspective is long-sighted and relationships are built on mutual adjustments over a period of time. Both parties should benefit from maintaining the relationship. The price variable is therefore not especially important, rather it is the ability to jointly find good solutions and so develop reciprocal trust (see Grönroos, 1994, for a discussion of transaction versus relationship marketing). In the application of relationship marketing, the strategic attitude is not principally built upon the consideration of how the marketing mix is to be managed (even if this is also important). Rather, the main things are the consideration of how certain relationships should be developed and how relationships should be managed (Axelsson, 1995). These latter aspects are clearly shown in the case under discussion, as the tourism manager's strategy was not focused primarily on how the marketing mix should be shaped, which, in any case, was impossible as he did not have control over all the variables in the mix. Therefore, we can assume that consideration was given to which relationships should be developed and how they should be maintained. Long-term relationships are needed to ensure that business can be done.

Using relationships in business is nothing new. For those people involved in business, the importance of handling relationships has probably been obvious, so why is it that this has not received earlier attention within marketing? There are probably no simple answers, but one explanation could be that the basic assumptions behind traditional marketing theory have been inspired by economics. A dominant assumption within this discipline is the idea of 'the economic man', i.e. the belief that economic parties act in a rational manner to maximize their own profit or benefits. This leads to the belief that every economic party one-sidedly looks after its own best interests and uses the marketing mix to position itself against its competition (the marketing mix is sometimes also called the competitive tools mix). The basic assumption behind this viewpoint is that markets are characterized by competition, and that it is this competition that enables the markets to work.

These theoretical ideas about markets have guided our way of thinking for a long time, but research shows that, in practice, markets consist of two fundamental parts, namely competition and cooperation (see Brunsson and Hägg, 1992). Maximizing profits is consequently not such an obvious goal for a company, rather it is survival and long-term development that is the ambition (Cyert and March, 1992). With these ambitions, cooperation with others can reduce uncertainty and so can be a conceivable and often necessary strategy (Pfeffer and Salancik, 1978).

Why Change a Winning Concept?

We have now come to the final question: why was it that the municipality went ahead with changes in the tourist industry in Älvdalen after thirty years of success? One opinion that we have heard during our interviews is that the municipality wanted to concentrate its investments upon the northern parts of the municipality, i.e. Idre and Grövelsjön. The natural prerequisites for winter tourism are found in this area, and development increased rapidly as alpine skiing grew in popularity in Sweden through the 1970s and 1980s. The development of tourism in the main town of Älvdalen, which would have been given a great priority in many other municipalities, was not considered to be sufficiently interesting compared to development in Idre.

Another reason could be that many people saw that the tourism manager was no longer a young man. The tourist industry had grown to such a point that it should have been taken over by someone capable of administering it. Many realised that the tourism manager, who was an entrepreneur, was not capable of doing this. At the same time, there were also questions about whether the tourism manager really worked in a professional manner. Few people, except those closest to him, understood how he worked and saw the strategic considerations he made. We must remember that this was a time when the concept of relationship marketing did not exist, which is why there was no generally acceptable term for his working method. Therefore, it was difficult for outsiders to understand how he worked as the methods were not recognized and legitimate.

At the same time, it is possible to maintain that the relationship network that the tourism manager built up was largely a network of strong bonds between individuals. Such personal networks are probably more common in service industries like tourism than in, for example, goods production. In goods production, physical resources are tied together and activities that transform these resources are linked in a way which means that a routine connection will develop between the parties, which does not make the relationship as dependent on individuals. In service industries, the resources often consist of the knowledge, contacts and experience that the separate individuals have 'in their heads' (Axelsson, 1995: 396). This makes activities that organizations do jointly very sensitive to personal changes. In Älvdalen, the tourism manager was the man who held together all the relationships, and when he was no longer around all the resources to which he had gained access through his different contacts also disappeared. These interpersonal contacts underpinned, more than anything else, the development of Älvdalen as a tourist destination: a success for relationship marketing *avant la lettre*.

References

Axelsson, B. (1995) *Professionell Marknadsföring*. Studentlitteratur, Lund.

Bauer, H. (ed.) (1996) *Dalarna 1997*. Svenska Turistföreningen, Stockholm.

Brunsson, N. and Hägg, I. (1992) *Marknadens Makt*. SNS Förlag, Stockholm.

Cyert, R.M. and March, J.G. (1992) *A Behavioral Theory of the Firm*, 2nd edn. Blackwell, Oxford.

Gunn, C.A. (1997) *Vacationscape: Developing Tourism Areas*, 3rd edn. Taylor and Francis, Washington, DC.

Gummesson, E. (1995) Relationship marketing: its role in the service economy. In: Glynn, W. and Barnes, J. (eds) *Understanding Services Management*. John Wiley and Sons, Chichester, pp. 244–268.

Grönroos, C. (1984) *Strategic Management and Marketing in the Service Sector*. Chartwell-Bratt, Cambridge, Massachusetts, pp. 38–40.

Grönroos, C. (1994) From marketing mix to relationship marketing: towards a paradigm shift in marketing. *Management Decision* 32 (2), 38–40.

Håkansson, H. (ed.) (1982) *International Marketing and Purchasing of Industrial Goods: an Interaction Approach*. John Wiley and Sons, New York.

Håkansson, H. and Snehota, I. (1995) *Developing Relationships in Business Networks*. Routledge, London.

Kotler, P. (1994) *Marketing Management. Analysis, Planning, Implementation, and Control*. Prentice Hall, Englewood Cliffs, New Jersey.

Lundström, E. and Sundgren, E. (eds) (1997) *Dalarna: Fakta och Perspektiv*. SCB, Luleå.

Pfeffer, J. and Salancik, G. (1978) *The External Control of Organizations: a Resource Dependence Perspective*. Harper and Row, New York.

Resurs A.B. (1997) *Rese o Turistindustrins Effekter på Ekonomi och Sysselsättning: Idre – Särna – Grövelsjön 1996, Älvdalen 1996*. Resurs AB, Stockholm.

Tynderfeldt, B. (ed.) (1991) *Dalarna*. Utbildningsförlaget brevskolan, Stockholm.

Part 3

The Sociocultural Context

Introduction:
The Sociocultural Context
as Dominant

Richard Voase
University of Lincoln, Lincoln, UK

On the surface, the four case histories in this final part may appear to have little in common. However, as will be shown in this introduction, there are unifying sociocultural themes. The key corollary of the 'new' tourism, representing a diversification of interest away from the normative beach holiday to the quest for experiences and environments which offer increasing challenge, is that nothing – from the folk culture surrounding league football in the United Kingdom, to rural life in Austria, to conservation issues surrounding an established coastal visitor site in western France – is exempt from annexation and commodification for the benefit of the tourist cause.

Finn's exposition of the transformation of English league football from sport to spectacle indicates how folk culture – for that is what it is – can be transformed into a generator of major revenue streams. An interesting facet of this case is that this particular aspect of folk culture was already professionalized, prior to the transformation charted by Finn. What in essence has happened is a two stage process: league football, already commercialized and employing paid players, was restructured to provide a commodity for televized output. In other words, commercialization and commodification, terms often used interchangeably, are not necessarily one and the same thing. The same dichotomy is evident in Baron-Yelles' exposition of the Pointe du Raz, but in reverse. The latter-day official interest in the site involved the *decommercialization* of the site at the same time as its *commodification* as a visitor attraction returned, in manicured form, to a pre-modern romantic state. Lohmann and Mundt valuably contribute to the picture by indicating how a range of demographic variables, of which levels of education proves to be the most salient, can be linked with a resurgence of interest in cultural experiences on the part of the German outbound market, Europe's largest. The pressure to return to the pre-modern, albeit in commodified form, is the central issue in Luger and East's contribution on youth culture and tourism development in an Austrian region. Here, commercialization and commodification proceed hand-in-hand; what the contributors succeed in adding, of great value, is an insight into the experience of living in a region re-presented as a pre-modern construct.

© CAB *International* 2002. *Tourism in Western Europe: a Collection of Case Histories* (ed. Richard Voase)

As with the introductions to the previous two parts, attention is drawn to three issues, in this case of a sociocultural nature, which are arguably common to all three contributions.

1. *The consumption experience as fashioned and as on offer is not 'as is', but 'as represented'.* Put simply, what characterizes the four cases is the shaping of the offer to fit the media representation. If the 'media' is taken to mean all vicarious representations of places and experiences, whether in literature, art, or more recently the cinematic and televisual media, the media are cited as shaping influences in each case. For example, Finn cites the revenue-generating potential of television as a transforming influence on the character and consumption of league football. Baron-Yelles shows how early romantic representations of the Pointe du Raz, in literature and art, have influenced its official re-shaping, accompanied by the demonization of mass tourism as that which had destroyed the potential of the site to be romanticized. We may well ask ourselves if the experience of visiting the Pointe was ever, in fact, as it had appeared in romantic literature. Similarly, Lohmann and Mundt cite early travel writings as the incipient reason behind the growth of the *Studienreise* and its latter-day derivatives, which we globally term 'cultural tourism'. In like fashion, cinematic exposure in *Heimatfilme* and major cinematic productions such as *The Sound of Music* have created a 'represented' view of what the experience of visiting rural Austria will be like.

2. *Commercialization and commodification are not synonymous terms.* In the Austrian region discussed by Luger and East, to commercialize, that is, to create a structured economy to generate revenue from tourists, involves attempting the simulation of non-commodity. The quest for the 'authentic', the seemingly but not necessarily real, necessitates the presentation of experience transactions which are perceived as faithful to the 'represented' mediated reality, but which nevertheless generate money. In Finn's exposition of football, the already-commercial but non-commodified game had to pass through a process of commodification in order to conform to the mediated, rather than the live, experience that is now definitive of league football. By contrast, the annexation of the Pointe du Raz to the cause of 'official' culture involved the removal of established commercial trading operations from the Pointe in order to create a commodified, in the sense of consumable, visitor experience of the romantic kind. The parallels with the intentions of the subvention scheme in Wales known as *Tir Gofal* (see Lewis' contribution) and the influence of the values of official culture as represented by the *service class* or, in Bourdieu's terminology, the 'new cultural intermediaries' (see first chapter) are clear.

3. *While environments can be made to simulate the pre-modern or the post-modern, people cannot.* In entirely opposite ways, the contributions of Finn and of Luger and East underline this point. Finn's football supporter, no longer a 'fan' but a 'spectator', has his or her responses to the action of the game pre-programmed in terms of vocalization and gestures (though Finn cites some contestation of this, inasmuch as spectators may choose to vary the lyrics of the pre-scripted songs!). To relate to football as folk culture becomes increasingly difficult. Similarly, in the

Austrian mountains, young persons experiencing the rites of passage associated with adolescence, such as fads in behaviour, dress and music, find themselves constrained by the pre-modern representation to which their locality must, for economic reasons, conform.

From Sport to Spectacle: the Emergence of Football as a Destination Attribute or *Look What They've Done To Our Game: the McDonaldization of Football*

8

Mick Finn
University of Lincoln, Lincoln Campus, Lincoln, UK

Introduction

Much evidence has accumulated over recent years demonstrating the extent to which major sporting events contribute to the tourism accounts of the communities which host them (see for example Destination Sheffield, 1996; Quinton, 1996; Gratton and Kokolakakis, 1997). Sport has acquired a new role, with urban communities competing to maintain their position relative to others through a period of structural economic change by developing consumable services based on leisure and culture in order to develop their quality-of-life credentials in the competition for inward investment and knowledge-based labour.

This chapter looks at just one of those sports, football. Taking as its starting point Euro '96, it will be argued that the staging of such a successful tournament in the United Kingdom represents a remarkably swift transformation in the game's fortunes from the dark days of incidents which incurred major loss of life at Bradford, Heysel and Hillsborough. Whether the steps taken to achieve that transformation will ensure the game's long-term health is, however, another matter. Central to the argument of this case study will be the gentrification of football and the transformation of the football supporter from fan to spectator.

It will be suggested that what was in 1970 a mass-market leisure activity watched by active supporters ('fans'), whose origins were largely working-class and who were embedded in football's culture, has mutated into branded entertainment watched by passive spectators ('customers') for whom retailing, merchandizing and corporate hospitality are important components. In order to change football's customer base in this way, the product has been re-packaged, homogenized, and sanitized in ways which have alienated much of the traditional support, and at the same time taken the game beyond the finances of those supporters. As such, the 'McDonaldization' of football has had salient impacts on the 'host' community.

There exists an intriguing similarity between the transformation of football from sport to spectacle, and the commercialization of heritage for tourist consumption purposes, where here too a range of broadly similar and expurgated attractions have been developed at which passive visitors are encouraged to gaze upon history as it 'really used to be'. This case briefly considers these similarities and examines this transformation, considering likely future outcomes, both from the point of view of football-as-sport and football-as-spectacle.

Inside a period of 20 years, football has been transformed from a position of apparent inexorable decline to a spectacle enjoying growing attendances and benefitting from lucrative television contracts. Whether this guarantees the long-term health of the game or whether, as some commentators argue with respect to the heritage industry, it will consume the authentic qualities which made it attractive in the first place, will be the final point for consideration.

In carrying out this analysis of football and, to a lesser extent, the heritage industry, reference will be made to Ritzer's McDonaldization thesis (Ritzer, 1996), and it will be argued that the components of McDonaldization – efficiency, calculability, predictability and control – help us in understanding the changes which have been made.

Euro '96 – the Year Football Came Home

Scene 1

On 22 June 1996, 75,000 spectators gathered at Wembley Stadium to watch England play Spain in the quarter-finals of the European Football Championships. As BBC television continued its build-up to the match, the cameras panned around the stadium and lingered on a group of spectators. Some were Spanish, some were English, some were male, some were female, some had their faces painted in their national colours, some were waving flags, and all were singing (word-perfectly it would appear) Three Lions, the Skinner/Baddiel/Lightning Seeds Euro-anthem. In that moment, one could not help but be struck by the orchestrated and homogenized nature of the football product. One also became fully aware of just how much football's audience was changing as it took its place in the family entertainment business.

To misquote Douglas Adams in the *Hitch Hiker's Guide to the Galaxy*, football is big, frighteningly big. At first glance it might appear strange to find a chapter on football in a book of tourism case histories. Wishing to avoid tedious debates concerning the definition of leisure and tourism, this chapter asserts that it is legitimate to consider football as part of the tourism industry. Each Saturday of our seemingly endless football season, thousands of fans criss-cross the country as they follow their team to away matches. Whilst it is true that many of them will return home straight after the game, many will spend money in public houses and restaurants, or will perhaps make a night of it and visit the local clubs for example; they may even take a short break and spend the weekend in the area, taking in the match on the Saturday afternoon. In terms of food and drink, transport, accommodation and attractions, football spectators each week contribute significant amounts to the tourism accounts of towns and cities throughout the land. It is, however, the major sporting events which are more naturally equated with tourist activity, and Euro '96 represented the biggest sporting event England has witnessed in the last 30 years. It is an assessment of the economic impact of this tournament to which we now turn to justify football as a legitimate area of tourism analysis.

In financial terms, Euro '96 was the most successful European Football Championship ever staged. The figures are impressive: ticket sales of £55m, television rights of £45m, sponsorship deals bringing £50m, and merchandising amounting to £120m. Total additional expenditure by the 280,000 visiting supporters was put at £120m, of which 35% went on food and drink, 21% on accommodation, 14% on travel within the host cities and 12% on shopping. This equated to 4131 full-time equivalent job years. In terms of the total tourism impact, it was estimated that Euro '96 produced an extra 3% on Britain's earnings from travel and tourism in the second quarter of 1996. Relating this to the whole economy, this equated to an extra 0.1% on Gross Domestic Product in the period April–June 1996 or 25% of the total growth of 0.4% for that period (Dobson *et al.*, 1997).

An HSBC Markets report (Loynes, 1996) includes some other fascinating information concerning the impact of Euro '96, for example, lager sales in supermarkets increased by 55% year-on-year for the second week of the tournament. That the nation was glued to the television set as England played West Germany in the semi-final is evidenced in figures from Domino's Pizzas, who reported an 88% jump in sales on that day compared with the week before. In addition, it is estimated that £60m was spent in bets on Euro '96. However, as the report points out, there was a downside to this expenditure, with other sectors such as restaurants, cinemas, and the National Lottery witnessing a corresponding fall in income for that period. Loynes estimates therefore that Euro '96 probably had a modest impact on *total UK consumer expenditure* (my emphasis), and that its most significant economic impact was the boost to exports arising from tourist expenditure.

This total impact of Euro '96 masks significant regional differences as matches were played in eight cities. Not surprisingly, London benefitted most with additional expenditure estimated at £34m compared with the lowest figure of £4m in Leeds. The next section takes a more detailed look at the impact of Euro '96 on just one of the eight cities, Sheffield.

66,723 visitors came to Sheffield for the three Euro '96 matches played there, of which 47.5% came from the UK, and 40% from Denmark (all three matches involved the Danish side). Direct expenditure was estimated at £5.83m, 56,759 bed-nights were generated, and 157 full-time-equivalent job years were created. Breaking these figures down, we find a broadly similar pattern to the national figures, with food and drink accounting for 32% of total expenditure, accommodation 17%, travel 12.6%, shopping 20.4% (this figure includes match programmes and Euro '96 merchandize), entertainment 12%, with other expenditure at 6% (Destination Sheffield, 1996).

As well as monitoring the economic impact, the research carried out for Sheffield City Council during the tournament also looked at visitors' perceptions of the city in order to improve marketing strategies. Overall they found that 66% of visitors had a more positive image of Sheffield as a result of their stay. This represents a sizeable potential market for future tourism campaigns, particularly as Sheffield is marketing itself as a city of sport. For, as the research showed, among the specific amenities offered by the city, it was the sports facilities and sports events coupled with the Meadowhall Shopping Centre which did the most to improve Sheffield's image.

A final interesting aspect of the impact of Euro '96 on Sheffield concerns the spin-offs from the media coverage. Destination Sheffield monitored press coverage of the city, and not the football, in Britain, Denmark, and other countries prior to and during the tournament. Their research revealed a total number of 625 press articles generating 20,044 single column centimetres. They concluded that this coverage was overwhelmingly positive. Their figures for broadcast coverage were less comprehensive, but did reveal a total of 92 broadcasts amounting to just over 5 h of transmission time.

In summary, Euro '96 was a major tourist event which had a significant economic impact. It brought large numbers of tourists to this country, spending £120m on food, drink, accommodation, travel, shopping, and entertainment. As the Sheffield case study shows, such events provide the host city with an opportunity to demonstrate its tourism product, to improve its image, and in so doing to encourage repeat visits. The Sheffield example also shows that Euro '96 brought a level of media coverage way beyond that which could ordinarily be achieved by the average promotional budget, and so the publicity potential of hosting a major sporting event is considerable.

From Footie to Footsie[1]: the Restructuring of Football's Finances

That football should come home so successfully and so rapidly since the World Cup was last staged here in 1966, represents a phenomenal turnaround in the image and fortunes of our national game. In the mid-1980s football had a problem: see Fig. 8.1.

These intervening years had seen the emergence of the football 'firms', with the hooligan in the ascendancy; the infiltration of extreme right-wing groups

---

[1] For the uninitiated, 'Footsie' is a game played with feet under a dinner table; it is also, as in this case, a para-acronym referring to the Financial Times Ordinary Share Index (FTSE).

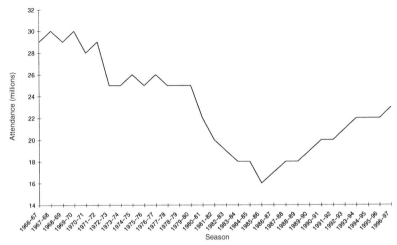

Fig. 8.1. League attendances since 1966. (Source: Rollin, 1997.)

spreading their racist ideologies; the deaths of 55 people in the Bradford fire of 1985, and 39 spectators at Heysel also in 1985; culminating in the deaths of 96 Liverpool supporters at Hillsborough in 1989. The years of neglect of the football supporter had taken a grim toll. As the decade ended, neutral observers wondered why anyone would want to attend a football match in this country. The game appeared to be self-destructing.

Ascribing cause and effect here is, however, a complex task. Whilst these high-profile tragedies undoubtedly contributed to football's decline, there were other factors in the wider society which impacted significantly: see Fig. 8.2. Although not a perfect correlation, there is a striking relationship between the graph showing league attendances and that depicting the unemployment statistics. The sharp decline in football attendances which began in 1980 is mirrored in the steep increase in unemployment which also began in that year. Both graphs start in 1966, which was a significant year for a number of reasons. Whilst it was the year England won the World Cup, it was also the year in which employment in manufacturing started to decline nationally for the first time since the Second World War. From the mid-1960s onwards there was a clear shift from the manufacturing sector to the service sector, thus transforming the structure of the workforce in this country. Whilst unemployment was rising, the segment of the workforce which was increasing the quickest was that including professionals, managers and administrators (Allen and Massey, 1988), a change which was not lost on football's administrators. The spatial characteristics of this economic change were crucial too. Cities were declining as centres of production, and these cities comprised football's heartland. In summary, football's traditional support amongst the working class were already being priced out of the game as a result of structural changes in the economy.

The situation at the end of the 1985/86 season was one where football attend-

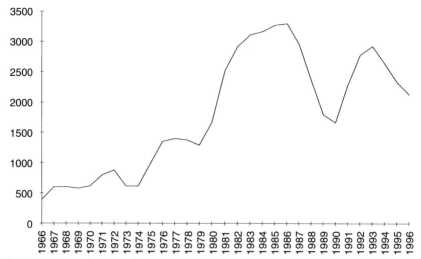

Fig. 8.2. Unemployment figures 1966–1996. (Source: Office for National Statistics, 1997.)

ances were at a post-war low. Any business contemplating the graph in Fig. 8.1 would have concluded that it was in serious trouble, and that, if immediate and drastic action were not taken, it would soon cease trading. Ten years on, the domestic game was enjoying year-on-year increases in attendance, and England was hosting Euro '96. So how had this remarkable change in fortunes been achieved? How was a post-war low in attendances in 1986 replaced 10 years later by a rejuvenated game and the staging of what most observers agree was a highly successful event? This section briefly considers the changes in three areas – the structure of the game, clubs and grounds, and players. A crucial fourth area is however missing, the experience of the spectators who at times did indeed feel as if they were invisible. We will return to the spectators' experiences later as they are at the heart of this discussion.

The strategy was a deliberate attempt to take the game up-market and to appeal to new market segments in response to the economic restructuring in the wider economy discussed above. The language and practices of the market entered football's vocabulary. As David Dein, vice-Chairman of Arsenal, said, football 'had a very strong brand image which really had not been taken to the market' (BBC Television, 1995). Football's marketing advisers made it clear that the way to maximize income was to create an elitist top division, which would appeal to television where the really big money was to be obtained, and so football was relaunched with the introduction of a Premier League for the 1992/93 season. In financial terms, the success of the Premier League was immediate and it now accounts for two-thirds of football revenue in this country (Boon, 1997). At the same time that the Premier League was launched, the media mogul Rupert Murdoch realized that if he was to penetrate the nation's sitting rooms with his satellite television service,

BSkyB, he would have to offer regular live football. As a result, the Premier League became awash with Murdoch's millions as BSkyB secured exclusive rights to live Premier League action, the 1992 deal being worth £200m over 5 years, and the new deal commencing in 1998 bringing in £670m. In summary, this strategy achieved what it set out to create: an elite caste of premier footballing clubs, fine to be part of, but well-nigh impossible to join.

The changes did not stop there, however. As a way of generating yet more revenue, many clubs (19 at the time of writing) chose to go public and float on the stock exchange. Some are considering taking this even further by looking at cross-shareholdings in European teams (Tooher and Phillips, 1997). This is a mechanism whereby European clubs would own shares in each other, and is a way of reducing the risk to investors of backing a single club (share prices can change dramatically with the result of a single game). Such a move would create opportunities for new marketing, merchandizing and television deals. As clubs go public, however, they come under intense pressure from shareholders to maximize their returns, and so in addition to cross-shareholding, leading European clubs are looking at cross-merchandizing, whereby club produce would be sold in each other's shops. A related phenomenon is that of companies owning several clubs in different countries. For example ENIC, an investment company listed on the London Stock Exchange, has, at the time of writing, ownership of AEK Athens along with stakes in Vicenza of the Italian Serie A, Slavia Prague from the Czech Republic and Glasgow Rangers (*Guardian*, 1997).

As a way of taking the game further up-market and maximizing its income, clubs also turned to corporate hospitality and merchandizing. Hospitality boxes were introduced, hermetically sealed units of corporate entertainment into which the atmosphere of the match could be piped at the flick of a switch. Club shops were developed, offering an extensive array of corporate merchandize with some clubs changing their strips each season, in an arguably cynical but successful attempt to grow the youth market for replica shirts.

Looking to the future, digital technology and pay-per-view is on the horizon, which will also be controlled by BSkyB. Some analysts predict this will bring a sum of money into the game double that currently provided by BSkyB. It is only a matter of time before BSkyB and the Premiership clubs utilize this technology to cover the complete league programme, so that any match can be watched on a pay-per-view basis. This already happens in France and Italy, and is likely to happen in the United Kingdom with the end of the BSkyB contract in 2001. One can only speculate what effect this will have on attendance levels, but if the American experience is anything to go by, the saturation television coverage will lead to dwindling crowds with attendances maintained by the corporate distribution of tickets. As Dell'Apa warns, this transforms a sports event into a business meeting, and produces a 'relatively uninterested and distracted audience' (Dell'Apa, 1992).

Football's finances would appear, at first glance, to be in a healthy state, with attendances rising and sponsors investing heavily in the game. However, closer inspection reveals that this picture of health is far from accurate. As the latest Deloite and Touche annual review of football finance shows (Boon, 1997), spiralling wage costs and transfer fees mean that many Premier League clubs are in serious financial trouble, with over three quarters of them in deficit, and the gap between the rich and poor clubs growing wider. In the season 1995/96, the English game as a whole made a pre-tax loss of £98m as players' wages rose by 22%, and clubs spent £250m on transfers.

Turning now to football stadia, the United Kingdom is now the possessor of an impressive array of comfortable all-seater grounds, welcoming to sections of society previously rarely seen at football matches (see below). That such changes were imposed on football by the Taylor Commission, which was established in the wake of the Hillsborough disaster and recommended all-seater stadia, is, however, a damning indictment of the indifference towards spectators which characterized football clubs and the game's administrators. The all-seater stadia have allowed clubs to introduce huge increases in ticket prices, thus taking the game up-market in line with football's strategy. Many of these new stadia have been developed in out-of-town locations away from the heart of urban communities from which local loyalties emerged. The traditional links between football clubs and their communities are disappearing, and so fans' identification with 'place' becomes even more problematic. Taken to its extreme, there was the case of Wimbledon (London) apparently considering a relocation to Dublin! The most important consequence of all-seater stadia, however, is that they have changed the experience of football fans, a point to which we will return later.

Players too have changed. Like actors and others in the entertainment industry, their affairs are handled by agents whose aim is to secure the best financial deal for their client. In the era of the football mercenary, the concept of traditional loyalty counts for little as players move from club to club picking up large signing-on fees, and taking home in their pay packets each week what most supporters would not earn in a year. All of this money brings new problems as stories of bribery, corruption, gambling, alcohol addiction, and drug taking appear with monotonous regularity in the press. This, however, is the experience of players attached to elite clubs. As wealth differentials within all aspects of the game increase, it is difficult to see how many of the smaller clubs will be able to survive in their present form, and it is likely that some will be consumed by bigger clubs, some will go part-time, and others will disappear from the scene completely. The effects of the residualization of football will be widespread.

From Passion to Fashion: the Fan's Perspective

Scene 2

8 March 1997, Molineux Stadium, Wolverhampton. Nationwide League Division 1, Wolves v Tranmere. As the crowd begins to grow, the surveillance cameras sweep the ground. At this all-seater stadium customers hand in their tickets and make their way quietly to their seats. To keep us entertained, a roving compere circumnavigates the ground broadcasting

messages, making presentations, and playing records. He is supported by a veritable menagerie of Disneyesque characters who 'amuse' the crowd by dancing, falling over, and joining in the pre-match kick-about with the players. At 2.50 p.m., the public address system broadcasts a tape of an American voice – 'ladies and gentlemen, please give a big Molineux welcome to the Wolverhampton Wanderers ball boys'. Tina Turner's 'Simply The Best' follows as the ball boys run on to the middle of the pitch, face the four stands in turn, wave, and receive polite and unenthusiastic applause in return. 2.55 p.m., Copland's 'Fanfare for the Common Man' rings out, a signal that the players are emerging from the tunnel. We stand and applaud our team. No sooner has this been done than 'The Liquidator' is played – the club tune, an instrumental to which the supporters have added their own lyrics. The 'official' lyrics are displayed on the video wall, but the supporters' version does not have the expletives deleted as reference is made to arch-rivals West Bromwich Albion. Indeed, some weeks the supporters are punished for their swearing by the withdrawal of 'The Liquidator', such is the penalty for departing from the script. 3.00 p.m. and the game starts. Attention switches between the pitch and the two video walls in opposite corners of the ground. A player is injured – we know this to be the case because the video wall shows a cartoon character in tears, followed by another cartoon character running on to the pitch with a sponge. 3.15 p.m., Wolves nearly score – we might forget to applaud this near miss, but fortunately we are prompted by the clapping hands on the video wall and the reminder that 'We Are Wolves'. 3.35 p.m., goal! What are you meant to do when your team scores? Thankfully the public address system comes to our rescue as James Brown's 'I Got You (I Feel Good)' is played, and so we can sing along and clap our hands to this for a few seconds. Half-time, and it's sing-along-a-compere time with Presley's 'The Wonder of You', Jeff Beck's 'Hi-Ho Silver Lining', and 'Wooly Bully' by Sam The Sham and The Pharaohs. It's always these three records, the lyrics, you see, can be adapted – The Wonder of Wolves, Hi-Ho Wolverhampton, with Wooly Bully referring to Molineux folk hero, Steve Bull. And so it goes on until 4.45 p.m. when the final whistle blows and we shuffle quietly out of the stadium and make our way home.

The re-packaging of football to optimize its commercial potential has so far been a success, at least if viewed by purely financial criteria, and from the perspective of the elite clubs, although even here, as argued above, this success is not quite as real as it appears. However, in so doing, it has fundamentally changed the nature of being a football 'fan' – the word itself is rarely used nowadays; we are spectators, customers, shareholders, club associates. Supporters used readily to identify with players, but how can the average supporter relate to a player earning twenty, forty, fifty thousand pounds a week, and who would disappear forthwith were a better financial deal to be offered elsewhere? More important, however, is the implication that this inflated remuneration has for the ability of the traditional fan to watch the game. In deliberately going up-market, football has attempted to attract a new class of customer by re-packaging the product at a structural level through the creation of the Premier League, and at a club level by carefully controlling the matchday experience: see Scene 2 above.

To achieve all of this, pricing strategies have been put in place which take the game beyond the reaches of much of its traditional support. The average admission receipt per spectator in Division 1 (then the top division) in 1987/88 was £4.26 (Football Trust, 1989). For the season 1993/94, this had risen to £9.18 for the Premier League (Football Trust, 1995), and to £11.01 for the 1994/95 season (Football Trust, 1996). The most recent figure is for the 1995/96 season, which shows an average ticket price for the Premier League of £15.11, with the range being £11.14–£19.10 (Williams, 1996). These are substantial increases, way beyond changes in the Retail Price Index and far in excess of the pay rises 'enjoyed' by supporters. For those watching football in Wolverhampton, the price of the cheapest matchday ticket for the 1997/98 season was 70% higher than it was 4 years ago; if a season ticket is purchased, this figure rises to 100% due to changes in the 'privileges' enjoyed by season ticket holders. During the same period, the total compound inflation rate was less than 15%. Given these figures, it is hardly surprising that the socio-economic composition of the football crowd is changing as many fans have simply been priced out of the game, whilst others, in some cases literally, have sold the family silver to pay for their addiction. These soaring ticket prices have ensured that those who do attend games also have the discretionary spending power to purchase the merchandize which is such a crucial part of clubs' commercial strategy.

Trend data is not available but it is reasonable to assume that the picture shown in Fig. 8.3 represents a crowd which is socially upwardly mobile in composition. At one level, this gentrification of the football crowd is no longer an issue; seating and pricing policies have achieved their intended objective. As Rick Parry, then the Premier League's chief executive said, 'I don't think clubs will be depressed about their increasing number of affluent supporters' (Rowbottom, 1996). Others point

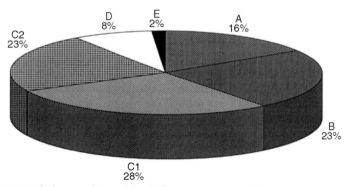

Fig. 8.3. Social class analysis of football spectators: 1995/96 season. (Source: Williams, 1996.)

to the complacency of this remark. As prices rise, as parents cannot afford to take children to games, football may be losing its next generation of customers.

It is, however, more than just a simple question of the price of a ticket which is alienating the traditional supporter. The mechanisms for obtaining a ticket have changed too. The majority of home seats at Premier League matches are now taken up by season tickets requiring an outlay of several hundred pounds: the average season ticket price in the Premier League for the 1995/96 season was £261.80, with a range of £126–383 (Williams, 1996). These tickets are often viewed as a means of convenience, allowing the holders to pick the matches they want to see without having to buy a ticket every time. Very few supporters are now able to simply turn up on the day and pay at a turnstile. Tickets need to be purchased in advance, which more often than not means access to a fax machine; it certainly means ownership of a credit card. It is more than just price discrimination, therefore, which is turning away the traditional supporter. As John Williams points out (Taylor, 1997), the democracy of the turnstile queue which characterized working class supporters' relationship with their club has disappeared. A similar point is made by King, who points out that prior to the Taylor Report, the following pertained:

> (most grounds) . . . 'had large terraces to which entry was relatively simple, involving
> payment of cash at the turnstile, and was almost always guaranteed. With the
> development of all-seater stadiums, access to the ground has become problematic.
> The reduction in capacity, the improvement in facilities and the cost of building has
> prompted a rise in ticket prices which has been quite unprecedented in football
> history.' (King, 1997: 334)

The social composition of the football crowd is changing as its established male support is turned away by sometimes overt and other times subtle mechanisms. King (1997) gives some interesting examples of ways in which the exclusion of traditional male support (the lads) is achieved at Manchester United. For example, he shows ways in which ticket allocation discriminates against local male fans, whilst at the same time supporter associations in Ireland experience little trouble in obtaining tickets. The reason, as these associations themselves acknowledge, is that the club knows these Irish supporters are big spenders in the club shops. Whilst not wishing to romanticize the past, it is important to acknowledge that 'the lads have constituted a very important part of football's support over the last thirty years and the restriction and, indeed, partial exclusion from the ground constitutes a profound social change' (King, 1997: 329).

In other ways, changes to the composition of the crowd are to be welcomed. A recent FA Premier League Fan Survey showed that women accounted for 12% of spectators. Trend data is again not available, but commentators agree that the percentage of women attending matches is growing, and the survey revealed that nearly 14% of females in the sample were 'new' to football. They are however clearly still under-represented as are ethnic minorities. The 1991 Census figure for the population of 'non-white' ethnic minority communities in Britain was approximately 5.5%, yet they account for 1.1% of football spectators (Williams, 1996).

Whilst the 'Let's Kick Racism Out Of Football' campaign is a laudable one, and whilst many clubs have introduced imaginative local initiatives, racism is still clearly an issue in football.

The spectacle described in Scene 2 above is played out each week at grounds up and down the country. Going to a game now is a highly predictable experience (apart from the score of course!). Football grounds in the higher divisions are places where one can 'spectate' in comfort. The word is used deliberately. *Chambers English Dictionary* defines a spectator as 'one who looks on', and to a large extent that is the contemporary experience of the football follower. The new stadia are certainly comfortable places to spectate, but the grounds now seem more like shopping centres with retail and fast food outlets, betting shops, fitness centres, banqueting suites and conference facilities. They are also 7-day-a-week businesses. They all have, however, a somewhat depressing similarity. Gone are the features by which different grounds could be recognized. The new generation of stadia share the homogeneity of design of the shopping mall.

Spectators now complain of the lack of atmosphere at grounds, and many yearn for a return to sections of terracing where it would be more 'acceptable' to sing. So acute has this situation become, that at a recent European Cup match between Manchester Utd and Juventus, a public announcement pleaded for more noise from the fans. Previously, it would not be uncommon for supporters to arrive at the ground an hour or 2 hours before kick-off in order to get a good view. The atmosphere built up as fans entertained themselves. Go to a game now, and the ground appears to be virtually empty 20 minutes before the start of the game as the spectators are out of sight in the bars, shops, restaurants, and betting offices. The old ritual of going to a game on a Saturday afternoon has also been broken. The demands of the television paymasters mean that games are now played on most evenings of the week, and at various times on a Sunday – yet further evidence of how football's culture is changing as supporters are required to dance to the commercial tune. The significance of this change should not be underestimated. As Taylor points out:

> 'It was the pulse-like regularity of the football season that helped make it so popular when the professional game was first born. Its almost biorhythmic attraction for city dwellers divorced from the natural cycle helped to maintain its cultural significance. Football rhymed with city life and work. Now it's arhythmically perverted by t.v. requirements, and removed from those who invested most in it.' (Taylor, 1997)

Being a supporter, a fan(atic), used to be an emotional experience which defied logic and rational explanation. Standing in a crowd was exciting, amusing, certainly frightening at times, but it was a spontaneous and creative experience. Today, it has been replaced by a carefully constructed package, homogenous in nature, and sanitized for passive consumption. Football has undergone a commercial rebirth, but where, one might ask, is its indefinable soul? The next section will attempt an analysis, utilizing and applying the paradigm of change known as 'McDonaldization'.

It Ain't Heavy, It's Just Theory:
The 'McDonaldization' of Society

This section is based on the work of Ritzer (1996) and his book, *The McDonaldization of Society*. In it he draws on Weber's work on the rationalization process and his assertion that bureaucracy is its ultimate manifestation. Ritzer argues that the fast-food restaurant has become the contemporary model of rationality:

> ' . . . although the fast-food restaurant adopts elements of its predecessors, it also represents a quantum leap in the process of rationalization. While McDonaldization is a logical extension of rationalization, McDonaldization is also a sufficiently more extreme form of rationalization to legitimize the use of a distinct label to describe the most contemporary aspects of the rationalization process' (Ritzer, 1996: 33).

So what exactly is McDonaldization? It is 'the process by which the principles of the fast-food restaurant are coming to dominate more and more sectors of American society as well as of the rest of the world' (Ritzer, 1996: 1). According to Ritzer, McDonaldization has four dimensions – efficiency, calculability, predictability and control. Taking these in order, *efficiency* means that, for consumers, eating a McDonald's is the most efficient way of satisfying one's hunger. From the perspective of the employee, the work systems in place at McDonald's ensure that each outlet operates at optimum efficiency. Efficiency is achieved through the streamlining of processes, and by getting customers to do work previously undertaken by staff. Relating the discussion to tourism, Ritzer argues that the design of theme parks for example is geared towards moving vast numbers of people through the park in the most efficient manner possible.

Quantification is crucial, and so *calculability* – stressing the quantitative dimensions of products or services – is the second dimension. Quantity equates to quality, i.e. large amounts of something or the rapid delivery of it means that it must be good. This is inevitable in a McDonaldized system as the quality of a product or service is not allowed to vary, and so quality has to be defined in quantitative ways. The concept of calculability can also be applied to customers as they calculate the time saved by eating at McDonald's as opposed to other ways of obtaining a meal, and also in terms of time saved which could be used in other ways. Applied to staff, the concept of calculability means that the quantitative rather than the qualitative aspects of the work environment are stressed, resulting in staff being expected to produce more, and more speedily at that.

Predictability is the third dimension, and this follows on from the earlier point about quality in that consumers can be confident that wherever or whenever they consume a McDonald's it will be the same product in the same setting. Customers also exhibit predictable behaviour and this, according to Ritzer, is assisted by three factors. First of all, they receive cues to expected behaviour: in the case of McDonald's this might be the existence of a large number of prominently placed waste bins, which indicate to customers that they are expected to clear away their own rubbish (another example of customers undertaking work previously done by staff). Secondly, there are the 'structural constraints', such as the drive-through system which, together with prominently displayed written instructions, give customers few alternatives, and finally there are the 'taken-for-granted norms' which are internalized by customers and which influence their behaviour. The example which Ritzer gives here relates to the earlier point about customers clearing away their own debris. Customers are not asked to do it, but it is widely understood and expected that this is what you do after your meal at McDonald's.

As Ritzer writes, 'The success of the McDonald's model suggests that many people have come to prefer a world in which there are few surprises' (Ritzer, 1996: 10). Staff too behave in a consistent way, and many of the interactions with customers are scripted. They are pioneers of the routinization of service-sector activity. The tourism industry is, of course, full of predictable and routinized products offering predictable experiences, such as attractions, package holidays and motel chains.

Finally, we come to *control*, which is achieved 'through the substitution of non-human for human technology' (Ritzer, 1996: 11) – the former being a technology which controls people, the latter a technology controlled by people. The problem with people is that they can be unpredictable and inefficient, and so any rationalizing process needs to look at replacing people through a process of control by technology. As a result, McDonald's customers are subtly controlled in order to achieve rapid turnover. Employees are controlled by being given a limited number of tasks to achieve in a consistent way, and by the application of non-human technology, i.e. the mechanization of much of the service-delivery system. Tourism offers many such examples, such as the Formule 1 chain of motels in France, which is virtually a staff-free environment. Access and payment is made by a machine situated outside a locked entrance. Food and drink are dispensed via machines, and the installation of self-cleaning toilets and bathrooms reduces the need for housekeeping staff.

These four dimensions of McDonaldization are, Ritzer argues, basic components of a rational system. However, in an endnote he reminds us that he is using the word 'rational' in a negative way, by which he means the denial of people to act and work in a creative way. The downside to McDonaldization is what Ritzer calls 'the irrationality of rationality', i.e. the notion that rational systems produce irrational consequences, and so, for example, customers and employees may perceive that they are part of an assembly line process. As Ritzer writes, 'Another way of saying this is that rational systems serve to deny human reason; rational systems are often unreasonable' (Ritzer, 1996: 13). Weber, too, pointed to the dark side of rationalization by alerting us to the dehumanizing impacts of rational systems. He used the term 'the iron cage of rationality' as he predicted a society formed of a series of rational structures, between which people would move and from which there would be no escape.

Ritzer offers a fascinating, extensive and highly readable account of ways in which these dimensions have been applied to other areas of human life, and he encourages readers to contact him with their own examples of McDonaldization in practice. In the following sections, an attempt will be made to link aspects of the McDonaldization process to our earlier discussion of football, and to the heritage industry. Before this is done, however, it is illuminating to note that Ritzer cites recreation as a classic example of McDonaldization, and so it is worth quoting him at length on this subject:

> Recreation can be thought of as a way to escape the rationalization of daily routines. However, over the years these escape routes have themselves become rationalized, embodying the same principles as bureaucracies and fast-food restaurants. Of the many examples of the rationalization of recreation, take today's vacations. For those who wish to visit Europe, a package tour rationalizes the process. People can efficiently see, in a rigidly controlled manner, many sights while travelling in conveyances, staying in hotels, and eating in fast-food restaurants just like those at home. For those who wish to escape to the Caribbean, there are resorts such as Club Med that offer many routinized activities and where one can stay in predictable settings without ever venturing out into the unpredictability of native life on a Caribbean island. For those who wish to flee back to nature within the United States, rationalized camp-grounds offer little or no contact with the unpredictabilities of nature. People can remain within their RVs and enjoy all the comforts of home – TV, VCR, Nintendo, CD player. These and legion other examples show that the escape routes from rationality have, to a large degree, become rationalized. With little or no way out, people do live to a large extent in the iron cage of rationality (Ritzer, 1996: 21).

Hamburger Heritage: the McDonaldization of Theme Park Britain

Scene 3

A tourist attraction, the Jorvik Viking Centre. The publicity brochure promises us the most exciting journey in 1000 years – 'now you can visit the Jorvik Viking Centre, step aboard a time car and be whisked back through the centuries on a journey to real-life Viking Britain. A bustling market, dark, smoky houses and a busy wharf have all been recreated in accurate detail so that you can experience in sight, sound and smell exactly what it was like to live and work in the Viking city of Jorvik'. 'Time is now stopped, history is frozen' promises the commentary.

Listen to the comments of the people leaving 'Jorvik', and more likely than not they will be about how it gave them a real feel for what life must have been like in a Viking village. But this is not real-life Viking Britain, but a simulation of it. In Jorvik the meaning of authenticity is challenged. Heritage centres mix ingredients from the worlds of the theatre and the museum and simulate a past environment in great detail, including the smells. Paradoxically, in these centres of hyper-authenticity, nothing is actually authentic (see Urry, 1990: 132).

The product, history, has been packaged for our convenience. We sit in our 'time cars' and are transported around a Viking village as we passively observe this sanitized and homogenized tourist product. Hewison likens Jorvik to a ghost-train which gives consumers no time to stop or to ask questions (BBC Television, 1989).

The non-human technology controls not only what you see but the pace at which you see it. The example is Jorvik, but the sentiments could have been applied to any number of attractions in 'theme park Britain': Beamish, The Black Country Museum, Ironbridge Gorge, Wigan Pier, Royalty and Empire, The Blitz Experience, The Welsh Folk Museum. They may be dealing with different eras, with different aspects of heritage, but the package is strikingly similar.

Elsewhere, instead of 'time cars', Walkmans are provided to direct visitors around the attraction, telling them when to move on and what to see. Visitor management techniques thus carefully control the tourist experience. At Wigan Pier ('The Way We Were') this is taken a stage further as actors are employed to play the part of the school master for example, with the public taking the part of his children, reciting lines from this carefully scripted performance. Control and predictability are thus key components of the heritage centre experience.

Merchandizing is vital to these attractions as well. The Jorvik gift-shop reckons it does as much business per square metre as the local Marks and Spencer's. However, there is a depressing similarity (predictability) about the products on sale. Calculability is also a factor here. From the perspective of the customer, visiting a heritage centre is perceived as a quick way of gaining 'knowledge'. Instead of having to engage in time-consuming research by reading books, for example, we can 'do the seventeenth century' in an hour, thus freeing up more time for other activities. And so, as the marketers get their hands on history, it becomes commodified as heritage, packaged and sold, as historical accuracy is sacrificed for profit.

Elsewhere, the application of the dimensions of McDonaldization to the tourism industry has taken a different perspective. Baum (1995), for example, addresses the contradiction apparent in two trends in the tourism industry. On the one hand, he points out, there is the move towards quality service products, differentiated and customized, requiring a management committed to internal marketing and staff empowerment. On the other hand, we have the McDonaldization of much of the tourism sector and all that it entails in terms of deskilling and the standardization and mechanization of the service delivery system. At the end of his book, Baum deals with these contradictory trends within his discussion of sustainable human resource management practices in the tourism industry.

The McDonaldization of Football

The similarities between the McDonaldization of 'the past' and its mutation into consumable 'heritage', and the parallel processes which have been applied to football and its consequences, are striking. Ritzer points out that McDonald's is a universally recognizable icon of Americana. Many of the ingredients included in the repackaged football product have been 'borrowed' from American sport: the use of animal mascots and cheerleaders, the master of ceremonies, the installation of video walls, and the playing of music (so loud incidentally as to prevent the crowd from generating its own atmosphere). All of these keep the crowd 'entertained'. There is little time to think for yourself at a football match nowadays, little spare time, as you are bombarded with sights and sounds. For spare time is danger-ous time, uncontrolled time, to be avoided at all costs. Further examples of Amer-icana can be found in the club shops stocked with baseball caps, college jackets and the like.

Let us now apply the four dimensions of McDonaldization to football, starting with efficiency. The mechanisms for purchasing tickets are now more efficient, or they are at least from the perspective of the club. As has already been argued, changes here have served to exclude areas of traditional support. Because your seat is guaranteed in this efficient way, there is now no need to take your place hours before the kick-off, which, as pointed out previously, contributes to the lack of atmosphere. Any spare time inside the ground can now safely be passed in spending money.

At the end of the game, efficient policing ensures that supporters, especially visiting ones, are swiftly transported away from the area and on to trains, the motorway or whatever. This is of course linked directly to the concept of control.

Elsewhere, clubs have been surprisingly slow in getting customers to do work previously undertaken by employees, although it will surely not be long before employee-operated turnstiles disappear and we gain entry to the ground through a ticket/credit card machine. Football clubs certainly now offer a much more efficient way of shopping, for instead of having to join lengthy queues at the club shop on match days, merchandise can now be purchased by mail order and over the Internet.

Calculability is more difficult to apply, although with the advent of pay-per-view television it is likely that many customers will balance the time, money, and inconvenience saved from watching a game on television against the atmosphere forsaken and calculate that spectating is best undertaken from the comfort of one's sitting room. The consequences of this for football have already been touched upon.

As Scene 2 and the subsequent discussion have illustrated, attending a football match is a predictable off-the-field experience. A carefully packaged product is provided for the spectator each week, which varies little and which is passively consumed. From the moment you arrive at the stadium to the time that you leave you know exactly what to expect from the package on offer. Even football pro-grammes are predictable, they contain few surprises, and even less in the way of content. They used to be packed with information, now they are glossy and expens-ive kitsch with little variety from issue to issue. A consequence of this is that dedicated fans have to resort to expensive 0891 telephone lines or the Internet for the sort of information programmes used to provide. Echoing Ritzer's comments, football off the pitch is a world in which there are few surprises. Cues to expected behaviour are provided all the time, from appeals in the programme not to swear to visual prompts on the video wall to applaud a near miss. The 'taken-for-granted norms' of being a contemporary football spectator have been internalized.

There are other ways in which football is predictable. Spectators wear the uniform of the replica shirt (different ones for home and away games of course). It is interesting to note that in King's study of Manchester United, 'the lads' were contemptuous of the wearing of replica shirts, viewing it as a symbol of the changes threatening traditional fandom. As has already been stated, grounds too are becoming predictable. Whilst the new stadia are comfortable places from which to spectate, they lack the atmosphere and distinctiveness of their predecessors. Describing these grounds just weeks after a visit is difficult, they have few distinctive points of reference. Even the outcome of matches has been rationalized, has become more predictable as cup competitions, instead of having replays until a result was achieved, are now decided on the day with the use of the penalty shoot-out.

In many ways the concept of predictability is linked to that of control. Sometimes this technological control of spectators is overt, such as the use of surveillance cameras. The video wall and the compere are perhaps more subtle forms of control as continuous audio and visual stimuli give spectators little opportunity to do their own thing. Seats too control spectators. Seated spectators are thankfully less likely to be violent spectators and are easier to control but it is also more difficult to sing and to create an atmosphere sitting down. This lack of atmosphere at grounds has been touched upon elsewhere in this chapter and the consequences for football have not been lost. As David Lacey has written, 'take away the fans' freedom of expression and there is not much purpose in playing the game as a spectator sport' (Lacey, 1997).

In an effort to tackle this problem of lack of atmosphere arising from the control of spectators, the Premier League carried out its own enquiry into crowd atmosphere. One of its suggestions is to introduce 'atmosphere areas' at grounds as well as welcoming the sort of musical bands which accompany the Dutch national side. 'Designated song leaders with musical instruments and amplification' (Lacey, 1997) should also be welcomed in its view. So in seeking to tackle the problem of a lack of atmosphere, which has arisen in large part from the tightly controlled nature of the football package, the proposed solution is yet more control through the designation of 'atmosphere areas' – a highly rational response with predictable consequences perfectly consistent with the principles of McDonaldization. As Lacey observes, whilst the Premier League proposals are well-meaning, they do not 'really address the lack of spontaneous reaction among Premiership crowds . . . ' (Lacey, 1997).

Of course football fans have always been controlled, but the forms of control have certainly changed. Previously it was a more crude and overt form of control by the police; today it is more subtle in the ways suggested above.

The Chapter Ends: Not with a Bang, but a Wimpey

By the mid-1980s, football was in crisis, both economically and in terms of its image, and the two were clearly related. The response was market-led with economic and other measures introduced to take the game up-market. The impact, however, has been a dramatic one on football's culture. This chapter does not imply some sort of romantic appeal to the good old days of the past. In truth, many of those days were far from good, and there was much that was deeply unattractive about football in the 1970s and 1980s. However, whilst Lord Justice Taylor pleaded in his report for prices to be maintained at affordable levels, traditional football supporters, those whose cultural allegiance to football is remarkably strong and who supported the game through the bad times, are being priced out of and turned away from their game. Even the Government has now recognized this as an issue, and its Football Task Force has been asked to consider amongst other things equitable ticketing and pricing policies and commercialism in order to ensure that clubs do not alienate the less well off from the sport they love.

As Rogan Taylor (1997) argues, football is engaged in a gigantic act of betrayal. Of course we cannot turn back the clock, nor should we. Football had to change but in so doing it has thrown away much that was good about the game. At the present time, football is fashionable. It is fashionable to talk about it at parties. Politicians, musicians, and television personalities have 'come out' and disclosed their football allegiances, but as it loses its traditional support the possibility is that the new supporter, not immersed in football's culture and fickle by nature, will tire of the game and move on to the next fashion promoted by the entertainment business. The research evidence is clear, as the third Football Association (FA) Premier League survey of fans showed, the lower a person's income the more important football is in his/her life.

Football used to be a way of life, it used to be referred to as 'The People's Game'; now it is increasingly becoming just another leisure pastime, and the new consumers have plenty of other attractions to choose from. The relationship which bound the supporter to the club was a social and cultural one; now the relationship between club and customer is an economic one. Clubs understand their supporters as a result of their consumption, but the consumer–producer relationship is far from being a stable one.

The changes to football's culture as experienced by the fan have been analysed using Ritzer's McDonaldization thesis. Of course, the one thing that cannot be rationalized in football is the result, although even here the nature of the result is not immune to commercial interference. When America hosted the World Cup in 1994, television companies tried to get the football authorities to widen the goals so that more goals would be scored, thus making the product more broadcastable. The unpredictability of the score is, however, football's last defence against McDonaldization. As John Williams wrote, 'Sport's one, still remaining, saving grace, however, is that the joys of performance and the excitement of unpredictable drama, still have the ability to transcend its own commodification' (Williams, 1994: 37).

Epilogue: Football Under the 'Tourist Gaze'

Somehow, amongst the commodification processes by which football has been transformed, the notion of the committed supporter survives, even in the promotional activity of BSkyB. A 1999 television advertisement for the company features a fictional father inviting his son to choose a team to support and watch on satellite TV. The paternal injunction is that, once chosen, the team is 'yours for life'. So, perhaps unsurprisingly, the committed fan/loyal customer still has a value, albeit in a commodified form. The difference is that fandom is no longer spatially defined, in terms of a community's support for a local team. The choice is made from a menu of teams whose status acquires them exposure on satellite television. In that sense, the choice is, if not exactly illusory, a product of commercial control. The choice is made from a 'menu' provided by the television station. Football has been McDonaldized.

More to the point, football has fallen under the 'tourist gaze'. As a commodified spectacle for passive consumption, it has joined other instruments of tourism development. That instrumentality may appear in three principal forms: as a 'hallmark' event which attracts direct visitation and revenues, as in the case of Euro '96; as a vehicle for achieving secondary exposure of a particular host destination, as in the Sheffield case described earlier in the chapter; and as a component of that sector of the tourism industry known as 'business tourism' of which one component, loosely described as 'incentive travel', is arguably inclusive of the role of football as an option for business entertaining and corporate hospitality.

Not only is football identifiable as a destination product attribute in these ways, it is also recognizable through its social impact on the host community. While the transformation of football from sport to spectacle may have been an essentially internal process, fuelled by external opportunities provided by the proliferation of televisual media rather than tourism itself, the social exclusion of the host community – through such measures as pricing mechanisms and, in the case of the Manchester example cited earlier, ticket allocations which favour visiting supporters in preference to local fans – has much in common with instances of tourism development where hosts become excluded from key areas of consumption by rises in prices of produce and services induced by an influx of tourists. The intriguing relationship with the elusive 'authentic', as alluded to in the above discussion of the heritage industry, argues a continuing role for the committed fan as a part of the commodified 'product'.

So, if the young boy in the BSkyB advertisement chooses a team 'for life' from the BSkyB menu, is he an authentic fan, or a simulation of one?

Acknowledgement

I am very grateful to my colleague and friend, Charlie Cooper, who, although a Sheffield United supporter, was still able to give valuable feedback on the first draft of this chapter.

References

Allen, J. and Massey, D. (1988) *The Economy In Question*. Sage, London.
Baum, T. (1995) *Managing Human Resources in the European Tourism and Hospitality Industry*. Chapman and Hall, London.
BBC Television (1989) The past for sale. *Chronicle*. BBC, London.
BBC Television (1995) Whose game is it anyway? *Kicking and Screaming*. BBC, London.

Boon, G. (ed.) (1997) *Deloitte and Touche Annual Review of Football Finance*. Deloitte and Touche, London.

Dell'Apa, F. (1992) England heading towards American nightmare. *Guardian*, 15 December, p. 17.

Destination Sheffield (1996) *Sport and Tourism – The Impact on Sheffield*. Media briefing summary, 6 November.

Dobson, N., Holliday, S. and Gratton, C. (1997) Football comes home. *Leisure Management*, May 1997, pp. 16–19.

Football Trust (1989) *Digest of Football Statistics, 1988 Edition*. Sir Norman Chester Centre for Football Research, University of Leicester, Leicester.

Football Trust (1995) *Digest of Football Statistics 1993–1994*. Sir Norman Chester Centre for Football Research, University of Leicester, Leicester.

Football Trust (1996) *Digest of Football Statistics 1994–1995*. Sir Norman Chester Centre for Football Research, University of Leicester, Leicester.

Gratton, C. and Kokolakakis, T. (1997) Financial games. *Sports Management*, July, pp. 12–15.

Guardian (1997) AEK Athens bought by company from London, 14 October, p. 26.

King, A. (1997) The Lads: masculinity and the new consumption of football. *Sociology* 31 (2), 329–346.

Lacey, D. (1997) Fans should always be in with a shout. *Guardian*, 27 September, p. 12.

Loynes, J. (1996) Euro '96: an extra kick for the economy? *Greenwell Gilt Weekly*, September, pp. 2–3.

Office for National Statistics (1997) *Economic Trends*, Annual Supplement 1997 Edition. HMSO, London.

Quinton, R. (1996) Sporting life. *Leisure Opportunities*, 22 July–4 August.

Ritzer, G. (1996) *The McDonaldization of Society*. Pine Forge Press, Thousand Oaks, California.

Rollin, G. (ed.) (1997) *Rothmans Football Yearbook 1997–98*. Rothmans/Headline, London.

Rowbottom, M. (1996) Proof that money dulls the passion. *Independent*, 14 November.

Taylor, R. (1997) *The Death of Football*. BBC Radio 5, 17 April.

Tooher, P. and Phillips, R. (1997) Football clubs may invest in foreign teams. *Independent*, 31 January, p. 20.

Urry, J. (1990) *The Tourist Gaze*. Sage, London.

Williams, J. (1994) *Sport, Postmodernism and Global TV*. Sir Norman Chester Centre for Football Research, University of Leicester, Leicester.

Williams, J. (1996) *FA Premier League Fan Surveys: General Sample Report 1996*. Sir Norman Chester Centre for Football Research, University of Leicester, Leicester.

Literature, Tourism and the Politics of Nature: the Making of a *Grand Site National* at La Pointe du Raz, Brittany, France

9

Nacima Baron-Yelles
Université de Marne-la-Vallée, France

Introduction

The principal aim of this contribution is to reflect on the specificity of the concept of *Grand Site* as it appeared more than two centuries ago in French culture, accompanying the development of tourism. In particular, we shall observe how this concept has evolved in the last decade under the influence of social, economic and political change. The aim is pursued through an examination of the emergence of La Pointe du Raz, a promontory in Finistère, Brittany, and a designated *Grand Site National*.

The symbolic importance of the *Grands Sites* in the fashioning of the French nation's self-identity is quite considerable, and a notable renewal of interest in them has been observed for the last 10 years, accompanied by a policy of preservation of the French coasts. The administrative procedure allowing the State to list a natural site as *Grand Site National* is still used only in exceptional cases, and it has not been applied to more than a dozen places, most of them located along the French coasts of the Atlantic Ocean, the Channel or the Mediterranean.[1] This procedure can be implemented only if different participants cooperate with a view to the

[1] The *Grands Sites* are 'most famous sites, essentially natural, but which acquire social consecration through their volume of visitation', suggests Andre Micoud in 'Les grands sites naturels et la geographie du beau pays de France', *Colloque Tourisme et Environnement* held in La Rochelle, 13 et 14 mai 1991, Paris: La Documentation Française. In 1998, five *Grands Sites* operations have been established, eleven are in progress, and fourteen are under consideration.

© CAB *International* 2002. *Tourism in Western Europe: a Collection of Case Histories* (ed. Richard Voase)

ecological conservation of the area, aesthetic improvement, and economic development in a holistic fashion in keeping with the philosophy of sustainable tourism.

The affixing of the designation *Grand Site* to the Pointe du Raz was not obtained easily. It was mooted for the first time in 1977, but the initiative was a failure because both the local community and the ecologists were radically opposed to an intervention by the State (see the chronology, Table 9.1). It was proposed again in 1988 by a new local representative of the State; this time the proposal succeeded, and led to decisions that changed in a significant manner the overall organization of the site, including the demolition of buildings and shops, the exclusion of access to some areas, and related measures. The authorities now consider the operation to be a success. For some people, the Pointe du Raz is considered to be the epitome of the French *Grand Site*, and an example of good practice for other French sites.

Historical research into the symbolic and material elaboration of the Pointe du Raz's *Grand Site* reveals concern for three fields: ecological, political, and economic. The aim in this exposition will be to explore three questions. First, what are the cultural values associated with the Pointe du Raz, and how are these integrated into a certain image of the province of Brittany? In order to answer that question, the successive stages involved in the elaboration of the image of the site have been studied, so as to illustrate the manifold social significance it bears.

Table 9.1. Chronology of the Pointe du Raz.

1794	Visit of Chevalier Cambry
1831	Visit of Jules Michelet
1851	Construction of a lighthouse
1865	Construction of the railway line from Paris to Brest
1920–1930	Construction of three hotels on the headland
1941	Listing of La Pointe du Raz as protected monument
1954	Construction of the Hotel d'Iroise
1955	Road to la Pointe du Raz is made accessible to the cars
1958	Accentuation of the protection of the site
1962	Construction of the first commercial hall
1977	Minister of the environment (d'Ornano) launches first 'Grand Site' plan
1980	January: dispute, protest and violence at la Pointe du Raz
1981	Proposed nuclear plant abandoned
1989	Minister of environment launches second 'Grand Site' plan
1991	Agreement between the state and the local administrative stakeholders
1991	Signing of the protocol agreeing 'de-development'
1996	Demolition of the Hotel d'Iroise
1996–1997	Opening of the restored 'Grand Site'
1997	ICOMOS (International Council of Monuments and Sites) visits the site and declares it an example of 'best practice'

Second, considering the controversies generated by the *Grand Site* project over three decades, what is the role of the social and political participants in defining the policy for the *Grand Site*? Indeed, if everyone agrees that the carrying capacity of the site has been reached (with almost one million visitors a year), there are none the less diverse views: for example, should the area be brought under total state control? Should the visitor-flows be channelled? Should admission remain free? And third, the present social and political context is an opportunity to study the nature of the site's operation and to evaluate some of its limitations in both the economic and ecological fields.

Artists and Writers and the 'Making' of the *Grand Site*

Topographical background

Because of its situation on the map, the Pointe du Raz has always been seen, falsely, as the westernmost point of France.[2] This rocky cape is located at the south-west end of Finistère, in the Cornouailles, and constitutes the very end of Cape Sizun, a remote peninsular area which remained, until the 1960s, a repository for the Breton culture. Biogeographically, this whole area is covered with a barren heath, ending in jagged cliffs about 200 feet high that fall down into a rough ocean channel 'Le Raz de Sein'. Sailing there has always been dangerous because of the rocks that surround the 'île de Sein', a few nautical miles away.

The Pointe du Raz runs out into the sea, and has never been a site of permanent human settlement except for a military camp in Roman times. For the traditional rural economy, the site provided varied, though modest, resources. The inhabitants of Plogoff, who lived 4 km inland, used to go there to gather heather (out of which they made litter for the cattle), to pasture sheep, to gather seaweed (to be used as manure), to pick up eggs laid by sea-birds, and to fish for crustaceans among the rocks. The site was nevertheless, and from very early times, ranked as the most scenic landscape of all Brittany, probably because it was shaped as the prow of a ship plunging into the ocean, and because it had remained wild and unpopulated. As such, it was widely recommended, then advertised, as a sight to be seen.

The 'discoverers' of the Pointe du Raz

These may conveniently be separated into two categories: the representatives of the State and artists. At the end of the 18th century, the very first discoverer had been sent by the State to draw up a socio-economic inventory of the region; as he travelled, he chose to describe the scenic landscapes that aroused his romantic spirit.

---

[2] The westernmost is la pointe Saint-Mathieu, also in Finistère.

This is how the Pointe du Raz was mentioned for the first time in 1794, in memoirs entitled *Travels in the Finistère, or the state of this département*, whose author was Chevalier Jacques Cambry. Alongside his practical considerations, the few lines Cambry wrote about the Pointe du Raz constituted the starting point for the representations of this site for the next two centuries:

> Here, on this wildest of rocks, when the sun plunges into the ocean, when the swell rises, roars, announcing a tempest: sublime spirits, profound philosophers, strong and melancholy souls, exalted poets, come and silently meditate . . . The Pointe du Raz is 300 feet high; from there you can see the ocean battering against the bare cliff and eating it away. The waves, pushed by a north-west wind, unfurl with incredible strength. The view from the Pointe du Raz is sublime, especially at sunset.
> (in Chevalier de Fréminville, 1836)

This text became quite famous in the salons and literary societies, and it prompted many people to follow in Cambry's steps throughout the first third of the 19th century. For instance, Brizeux wrote a book about Finistère,[3] and was followed by others: J. Janin and C. Boulain. Even though these early and fiery descriptions of the Pointe du Raz cannot compare with Anglo-Saxon romantic literature and Byronism, they generated considerable attention: from the 1830s to the 1860s, there were visits from inspired travellers, aesthetes, dandies, writers and painters seeking poetic inspiration or wishing to make a rough sketch. The site became quite famous thanks to the visits and the literature of regional writers, from Brizeux to François Menez.[4]

The *Grand Site* as a literary motif

The Pointe du Raz progressively acquired, at the same time, the status of literary object and a specific geographical significance within a French nation which was then in the process of sociological and political transformation. In people's minds, the Pointe du Raz represents the end of Brittany, the most Celtic among the French regions and the western limit of the country. Of course, the site ranks alongside similar extremities in Europe: Cape North, Cape Finisterre, Land's End in British Cornwall. The most prominent 19th century French writers, Victor Hugo, Michelet, Flaubert, after visiting the Pointe du Raz, chose it as the backdrop for some of their books, making that legendary 'fin de terre' (meaning Finistère) pregnant with meaning. One of the major literary texts about the Pointe du Raz was written by G. Flaubert and M. du Camp in *Par les champs et par les grèves* ('Through fields and beaches'), which relates their travels and was written in 1847:

---

[3] Brizeux, *les Bretons*. The seventh song is dedicated to Cape Sizun (Janin, 1862; Boulain, 1895).

[4] A regionalist movement appears in the arts and literature from the 1880s to the First World War, led by the first Celtic historians (De La Villemarque, le Barzaz Breiz) and continued by poets and painters.

At our sides was the gaping, unfathomable, dreadful abyss, in which, 500 feet beneath, the sea was howling; if one of us wanted to watch it, he would lie down on the ground while the other seized his legs and held him back using all his strength, which had to be done because all hope would have been lost had one fallen from the cliff . . . In some places the rock burst open, revealing its dark, black and green entrails. In others it was hollowed in resonant caves, or was soaring like the arch of a bridge, or it raised as a monstrous monolith, or again gradually receded like the steps of a Roman amphitheatre. At the bottom of the cliff the sea was pounding, now seething into froth and now so transparent that one could see the rocks lying on the sand, immobile, pale and turning bluish under a rich cover of wrack, fucus and seaweed. (Flaubert and du Camp, 1907)

In this manner Flaubert, through his writings, contributed to the site's strong cultural resonance. Later the famous historian Michelet, who visited the Pointe du Raz in 1856, followed in his steps. On the one hand, the Pointe du Raz is presented as the most magnificent coastal landscape in France, a view that partakes of the sublime. On the other hand, the Pointe du Raz can be considered as the epitome of the Breton regional identity, which was then in the process of being constituted by regionalists, artists and folklorists. J. Michelet, in particular, researched and obtained information from the writer E Souvestre, a folklorist who took part in the Breton regionalist movement.[5] In the area of the Pointe du Raz he situated Celtic legends such as that of the city of Ys, said to have been engulfed by the sea.

As the writings of these authors were disseminated, the Pointe du Raz attracted more and more visitors, and it became a necessary item in the catalogues listing sites and landscapes which were then circulated in the best society. The first lithograph of the site, made in a workshop in Nantes, was published in 1856 in Felix Benoist's *Contemporary Brittany*, subtitled 'Picturesque sites, monuments, costumes, stories, legends, traditions and customs in Brittany.'

A sublime seascape

If the Pointe du Raz has such a special place in French sensibility and imagination, it can be accounted for by the artistic interpretation of the coastal landscape defined very early by these writers, and faithfully maintained up to now. Indeed, both texts and pictorial representations convey a symbolic dimension to the site. First of all, seeing the foreland and the strikingly beautiful view of the ocean for the first time is a strongly aesthetic experience. Descriptions of the area most often focus not on the headland itself, but on the sight of the sea. What makes the site exceptional is the openness, the height and the depth of the field of vision offered by this rocky horn of land confronting the infinite ocean.

---

[5] He said: 'Talking about Brittany, I should have mentioned Cambry's book, which gave me a first insight of the place. One has to read the édition Souvestre beautifully enriched with notes and notices. In several short novels, which are marvellously true to reality, Souvestre drew the best portraits (we have ever had) of our west coasts'.

Thus, the Pointe du Raz is both a spectacle and a receptacle into which feelings freely flow with true romantic pathos. If it allows the expression of passions, the Pointe du Raz is also used as a pretext for exercising one's writing abilities. The place becomes a theatrical stage, for instance when tragic Celtic legends are situated precisely in the area. That wild spot, antechamber to another world, bears witness, in the event of a tempest, to the fantastic raging of the elements, reminding any witness of the origins of the world and illustrating the incessant attrition between ocean and land.

Thus, the phase during which the Pointe du Raz was invented as a picturesque *grand site* lasted throughout the 19th century, and its most direct manifestation was literary exaltation. The Pointe du Raz was made the tourist emblem of a region that was linked to the rest of the regional territory by railway after 1865, and at the same time it became its scenic and cultural symbol. At that period, though, the number of visitors was not important enough to require the creation of specific facilities on the foreland.

From Literature to Tourism: the First Phase of Commodification of the *Grand Site*

The first tourist-oriented activities

Crowds of visitors flowed to the Pointe du Raz from the moment when guide writers started incorporating the literary motifs into guidebooks. Several guide-books, often published by the main railway lines, appeared during the Second Empire: among the most famous, those by Joanne and Baedeker. The direct models for these guidebooks were travel accounts. Anatole Le Braz, a prominent folklorist, is himself the author of the preface to one of these guides,[6] which as a rule emphas-ize the picturesque sides of the Pointe du Raz. Moreover, they are intended for readers who will visit the area, and not for those spectators who merely imagine it from afar. This is why the discovery paths are meticulously described, providing a progressive approach to the site. The risks one runs are also mentioned by the authors, who advise women and children not to approach the cliff and not to climb the rocks either:

> Some advice for tourists: this is how people usually proceed for a complete walking tour of the Pointe du Raz: they go to Lescoff, where they take a path that soon leads to the Baie des Trépassés. From this place, another path leads along the cliffs to the northern end of the foreland; the tour ends up with walking round the headland to reach the old lighthouse, where the carriage can conveniently be waiting for the visitors (who had disembarked at Lescoff). Walking round the headland, beyond the

---

[6] A. Le Braz is the author of the tourist Blue Guide 'Brittany' in its 1924 edition. Moreover, the image of *Grand Site* begins to be largely disseminated thanks to tourist posters painted for the railway line. The official poster of la Pointe du Raz was published in 1930.

awe-inspiring Plogoff, consists in clinging to the rocky cliffs rising above the ocean, and which fall away to the pounding waves below.

A tourist awakening, locally initiated

The Pointe du Raz happened to be situated within the sphere of influence of a whole cluster of small Breton towns and harbours around Cape Sizun. The site was advertised as an interesting day-trip for the visitors staying at the resorts of Quimper, Douarnenez-Treboul and Audierne, which themselves relied on the two railheads: Quimper (line between Paris and Orleans) and Brest (line belonging to the State network).[7] Those who were in the accommodation business (hotels or boarding houses/*pensions*) and those whose job was linked to the transport of passengers were those mainly responsible for the development of the headland.

For instance, the tourists who intended to visit the Pointe du Raz were thus directed to the Hôtel de France in Audierne, where light horse-drawn carriages (the roads were quite rough) were available, and guides could be found. Progressively, the hotel-keepers who regularly organized horse-drawn trips set up some basic facilities on the headland[8]: stables to change horses, a building for the guides, outdoor stalls displaying small objects (lace) and offering fish for sale. A visitor centre was opened in Audierne in 1912, but the real tourist take-off of the Pointe du Raz occurred during the inter-war years.

The tourist development of the Pointe du Raz became more intensive soon after the Second World War. At this time, the Pointe du Raz was mentioned in every single tourist leaflet on Brittany, and never failed to be visited by organized tours, be they by train, by car or by motor coach. Hotels were built on the headland as branches of the hotels from Audierne or Quimper, each one of them offering at least 20 rooms.[9]

The tourist exploitation of the Pointe du Raz was by now a serious business. Promotion was ensured by ever-increasing numbers of tourist guides, by a magazine entitled *Tourism in Brittany*,[10] by the development of visitor centres, and by writers too: Anatole Le Braz used the Pointe du Raz as the setting for one of his 'bestseller' novels, *The Fire-Keeper* (1929). In 1928, an obscure variety-show author created an opera about the headland.[11] As a consequence of complaints from tourists

[7] The railway line opened in 1865.
[8] Several shops in Quimper profited from the visits to the Pointe du Raz: the bookshop sold some materials for painting, three hotels organized excursions (Hôtel du Parc, Hôtel du Commerce et Hôtel des Voyageurs) and four garages hired out carriages.
[9] The hotels of la Pointe du Raz were the Atlantic hotel, the Hôtel de la Pointe, and the Hôtel du Raz. Rooms cost from Ffr 5 to Ffr 25 in peak season.
[10] 'La Bretagne touristique, revue mensuelle illustree des intérêts moraux, économiques et touristiques de la Bretagne' was published by Octave-Louis Aubert in the 1920s and the 1930s. It was an efficient support for the tourist promotional material which used literature and painting.
[11] This opera by Sylvio Lazzari is entitled 'La tour de feu'. It is discussed by Le Grand Velin, La pointe du Raz à l'opera, *Cahiers d'Iroise*, 1983, pp. 154–155.

Fig. 9.1. Railway poster.

defrauded by all too greedy guides, prefectoral inspections had to be instigated, and the authorities had to establish an official guide company whose guides would be identifiable by wearing an armband.

First efforts to regulate the tourism

The development of the Pointe du Raz, from the inter-war years to the 1960s, meant easier access for ever-increasing numbers of tourists. A road suitable for motor vehicles was opened in the late 1950s, and a jetty was built for trips to the isle of Sein. Although the number of tourists increased, the mythical resonance of the site was not undermined. Generations of writers followed the previous generations, from Suarez to Colette, and from Julien Gracq to Simone de Beauvoir.

> What I found here is an impressive, ragged coastline – a purple and green ocean foaming against the rocks; and I was deeply moved. (Simone de Beauvoir)

> There surges a profound desire, once on this last advance of the land, to reach towards the place where the sun sets. (J. Gracq)

Even though tourism at the Pointe du Raz underwent a destructive drift, the site retained its literary appeal and remained a place of tourist and republican pilgrimage: after the Second World War, during which the headland was severely bombed because the Germans used it as an advance post in their Atlantic defences, the inhabitants of Plogoff intensified their commercial hold on the Pointe du Raz, so that they might derive benefit from the crowds of tourists who came during the years of economic growth. Thus were light carts, caravans, market stalls, wicker baskets laid on the ground or on stands, displayed for visitors as far as the cliffs. As the car industry developed, car parks were improvized on the heath. In the 1950s, new hotels were built on the outskirts of the preserved area: the Iroise (ten rooms) in 1954; however, that did not prevent the development of unregulated camping.

The image of the Pointe du Raz became progressively tarnished, and tourism started being presented as incompatible with the aesthetic dimensions of the site. The first recriminations about aesthetic damage were formulated as early as 1935, both by journalists and by artists, but such complaints became frequent and commonplace soon after the Second World War. The alarm was given by the new generation of regional writers in the name of a certain idea of Brittany. Henri Queffelec wrote:

> The Pointe du Raz, a tragic landscape devoted to meditation, but which the crowds of visitors, during the infernal summer months, turn into a souvenirs fairground, into a watershow, into a cliff-rally, into a promenade for legions of photographers . . . (Queffelec 1956)

The Pointe du Raz was the site for various informal activities, differing from those of the 19th century romantic artists. A trip to the Pointe du Raz involved watching the sea, having a picnic or using the rocks for playful but potentially dangerous activities. During the 1960s, tourism was mainly family-oriented and people would come from the Île-de-France, the Rhône-Alpes region or the western part of the country. The Pointe du Raz acted as a magnet for visitors from continental France and for tourists of more germanic origins (Germans, Swiss and Belgians), because the site occupied an essential position in their mental geography of Brittany (Vourc'h, 1999). However, since cars were an easy way to get to the Pointe du Raz and away from it, the visits were mostly short ones, the average time spent on the site being approximately 1 h. The ecological effects in terms of soil erosion were becoming more and more evident.

Fig. 9.2. Barren landscape.

When, in 1960, a new mayor was elected in Plogoff, the situation changed: for the first time, both an ecological and a financial solution was found. It consisted in reducing the number of cars on the headland and concentrating the traffic flows so that the soil might be protected. Thus two large car parks were established, the use of which was not free of charge, and which were placed under municipal supervision. A cement-and-granite commercial hall was also built to regroup all the so far disparate commercial undertakings. It was the municipality which, against the traders' wishes, carried out that first management programme, buying parcels of land suited to the construction of the car parks and the hall. Functional and modern, the hall, built by a local architect, was then considered by the authorities to be the best solution, aesthetically, ecologically and financially. The commission for monuments and sites, the representative of the State, endorsed the project.

Ethical and political controversies

That first initiative from the authorities could not solve the problems linked to the overabundance of tourists on the Pointe du Raz, and it also caused people to protest. Once the symbol of a sublime and untouched landscape, the Pointe du Raz became, on the contrary, the symbol of a denatured site. The guides themselves changed opinions. It was now both common and fashionable to say that tourism had deflowered the headland, and ecologically damaged the site. Indeed, so serious were the consequences of excess pedestrian use that the Armorican heath had been wiped out over 15 acres at the end of the headland, resulting in a 1-foot erosion of the upper layer of soil.

As early as the mid 1960s, the negative consequences of tourism on the Pointe du Raz started to be exposed by the media. The site was presented as both the symbol and the anti-symbol of Brittany, that of a soiled purity, of a prominent cultural site corrupted by tourist and financial interests. The inhabitants of Plogoff, who had accepted, a few years earlier, the setting up of a commercial hall, started protesting against the 'invasion' by tourists and against the State. The protest reached its violent climax during the months of February and March 1980. The protestors were also willing to undermine the decision to set up a nuclear power station in the direct vicinity of the *Grand Site*.

Some violent encounters between the protestors and the police took place at the Pointe du Raz. For a few weeks, Plogoff acquired the status of an 'ecological Mecca', gathering Woodstock-type crowds who organized pacifist marches. Inside the commercial hall, concerts with exclusively Breton traditional music, featuring the singer Alan Stivell, were held by the group 'Plogoff alternatives' and offered as a symbol of both the recovery of the site by the regionalist movement and the renewal of a regionalist counter-culture opposed to authoritarian and centralized government. When President Mitterrand, in 1981, officially gave up the idea of setting up the nuclear power station, the ecologists celebrated the event on the Pointe du Raz.[12]

What happened during the time from the inter-war years to the beginning of the 1980s thus seems to show that the Pointe du Raz, even though subjected to ever-increasing crowds of visitors, remained a place associated with the regional identity, and a site laden with imaginary significance. Despite its overcrowding, the Pointe du Raz retained its attractive power for tourists, who came from ever-broader horizons to visit it. However, something else was at stake. In so far as the State was accused of carelessness in relation to the increasing tourist development of the coast between the 1980s and the 1990s, the Pointe du Raz was chosen, once again, as an exemplary site. The rehabilitation of the headland, which started at the beginning of the 1990s, showed that the State was once again taking the lead to impose its own conception of a *Grand Site National*.

The Political Redefinition of the *Grand Site*

Re-establishing the Pointe du Raz as a *Grand Site National* can be interpreted as a three-dimensional operation. There was, first, an ecological dimension: tackling the issue of the excessively numerous visits by appropriate visitor management techniques. There was also a financial dimension: how to obtain the highest revenues from the site with a view to supporting the development of a rather poor, isolated agricultural area. Last, but far from least, came the political dimension, the aim

---

[12] Plogoff la revolte, Archives departementales du Finistère, Q 4 bb 208. See also Pichavant, 1980.

being to tame this socially troubled region, and to restore this 'jewel of nature' back
to its position of pride within the national heritage of France.

New representations of the *Grand Site*

During and after the 1980s, the authorities, in order to regain the initiative concerning the Pointe du Raz, addressed the question of 'ecology', presenting themselves as the most expert on the site, hence best able to protect it.[13] They declared
a concern that the reality of the Pointe du Raz might fall short of the tourist's
expectations for so mythical and emblematic a site: 'The visitors are generally
offered quite poor, unsatisfying conditions of discovery, which, considering how
prestigious the place is, should not be the case'. They intended to give themselves
the power to raise the standard of the site to the visitors' expectations. Diagnosed
as 'sick' as a conquence of its own success, the Pointe du Raz, in the eyes of the
Prefect who started the operation, deserved public works on the largest scale.

This whole issue of a so-called 'sudden awareness' of the negative consequences
of tourism on the Pointe du Raz deserves further analysis. It came to a head in
1991, when the famous French weekly *Le Point* organized on a national scale a
campaign for the preservation of the coast. This campaign enabled the 'Conservatoire du littoral' to purchase the Pointe du Raz, which had by that time become
synonymous with 'tourist havoc' on the French coasts. It was the starting point for
a deprecating discourse of the Pointe du Raz, now a symbol of the damage caused
by tourism. Journalists, be they from Brittany or from the rest of France, presented
the excessive number of visits and the disfigurement of the site as established facts.
They metaphorically posed the Pointe du Raz as a victim of these phenomena,
spreading the image of a natural area symbolically raped by tourism, as well as
symbolically rescued or morally redeemed by the 'Conservatoire du littoral'.

While once wonderfully pure and beautiful, in 'a green dress of moor lined
with pink heather and adorned with golden jewels, the gorse',[14] the Pointe du Raz,
continuously compared to a woman, was now presented in the press as doomed to
defacement. The idea was that nature had lost its virginity under the action of the
tourists' physical aggression: trampling on the heath, destruction of the vegetation,
soil erosion, stones laid bare ... The Pointe du Raz was said to be 'in danger',[15]
'disfigured',[16] 'ruined',[17] it '(had) lost its soul'. 'The Pointe du Raz can please no
more, the site is worn out'; 'the listed site was losing its beauty and its soul'. To
the physical damage was added insult, moral aggression towards the supernatural:
the Pointe du Raz, a rocky horn rising immediately out to the pounding sea and

---

[13] The French Ministry of Environment, under D'Ornano's supervision, envisaged a *Grand site*
procedure which as early as 1977 proposed the demolition of the commercial hall to rebuild
it elsewhere, and a better distribution of the revenues to the hinterland.
[14] *Ouest-France*, édition Brest, 18 July 1991.
[15] 19 *Le Télégramme de Brest*, 3 October 1989.
[16] *Ouest-France*, édition Brest, 30 September 1989.
[17] *Combat nature*, November 1991.

defying it (according to the standard description of the site in romantic literature), was able to resist the ocean over centuries, but it could not resist man. The issue now was to protect the site, to allow nature to 'recover its (own) rights'.

> Last year, 600,000 tourists came to the Pointe du Raz, drawn by the wild beauty of the struggle between ocean and rock just as moths are drawn to light. But tourism can be quite wild too. The Pointe du Raz is currently disfigured by the presence of souvenir sellers, bars for tourists and hotels 'with a view'. Even worse, a car park and a wide trail of red asphalt leaves a scar on the foothills. The tourists' trampling has made a desert out of the place: vegetation won't grow anymore, and soil erosion has been so severe that one fears for the preservation of the site.[18]

These interpretations, initiated by the 'Conservatoire du littoral' and then commonly circulated in the press, were the first indication of a new institutionalized belief rooted in the ideology of environmentalism. The Administration and the politicians, who originated this new reading of the *Grand Site*, metaphorically presented themselves as the medical doctors who would perform an ecological treatment on the Pointe du Raz. The emblematic and 'moral' status of the site in the context of national heritage made such treatment an absolute necessity: 'It is our duty to return to that awe-inspiring but defaced site its former beauty, its former virginity. Nowadays, it is of paramount importance to protect our environment', said the prefect who started the restoration operation on the Pointe du Raz.[19]

The fact that the 'Conservatoire du littoral' should participate was more or less presented as a miracle: the Conservatory, (nick)named 'the guardian of our shores', was said to 'spread its protective wings' over the Pointe du Raz, which thanks to its action would 'regain its beauty',[20] and 'start all over again'.[21]

Controversies surrounding the 'naturalness' of la Pointe du Raz

The 'Conservatoire du littoral' had, among its responsibilities, to buy back the *Grand Site* lands and to lead a policy that might reconcile the protection of the environment with tourist visitation. Practically, it led to the signature of an agreement with the commercial traders for them to move: the commercial hall was demolished to be rebuilt half a mile inland. The demolition of the last hotel to be built on the headland, the Iroise, which had opened in 1954, was also mentioned. The controversies about the demolition of the buildings, which according to the representatives of the State was necessary in order to give its natural character back to the site, once again hurt the feelings of the locals. Another rebellion arose, fuelling a wave of protest against the authorities. The tourists drew up petitions so as to retain car parks and hotels at their disposal, as did the inhabitants of Plogoff and local ecologists.

[18] *Le Point*, 10 June 1991.
[19] *La Vie*, 27 June 1991.
[20] *Le Télégramme de Brest*, 3 February 1994.
[21] *Le Télégramme de Brest*, 26 June 1992.

'We don't come here to see hills covered with barren heath, which we could do anywhere in Brittany, but to admire the Raz, namely an awe-inspiring sight', one visitor wrote in 1995.[22] He implied that the Pointe du Raz, as a site important for both its landscape and its culture, should be equipped to favour tourism, and not become a nature reserve closed to the public and in which no man-made building should stand. With similar concerns, numerous tourists entered the fray, using the press as a medium, to prevent the demolition of the Iroise hotel, which they referred to as 'the meeting-place for *true* nature lovers'.[23] That building was 'the missing link between man and the landscape' they wrote in comments sent to the 'Conservatoire du littoral'.[24] Far from accepting the Conservatoire's decree according to which the hotel had to be demolished since it had 'no architectural value', the tourists answered back, both to the 'Conservatoire du littoral' and to the major national and regional papers, that:

> . . . the Iroise is a touch of happiness lying on the heath. A thousand painters have chosen to paint it. A man-made work seldom finds its place in the landscape, and hardly ever induces reverie while surprising the spectator as it does.[25]

The old lady with a Breton-sounding name who was running this diminutive hotel facing the sea became an heroic figure of the resistance to a behemoth-like Administration, ecological but inhuman. The hotel was presented in the press from two quite different, contradictory points of view. For those who favoured its existence, it was a symbol of a reassuring permanence in the surrounding space, 'a refuge in the moor, heat and peace in the heart of hostility'; 'were it not for the hotel, the landscape would be flat and grim; it is the small house that gives the scale'.[26] But for the others, it stood out against the completely natural space as an ugly man-made building.

The controversies provoked by the *Grand Site* operation, in which the State and the regional and the departmental organizations participated, revolved around two major points: how the coastal nature was perceived, and how the tourists themselves were considered. According to the people now in charge of the treatment of the *Grand Site*, responsibility for the damage to the area would fall to mass tourism; and indeed the tourists were presented as devils (dirty, swarming, teeming), and compared to 'processionary caterpillars', to 'hordes', to 'invaders'. Considering this image fostered by the protectionist institutions, the tourists' response was, once again, to defend themselves: 'I will not subscribe to the propaganda image spread out by the guides' bureau, according to which we tourists would be cliff destroyers and rubbish leavers',[27] a visitor wrote in a spontaneous letter to the 'Conservatoire du littoral'. In fact, most tourists were treasuring, and

---

[22] Source: complaints notebook left for tourist use at the guides' reception at La Pointe du Raz, consulted at the headquarters of the Conservatoire du Littoral.
[23] See note 22.
[24] Letter to Conservatoire du Littoral, Saint Brieuc, consulted at their headquarters.
[25] See note 24.
[26] See note 24.
[27] See note 24.

willing to preserve, the image they had of themselves as romantic travellers, following in Flaubert's, or Michelet's steps. They kept repeating to the authorities, in as bombastic a style as can be found in the early travel accounts, that their visit to the place was embued with symbolic dimensions.

> Let's hope the authorities will understand that this little hotel's façade, white and delicate, becomes for the stroller the white screen upon which he/she projects his dreams: dreams of nature, of purity, of sea, land and sky eventually meeting.[28]

In these conditions, the movement for environmental protection at the Pointe du Raz was not an even process. Models and counter-models for an appropriate administration of coastal nature were opposed in the name of historical values and human parameters, but without stopping the dynamics of ecological restoration.

Ecological engineering for tourism

The restoration programme for the Pointe du Raz consisted of a series of technical responses with an obvious purpose: showing care and respect for the site by the restorers. In 1988, the Prefecture du Finistère launched a new *Grand Site National* project with a view to finding solutions for the management of the site. A joint association of communes was organized in 1991 to manage the works. The 'Conservatoire du littoral' acquired 250 acres on the Pointe du Raz itself.[29] The State financially supported the project, helped by commercial sponsorship: apart from 'Gaz de France', the only national partner, two regional partners and a dozen local partners made it possible to add about 8 million francs to the budget of 40 million francs. In September 1997, the *Grand Site* reopened, and it looked quite different from its previous appearance (see Fig. 9.4).

The Pointe du Raz under its new appearance reflects the 1990s ideologies concerning the equipment of natural sites, in France and more generally in Europe. Indeed, the options had their source in the treatment of other sites, in France or abroad (the coastal site of the Lizard peninsula and that of Land's End, both in Cornwall, Great Britain, were taken into account). Two major principles were followed in the treatment of the Pointe du Raz. First of all, moving away any commercial undertaking that might so far have been taking place on the headland was considered indispensable to the re-valuation of the site. In accordance with that principle, the commercial hall was moved half a mile inland and relocated in a small valley, while the small Iroise hotel was demolished. Second, directing the visitor-flow, as opposed to allowing free rein of the site, found its justification in the necessary restoration of both the soil and the plant life. In this respect, it was

---

[28] See note 24.
[29] What makes it difficult for the conservation agencies is that the Breton littoral is mostly divided into very small parcels whose owners have sometimes disappeared. For the purchase of the Pointe du Raz, the 'Conservatoire du littoral' had to trace some 300 owners.

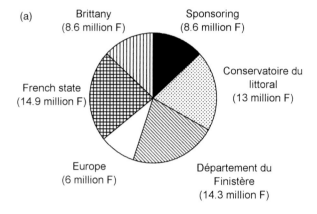

(a)

Fig. 9.3. Financial budget of the Grand Site Plan: (a) by sponsor; (b) by site income and expenditure.

(b)

Expenses		Incomes and Profits	
Wages	826,000 F	Carparks	2,349,000 F
Maintenance of the site and of the buildings	200,000 F	Guiding	25,000 F
Shuttle to the headland	540,000 F	Slides and films	34,000 F
Promotion of the site	170,000 F	Real estate income	13,000 F
Liabilities interests	95,000 F		
Taxes and other expenses	420,000 F	Total incomes	2,424,000 F
Earnings from the carpark	750,000 F	Subsidies	104,000 F
Total	3,012,000 F		

decided that pedestrian traffic would be strictly channelled through a series of paths, some wider than others, with indications of the proper way to visit.

René Leberre and Bernard Lanctuit, two regional architects, designed a new commercial hall surrounded by car parks with a capacity for 800 cars (the same number as before), conceived to merge into the environment. Of rectangular shape, it is hidden away in a small depression, making it almost invisible. Not only could it accommodate all the traders from the former hall, but it also allowed them to considerably increase the comfort and the quality of their commercial services. The new car parks themselves were the object of thorough aesthetic research: they are hidden behind dry stone walls almost 2 miles in length, which stop the Atlantic wind and are sympathetic to the Breton heath landscape.

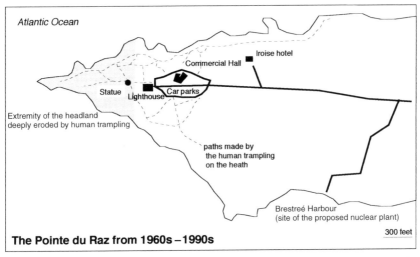

The Pointe du Raz from 1960s–1990s

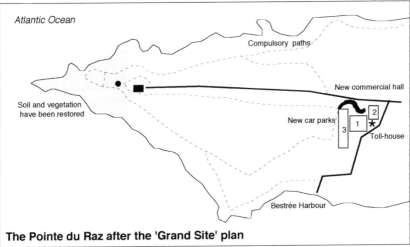

The Pointe du Raz after the 'Grand Site' plan

Fig. 9.4. Cartography of before/after site plan.

The choice of the experts and the administrators was to dispense with the idea of any urban type of equipment (such as benches, or urban surface materials, or multiple explanatory signs) while still offering an easy visit to large flows of tourists: 1600 to 2000 people per hour. The main trail, which leads from the shuttle's terminus to the extremity of the headland, is a paved way, 4 yards in width, built out of materials quarried on site during the treatment works. Not only does it allow access for disabled visitors, but its cost was quite reasonable (Ffr 250 per metre). Despite these advantages, some people are dissatisfied: not only those who would have favoured the more-comfortable asphalt, but also those who consider it as already too artificial to be established in a natural site.

Fig. 9.5. New pathway.

Favouring the regrowth of vegetation by treating soil and damaged heath surfaces was the most technically innovative part of the restoration project. With the
help of various ecological studies led by the Université de Bretagne Occidentale,
Christian Celton, responsible for the landscaping, sowed eroded surfaces with seeds
taken from plants growing in the 'sound' heath: gorse, plantain, armeria maritima,
heather, festuca, etc. Sophisticated methods were used to gather the seeds and to
prepare the soil: levelling, scratching the utterly bare soils, spreading of a heath
substrate. The results are actually quite satisfying: the coastal grass, gorse and heath
is now restored.

If appropriate responses in terms of ecological protection and administration
were finally being found (despite the objections, inevitable though they were, raised
by the advocates of a non-intervention policy), new issues had to be addressed. In
order to provide reception facilities for the tourists, 14 people are employed in the
high season. This represents a source of expense that has to be covered by receipts.
The Ffr 10 per car and Ffr 50 per coach access fees to the new commercial hall's
car park rekindle the old debates between those who advocate a free access to nature
and the defenders of 'commercial realities'. We will probably have to wait a few
years before knowing if this *Grand Site* is economically viable. However, from a
wider point of view, nobody can deny the role the *Grand Site* had in the aesthetic
valuation placed on the Cape Sizun area. The Pointe du Raz, being famous,
becomes the cue for all sorts of activities, be they tourist activities such as the
'alternative' festival mentioned earlier, or otherwise. Moreover, another dimension
is already envisaged: not only will the *Grand Site* be a natural object, but also a
vehicle for interpretations of human heritage; a historical exhibition of the *Grand
Site* in Gallo-Roman times is currently under study.

The question of the tourist viability of the site

The investments made by the government are undoubtedly important, but the expenses incurred year after year in the maintenance of the *Grand Site* and in the follow-up of the ecological restoration operations are quite considerable. The problem is that, while it is fairly easy to get investment to rehabilitate a site, it is not so easy to obtain stable public subsidies for its maintenance. That is why the financial viability of the site is an issue. For the present, the greatest share of the revenues derived from the Pointe du Raz's car park fees go to the village of Plogoff, while the largest part of the operational expenses of the site are assumed by the State. That is perhaps a source of intractable problems of the *Grand Site* programme.

Conclusion

The Pointe du Raz is a powerful image which appeared and developed in the sensibility and the imagination of the romanticism of the 19th century, and which corresponds to the growth of tourist interest. The tourist image of the Pointe du Raz was built concurrently with the tourist image of Brittany, with a view to serve it. That first-rate site was commercially exploited very early, and more and more intensively as time went by, without the slightest reservation either by the local society or by the local advocates of conservation of the littoral, until crowds of tourists had caused severe ecological damage. The Pointe du Raz, as a matter of fact, was not perceived, in the area, as a natural site, but as a symbolic place, bearer and catalyst of a regional identity somewhat negated, in these years of economic growth, by a centralized State. Nowadays, the realization of the *Grand Site* procedure is grounded on new values, among which are ever-more prevailing ecological imperatives, perceived as a means to regain the political initiative over the area, and to give it an economic boost.

Today, the *Grand Site* is mostly a grand problem, and the Pointe du Raz, the conservation of which was decided very late and after much debate, has a place of its own among the protected areas on the French coasts. 'What defines a *grand site* is neither its size nor the number of tourists it receives, but a common set of problems linked with the presence, in a fragile site, of visitors attracted by its fame' (Vourc'h, 1999). Those who were responsible for the treatment of such a place had to realize that it could not be limited to technical measures, because what is at stake is a deeply cultural approach to the status of natural spaces in a modern society. What makes this *Grand Site* and the history of its treatment particularly interesting is precisely the fact that the different opinions on coastal conservation, on public access, and on how to deal with the tourists, were expressed and they conflicted more openly here than anywhere else in France. These emblematic spaces, thus 'consecrated' by public opinion, most probably represent the elaboration of a new approach, perhaps even a new ideology, concerning the role of tourism in natural spaces.

References

Annales Economie, societe, civilisations (1992) Patrimoine en debat: construction de memoire et valorisation du symbolique, numero spécial 9.

Ardouin-Dumazet, N.B.Y. (1901) *Voyage en France: la Bretagne peninsulaire*. Berger-Levrault, Paris.

Baring-Gould, S. (1902) *A Guide Book of Britanny*. Methuen and Co., London.

Benoist, F. (1845) *La Bretagne contemporaine, sites pittoresques, monuments, costumes, scènes de mÏurs, histoires, legendes, traditions et usages des 5 départements de cette province*. Champestre éditeur, Nantes.

Boulain, C. (1895) *Souvenirs de la basse Cornouaille*. Chez P. Le Gloaziou, Guinguamp.

Brizeux, J. (1845) *Les Bretons*. Magana, Paris.

Brousmiche, J. (ed.) (1977) *Voyage dans le Finistère 1829–1830–1831*. Morvran, Quimper.

le Mercier d'Erm, C. (1927) *La Bretagne pittoresque et artistique vue par les écrivains et les artistes*. Rasmussen and Co.

Chevalier de Freminville (1836) *Bicentenaire du Voyage de Cambry dans le Finistère ou État de ce Département en 1794*. Brest.

Corbin, A. (1988) *Le Territoire du Vide, l'Occident et le Désir de Rivage*. Aubier, Paris.

Dupouy, A. (1947) *Michelet en Bretagne*. Horizons de France, Paris.

Flaubert, G. and du Camp, M. (1907) *Par les Champs et par les Grèves*. Fasquelle, Paris.

Helias, P.-J. (1966) *Légendes de Raz et de Sein*, Coll. Bretagne vivante. J. Le Doare, Chateaulin.

Janin, J. (1862) *La Bretagne*. Bourin, Paris.

Joanne, A. (1888) (edition 1902) *La Bretagne*. Coll Itineraire general de la France. Hachette, Paris.

Le Braz, A. (1925) *La Bretagne*. Laurens, Paris.

Lebesque, M. (1970) *Comment peut-on être Breton?* Le Seuil, Paris.

Mérimée, P. (1836) *Notes d'un Voyage dans l'Ouest de la France*. Fournier.

Michelet, J. (1892) *La Mer*. Calmann-Levy, Paris.

Monmarché, M. (1900) *Livret Guide Officiel des Chemins de Fer d'Orleans – La Cornouaille*. Hachette, Paris.

Monnier, E. (1880) La Bretagne artistique, pittoresque et littéraire dans les départements de l'ouest. *Courrier de l'art et de la curiosité*, le année, vol 1, juillet-decembre.

Philipponeau, M. (1970) *Debout Bretagne!* Presses Universitaires de Rennes, Rennes.

Pichavant, R. (1980) *Les Pierres de la Liberté, Plogoff 1975–1980*. Éditions Morgane, Douarnenez.

Pinot, J.-P. (1988) Comment les romantiques percevaient la dynamique du territoire dans les pays celtiques. *Melanges offerts à Le Guillou, Bretagne et romantisme*, Université de Bretagne occidentale, pp. 112–116.

Queffelec, H. (1956) *La Bretagne*, coll. Les guides bleus. Hachette, Paris.

Revue du Touring Club de France (1924) Journées du comité des sites et monuments de Bretagne, no. 359, août/septembre.

Serant, F. (1970) *La Bretagne et la France*. Fayard, Paris.

Vidal de la Blache, P. (1908) *Tableau de la Geographie de la France*, In: Lavisse, E. (ed.) *L'Histoire de la France*, Vol. 1. Hachette, Paris, pp. 1–55.

Vouc'h, A. (1999) 'Vaut le détour!' Les grands sites, *Urbanis*, Atelier Technique de l'Environnement-ICOMOS Section Française, p. 76.

Maturing Markets for Cultural Tourism: Germany and the Demand for the 'Cultural' Destination

10

Martin Lohmann[1] and Jörn W. Mundt[2]

[1]Institut für Tourismus- und Bäderforschung in
Nordeuropa, Kiel, Germany; [2]University for
Cooperative Education/Berufsakademie, Ravensburg,
Germany

Tourism and the Understanding of 'Culture'

Culture and curiosity have been major drives for the development of tourism in Germany. Johann Wolfgang von Goethe's trip to Italy 1786–1788 was the blueprint for classical journeys by generations of educated German travellers who wanted to experience the country in his footsteps. Even though Goethe himself was travelling in an old German tradition, he not only was the most prominent tourist but also changed the pattern of these trips from broad educational projects to the dominance of subjective experience. By doing this, he utilized the 'invention' of ancient Greece (Friedell, 1927) by Johann Joachim Winckelmann, the German archaeologist and antiquarian (1717–1768) who lived in Rome and was one of the founders of the long tradition of German philological humanism. Hence the tourist gaze changed its subject from the contemporary situation to an idealized past:

> Italy became the stage for Hellenic spirit and Greek art. . . . A new chapter had begun. Not studies dominated any more but experience, not the collecting intellect but the seeking soul, not encyclopaedic knowledge but selective feeling. The primacy of aesthetics began. (Müllenmeister, 1997: 110)

Even though there seems to be a bit of a misunderstanding, this kind of tourism has been dominated ever since by visiting monuments and excavations of ancient cultures, accompanied by knowledgeable explanations of philological thoroughness. The classical *Studienreise* (study trip) typically is a guided tour, organized by a tour operator specialized in this kind of tourism. The tour guide normally will have an academic background and be a specialist in the history of the country visited or an archaeologist with a sound knowledge of the ancient sites included in the tour. Also, the *Studienreise* may be a trip to visit cathedrals and museums to see the architecture of different epochs and the artwork of old masters. The different landscapes and natural habitats which have been reflected by history, paintings and literature also play a role as environmental factors to complement the travellers' picture of past times.

Before his trip to Italy, Goethe, who erroneously deemed himself to be more a natural scientist than a writer, had made various trips through Germany in order to experience nature. People were using his papers as guides and followed his travel paths in order to repeat his encounters with landscapes and nature. Being a cabinet minister in Weimar, he could support the development of infrastructure to support tourism to the *Thüringer Wald*, a mountain range in the centre of Germany, one of his favourite spots. A particular valley in which he stayed quite often became very attractive to many people who admired him. It was visited by courtiers from Weimar, writers, and well-off citizens from Frankfurt am Main and Leipzig. The resulting number of hotels and inns was unprecedented in the 18th century (Berktold-Fackler and Krumbholz, 1997: 35).

It therefore was not only a matter of financial and organizational restraints, but also of reminescence, that the prototype of the now classical *Studienreise* was a domestic trip to another German mountain range, organized by Dr Hubert Tigges in 1928 who started his business as a tour operator with this journey (Dietsch, 1996: 74). As a brand name, 'Dr. Tigges' is again being used by the study-trip branch of TUI, Germany's biggest tour operator.

The emerging tourism for broader social groups after the First World War soon diminished in the wake of the 1929 world economic crisis and during the Nazi government in Germany from 1933, and came to a standstill during the resulting Second World War (1939–1945). For the inhabitants of 'communist'-ruled East Germany, travelling was restricted until 9 November 1989, when the opening of the Berlin wall marked the downturn of the so-called German Democratic Republic, which finally in October 1990 became part of the Federal Republic of Germany.

For West Germans, however, it was soon after the war that the classical study trip, in accordance with the general development of tourism, grew to an important market size. It was not by pure chance that the long-standing market leader in Germany for study trips, Studiosus Reisen, emerged from the activities of a university student, organizing trips to Italy for the student union. He soon realized the potential of the market and, in spite of finishing his study, founded the tour operator in 1954 (Roth and Langemeyer, 1996: 176–178). Clients mainly had a background of higher education, which at that time included at least Latin. As study trips, in contrast to those in the emerging market for mass tourism, were rather expensive, the audience for these package tours tended to be middle-aged with a respectable income. Destinations for these journeys were mainly situated in Italy and Greece, but Spain, Turkey, Egypt, and, more recently, countries like Mexico, India, China, and South Africa also became within reach for study trips.

Apart from the economic upturn since the 1950s in West Germany, which facilitated travelling generally in an unprecedented way, there were two main factors supporting the rising importance of cultural tourism:

1. Better availability of education and the resulting larger proportion of the population with A-level or university backgrounds;
2. A broader understanding of culture.

The thorough change in the output of the German educational system is reflected by the number of people with tertiary education. In 1960, around 700,000 employees in Germany had an academic background, now the number is around 5 million. The first generations of Germans having taken advantage of the expansion of tertiary education are in their 40s and 50s at the turn of the century, and therefore are likely customers for suppliers of tourism.

In parallel to what Aurelius Augustinus stated for 'time', one might formulate for 'culture' the statement that 'when I don't think about it, I tend to know what culture is, but when somebody asks me I don't know how to define it'. Even though it is very difficult to define 'culture', it is evident that in the past decades there has been a significant shift towards a much broader understanding of its meaning. Traditionally, the term 'culture' had a connotation of high value and esteem when it had been restricted to fine arts. In tourism, it was primarily confined to visiting remnants of ancient times, sites being relevant in terms of art history (cathedrals, castles, art museums) and to the experience of the 'aura' (Benjamin, 1936) of the originals and the genuine places associated with them.

The term 'culture' lost some of its philological touch when, in the past decades, dead languages, even at German grammar schools, became less important. Universities, for example, in contrast with their practice until the 1970s, do not require their new entrants, irrespective of the subject, to have Latin qualifications at advanced or even ordinary level any more. Also, a growing number of subjects are now being taught in tertiary education (e.g. tourism itself). This also has enlarged the general scope of people's interests and contributed to a broader understanding of culture.

However, the word 'culture' has also become rather unspecific over the years, as almost everything these days is deemed to be 'culture' in one way or another. Mostly, the term is used in relation to arts and music, but there is a growing list of exceptions. Apart from traditional culture and pop culture, there is also a political culture and now even a 'corporate culture' that qualifies the way in which companies deal with clients, their staff and relate to other businesses. Often the term 'culture' is also used in the sense of 'civilization' and generally describes the complete social heritage of a society.

The understanding of culture in tourism has changed accordingly. This may be illustrated by a rather recent example. The decline of industrial production as the key to economic development and the closing of old industries like coal mining and steel production has left areas in Germany like the *Ruhrgebiet* with remnants of a time when, until the 1960s, this region was the very centre of the national economy. What used to be an exemplification of pure work, signs of non-culture and the 'symbols of exploitation' (Soyez, 1993: 50) turned into monuments for a working-class culture that has faded away with the rise of the computer and service industries. As in Britain, old industrial sites and buildings are changed into museums to document life under the rule of the old industries. It seems that generally 'technical works only have a chance to be appraised when they have become coated with as much rusty patina as the Eiffel Tower' (Müllenmeister, 1993: 148).

However, cultural tourism is not restricted to historical sites and art museums any more, but also includes destinations of contemporary importance. The topics being dealt with on these trips also relate to social and political aspects of everyday life. The current political situation and the relationship with neighbouring countries, for example, may be the most significant part of a visit to Israel. Meetings with politicians, sociologists, political scientists and historians complement the impressions tourists get on their guided trip around the country.

Traditional study trips already offered the opportunity to learn about national and regional cuisine. This used to be only one, though interesting, side-aspect of visiting a destination. Now one can offer study trips just to experience and learn about particular ways of cooking. Together with wine, it is regarded as an important part of culture worth exploring on special trips. Literature also became an important topic of cultural tourism. Trying to follow the paths of characters from novels (like Molly Bloom in Dublin) or experiencing the literary aspects of a region (like the one formed by three different countries around Lake Constance) are just examples. Trips to festivals, like the ones dedicated to classical music, opera or to particular composers in Glyndebourne, Salzburg, Savonlinna or Bayreuth, form a significant part of cultural tourism. Short or weekend trips to musicals or to performances in famous opera houses like the Metropolitan Opera in New York, Covent Garden in London, La Scala in Milan or the Bastille opera house in Paris add to the various possibilities of new forms of cultural tourism.

Study trips alone, therefore, do not make for cultural tourism. Even though they have been modernized by offering a variety of new contents, many cultural activities can be part of other than study trips. The German *Reiseanalyse*, an annual representative survey on the travel behaviour of the German population since 1970, shows that culture forms a significant element of main holiday trips. The figures given in Table 10.1 indicate that many of these actions are not exercised solely, but are part of a broader cluster of various cultural activities. This is in some contrast to the stereotype of particularly sun-and-beach holidaymakers, who generally are considered to develop no interest in the host countries at all. Yet beach holidays at the French *Côte d'Azur*, for example, may be combined with visiting some of the various art museums dedicated to painters like Fernand Léger, Pablo Picasso, Marc Chagall, Auguste Renoir, or artists like Jean Cocteau, who all lived there for quite some time. Even the world's number-one destination for mass tourism, Mallorca, apart from the Cathedral in Palma, offers lots of cultural spots like the monastery at Valdemossa, in which George Sand together with Frédéric Chopin spent a winter on the island, Joan Miró's studio in Cala Major, designed by the Catalan architect Josep Lluis Sert (who also designed the stunning museum of Fondation Maeght in St Paul de Vence in southern France), or the medieval walled town of Alcudia.

Table 10.1. Ranking of cultural activities during the 1995 main holiday trip.[a]

Rank	Activity	Incidence % of holiday-makers	Intensity Mean (1 = very often – 4 = rarely)
1	Attending sightseeing tours	66.1	2.6
2	Visiting historical buildings/churches	64.4	2.7
3	Visiting historical landscapes	46.9	2.8
4	Visiting heritage museums	44.0	3.2
5	Visiting folkloric events	37.0	3.1
6	Visiting archaeological sites	34.6	2.9
7	Visiting exhibitions	36.1	3.2
8	Visiting art museums	32.8	3.2
9	Visiting theatres – plays, operas, musicals	19.4	3.3
10	Visiting technical museums	17.0	3.3
11	Visiting festivals	15.6	3.4
12	Attending recitals of classical music	14.1	3.4
13	Being creative (painting, drawing, etc.)	12.1	2.6
14	Attending rock or pop concerts	11.0	3.4
15	Making music	8.1	3.0

[a] In case people have made more than one holiday trip of at least 5 days, this is the most important one to them. It tends to be the longest and most expensive journey and the destination normally is farther away than for additional holiday trips.
Source: F.U.R (Forschungsgemeinschaft Urlaub und Reisen e.V.) Reiseanalyse 1996 (unpublished).

Even the lowest-ranking activities like 'being creative' or 'making music' were reported by some 5.9 and 4.0 million tourists, respectively. The intensity of the activities generally seems to be associated with their occurrence but there are some exceptions. Creative activities like painting and drawing would rank first in terms of intensity, together with 'attending sightseeing tours', while visiting archaeological sites seems to be an activity on main holiday trips that does not seem to be confined to just one location.

Apart from holidaymakers, there are about 1 million travellers in Germany who occasionally combine a business trip with a private holiday and by this often also become cultural tourists: 20% of them reported visiting monuments during their stay (SPIEGEL, 1994: 77).

At this point it becomes obvious that it is necessary to distinguish between different types of cultural tourists:

1. Tourists who are motivated by culture and whose trips are formed by their cultural interest;
2. Tourists who are also interested in cultural aspects of their destinations.

In terms of research conducted by the Irish Tourist Board and Brady Shipman Martin (1988) for the European Commission, the first group consists of 'specific cultural tourists' whereas the second is made up of 'general cultural tourists'. Of all arrivals within the then European Community, 24% were attributed to cultural tourism in this study, 90% of which were by general cultural tourists.

During the 1990s, cultural aspects tended to become more significant as a tourist motivation (cf. Table 10.2). Already in the 1980s, this motive gradually seems to have gained more importance. Until 1992, however, respondents could only indicate this motive as having been important for the holiday trip; since then they can also qualify its importance. Therefore, it is not possible to form a time series that goes right back through the 1980s.

Table 10.2. Culture as motivation for holiday travel.

Percentage of holidaymakers for whom this motive for the main holiday trip was particularly important	1992	1994	1995	1996
To broaden the horizon, doing something for culture and education	17.5	19.1	20.0	20.1

Source: F.U.R (Forschungsgemeinschaft Urlaub und Reisen e.V.) Reiseanalysen 1993 – 1997 (unpublished).

As there has been a general tendency to list more motives for travelling since the 1980s, it is hard to decide whether these figures really indicate a genuine growth of interest in cultural aspects of travel. However, it may be argued that, with the growing travel experience of German tourists, other aspects of holidaymaking rather than just relaxing, enjoying beach, sun and the occasional walk become more relevant. From this perspective, it appears logical to assume there is a real growth in interest for cultural activities on holidays. This is supported by a general trend within Europe which led to increasing activities on the supply-side of tourism. 'Such is its growth that even in the heritage richness of Europe over 70% of all cultural heritage attractions have been created in the last 30 years' (McNulty, 1993: 13).

Types of Cultural Travellers

Referring to the tradition of study trips mentioned above, for Germany a slightly more differentiated view of cultural tourism is needed. If *Bildungsreisen* (educational trips) are also taken into account, another type of cultural travel is introduced. Even though the terms '*Studien-*' and '*Bildungsreise*' sometimes tend to be used synonymously, most people will recognize the difference. The term 'educational trip' will be reserved e.g. for language studies abroad or generally for any kind of trip associated with systematic learning. This is supported by respective regulations in most of the states (*Länder*) of the Federal Republic of Germany which, in the 1970s, introduced legislation on educational leave (*Bildungsurlaub*; Arbeitsgruppe am Max-Planck-Institut für Bildungsforschung, 1979: 254–259). This entitles employees to extra paid leave of some five days per annum (depending on the state) for general educational purposes. Accordingly, many people tend to think of trips related to educational leave when talking of *Bildungsreisen*.

Therefore, there are roughly six types of cultural travellers to be distinguished:

1. People on strictly educational trips (*Bildungsreisende*; e.g. for learning languages, to speak with confidence, becoming computer-literate and also for attending courses in painting, drawing or photography);
2. Travellers on classical study trips (*Studienreisende*);
3. Cultural tourists (*Kulturreisende*): people travelling in order to take part in cultural events (e.g. festivals, theatre performances, recitals, art exhibitions, etc.);
4. People whose motivation to travel is to (also) have cultural experience (cf. Table 10.2);
5. Holidaymakers who are also interested in culture and visit cultural sites and/or events during their holidays;
6. People on business trips who take the opportunity to develop some cultural activities.

With regard to such a typology, it is important to make it quite clear that typologies generally do not stick to tourists like labels and therefore should not be confused with personal characteristics. At least two arguments speak against such assumptions: (i) Tourists are very likely to make different types of trips at different times, e.g. a study trip and a pure package-tour beach holiday with no cultural flavour whatsoever; (ii) The personality-approach to such typologies often would imply tourists to be single travellers. However, most people tend to travel with partners who may well be of different character. As people with different personalities and lifestyles therefore show the same travel behaviour, and vice versa, it is evident that such an approach would not be of much use (Lawson, 1991). These limitations make it quite clear that typologies of this kind are always temporary: they do not last much longer than the latest trip.

Not surprisingly, education is the most important variable to determine the propensity to any kind of cultural tourism (cf. Table 10.3). This is particularly true for educational travellers and people who have been on a study trip in the last 3 years. Generally, it may be stated that formal education gradually becomes less relevant as a determining factor for cultural activities associated with travel from types one to five. The ratio between highest and basic educational levels for the respective types declines gradually, from educational travellers to tourists attending cultural events. The typology of tourists, therefore, reflects an underlying scale based on the intensity of cultural activities from strict learning to occasional participation in cultural events.

It is an interesting aspect in the demographic data presented in Table 10.3 that the 30–39 age group is generally less interested in culture than other age groups. A more-detailed look at the data reveals that this is due to couples with

Table 10.3. Social and demographic data of different types of tourists.

Types of tourists (%)	1 Educational travellers*	2 Study trip travellers[a]	3 Cultural tourists*	4 People with cultural motivation for tourism	5 Tourists attending cultural events[b]
German population (columns 1–4); holiday travellers (column 5)	2.0	4.4	3.6	20.2	30.1
Age groups:					
14 – 29	4.3	6.9	3.5	20.0	27.4
30 – 39	1.8	2.1	3.1	15.8	25.6
40 – 59	1.4	3.9	4.3	20.5	31.4
60 +	0.7	4.4	3.2	14.6	34.1
Monthly net income by household:					
0 – 2999 DM	1.8	3.3	2.4	13.9	28.3
3000 – 4999 DM	1.3	4.1	3.6	18.0	29.5
5000 DM +	3.7	6.5	5.6	24.5	32.8
Formal education:					
Basic	0.5	1.6	2.0	13.4	27.9
O-level	1.6	4.1	3.7	18.4	30.8
A-level/university	6.4	12.1	7.7	29.2	32.8
Ratio between highest and lowest educational level	*12.8*	*7.6*	*3.9*	*2.2*	*1.2*

Note: The definition of the different types of tourists is given in the text; business tourists (type 6) are not surveyed by Reiseanalyse. Columns 1–4 are based on the German population aged 14 and above, column 5 is based on holiday travellers 1996 aged 14 and above.
[a] People who have made such a type of trip during the past 3 years irrespective of trip length;
[b] Tourists referring to their 1996 main holiday trip of 5 days and more.
Source: F.U.R. (Forschungsgemeinschaft Urlaub und Reisen e.V.). Reiseanalyse 1997 (unpublished).

children aged up to 13 years. It appears that the 'full nest' phase (Wells and Gubar, 1966) in the family life cycle leads to the dominance of other motives and activities rather than culture-related ones. Generally, there is an impact of children on travel behaviour: the younger the children, the more likely parents are to sacrifice travelling (Mundt, 1998: 73). Those who still take holidays will 'become more organizational and less geographical' (Cooper *et al.*, 1993: 37) and therefore any other aspect of travelling, including cultural activities, tends to become irrelevant.

Study Trips vs. Cultural Trips

The broader meaning of the term 'culture' appears to have an impact on the development of the traditional study trip. It seems that, for many people, study tours have an image of being old-fashioned, school-type holidays for older people, particularly when organized by a tour operator. This at least is the perception of study tour operators in Germany (Lettl-Schröder, 1998). It might explain why generally there has been a shift away from study trips towards cultural trips. This is true both for the experience of the past 3 years and for the interest in participating in

Table 10.4. Type of holiday chosen by the German population aged 14 and above.

Type of holiday	January 1992 (%)	January 1997 (%)
Study trip (*Studienreise*[a])	7.3	4.4
Cultural trip (*Kulturreise*[a])	2.7	3.6

[a]Self definition by respondents.
Source: F.U.R. (Forschungsgemeinschaft Urlaub und Reisen e.V.) Reiseanalysen 1991 and 1997 (unpublished).

Table 10.5. Interest in types of holiday (percentage of population aged 14 and above who wants to make such a holiday trip during the next 3 years 'quite definitely' or 'probably').

Type of holiday	January 1992 (%)	January 1997 (%)
Study trip (*Studienreise*[a])	13.2	10.2
Cultural trip (*Kulturreise*[a])	8.9	10.8

[a]Self definition by respondents.
Source: F.U.R. (Forschungsgemeinschaft Urlaub und Reisen e.V.) Reiseanalysen Urlaub + Reisen 1991 and 1997 (unpublished).

these forms of travel during the coming 3 years (cf. Tables 10.4 and 10.5). In contrast to the tour operators' opinion, younger people can be found significantly more often amongst these two types of tourists than other age groups (cf. Table 10.3). Most study trips, however, are organized individually and so there seem to be marked differences in the social and demographic composition between the tour operators' clients and other study trip travellers.

The Entertainment/Culture Interface: the Staged 'Musical'

The data presented in Tables 10.4 and 10.5 are not limited to holiday trips of at least 5 days but also include weekend and short trips, which have become particularly relevant for cultural trips. This has much to do with the success of sit-down productions of single musicals performed *en suite* for several years in purpose-built theatres and/or entertainment centres (cf. Roth and Langemeyer, 1996: 170–171). Therefore, musicals are a good example for the changing patterns of cultural activities. By traditional cultural standards set, for example, by operas, they are perceived as pure entertainment: simple, superficial and undemanding. Qualitative research, however, has shown that the experience of visitors is completely different and much to do with the classical perception of theatre forming a moral institution (*Theater als moralische Anstalt*) that has the power to enlighten and change the lives of people in the audience.

> Seeing musicals can become a significant incidence in visitors' lives and can have a lasting impact on their life-style, their social engagement and their self-perception. ..(..).. Paradoxically it is just those characteristics of musicals which are smiled at by supporters of serious culture as being superficial which are responsible for the psychic explosive nature and dynamics of visiting a musical performance. (Dorn, 1997: 52)

Referring to Dorn's results, it is in particular the mix of fiction (e.g. singing cats) and very real things happening (e.g. actors appearing from the audience or parts of the set swinging into the direction of the audience) being responsible for the emergence of what can be seen as a liminal experience for the audience. By 'theming' the foyer, or even the whole building, with parts of the set, props, costumes and photographs of the performance, the plot also becomes part of the interval, the arrival and the departure. The feeling of crossing borders through this web of facts and fiction is supported by the touristic character of the visit: as each musical is performed in only one location in Germany, most people have to travel and are away from home for two or three days. Unlike going to the cinema, the theatre or a recital, this is rather time-consuming and requires some planning well in advance of the event. Very often people opt for organized bus tours. With this temporary divorce from their everyday environments, and the joining together of a new group of people sharing the same interest in the musical and an expectation of going to experience something extraordinary, Dorn's research suggests they are similar to pilgrims. In both cases, the journey there is a significant part of the experience.

It may be argued, therefore, that with adding 'travel as performed art' (Adler, 1989) to the performance of a musical, one may come close to a '*Gesamtkunstwerk*'. The opera, with its integration of music, literature, painting and acting, was the prototype for such synthesis of arts. Musicals stay within that tradition anyway, and it seems that tourism now complements it on a very subjective level. This is because travel in general can be perceived as the staging of a drama:

> Not only are the situations in tourism destinations more or less arranged for the tourists' gaze, touristic experience is always the result of arrangements like the stage-management of a drama. The possibility of choosing the destination,

determining the length of the trip, deciding the means of transportation and having significant influence on the selection of travel companions make a trip appearing like the realization of a "screenplay" that is produced by the tourist through the selection from these different options. (Mundt, 1998: 188)

Dorn in his research found that the liminal experience of musicals often also led to people becoming more interested in other forms of cultural activities, sometimes even becoming regular visitors to all kinds of 'serious' cultural events. Whereas for musicals there appears to be no specific target-group, people making short cultural trips of 2–4 days are typically either older or young and unmarried – another analogy with pilgrimage.

Tourism as culture

Tourism has been a significant agent of change in various aspects. It has changed the societies of countries from which tourists come and of countries they visit. The change is not confined to economic and political situations, but also affects the respective cultures of the societies exposed to tourism.

> In the name of tourism, capital and modernized peoples have been deployed to the most remote regions of the world, farther than any army was ever sent. Institutions have been established to support this deployment, not just hotels, restaurants, and transportation systems, but restorations of ancient shrines, development of localhandicrafts for sale to tourists, and rituals performed for tourists. In short, tourism is not just an aggregate of merely commercial activities; it is also an ideological framing of history, nature and tradition; a framing that has the power to reshape culture and nature to its own needs. (MacCannell, 1992: 1)

This has been the case at least since the days of Goethe, whose trip to Italy has been taken as an example for generations of German tourists. His perception of Italy as a stage for ancient Greek culture has, through his followers, had a significant impact on the presentation of the country to tourists motivated by cultural interest.

Yet tourism does not only, as MacCannell notes, reshape culture; in fact, it has always been an essential element of its formation. In a very real sense, there is no such thing as an indigenous culture. The deduction, for example, of Greek, Mesopotamian, Egyptian, Roman, Irish or Norman influences from German culture, like the subtraction of Jewish, Islamic or Christian elements, would leave virtually nothing. Without the contact facilitated through travel, European cultures, as known today, would not exist. They comprise many ingredients from different areas in the world; this includes their religions. This mobility of cultural ideas takes place by means of the mobility of people, which is the essence of travel and tourism.

Travel and tourism are themselves, therefore, constituents of culture. With travel becoming more accessible during recent decades, it turned from being something extraordinary, experienced by very few people only once or twice within a lifetime, to being an integral part of each year's time structure. Even when most of this additional travel is not motivated by cultural interest, it still is a significant cultural factor. Like the mass media, it has a significant impact on the individual's perception of the world, but one that is based on individual activities and experiences.

References

Adler, J. (1989) Travel as performed art. *American Journal of Sociology* 94, 1366–1391.

Arbeitsgruppe am Max-Planck-Institut für Bildungsforschung (1979) *Das Bildungswesen in der Bundesrepublik Deutschland.* Rowohlt, Reinbek, bei Hamburg.

Becker, C. and Steinecke, A. (eds) (1993a) *Megatrend Kultur? Chancen und Risiken der Vermarktung des kulturellen Erbes.* (*ETI-Texte*, Vol. 1) Europäisches Tourismus Institut (ETI) an der Universität Trier, Trier.

Becker, C. and Steinecke, A. (eds) (1993b) *Kulturtourismus in Europa: Wachstum ohne Grenzen?* (*ETI-Studien*, Vol. 2) Europäisches Tourismus Institut (ETI) an der Universität Trier, Trier.

Benjamin, W. (1936) *Das Kunstwerk im Zeitalter seiner technischen Reproduzierbarkeit* (reprinted 1977; first published in a French translation in *Zeitschrift für Sozialforschung*, Vol. 5, 1936). Suhrkamp, Frankfurt am Main.

Berktold-Fackler, F. and Krumbholz, H. (1997) *Reisen in Deutschland. Eine kleine Tourismusgeschichte.* Oldenbourg, München und Wien.

Cooper, C., Fletcher, J., Gilbert, D. and Wanhill, S. (1993) *Tourism: Principles and Practice.* Pitman Publishing, London.

Dietsch, K. (1996) Studienreisen. In: Dreyer (ed.) *Kulturturismus.* Oldenbourg, München und Wien, pp. 71–99.

Dorn, J. (1997) Musicals – die Renaissance der Wallfahrt. *Planung und Analyse* H. 6, pp. 52–53.

Dreyer, Axel (ed.) (1996) *Kulturtourismus.* Oldenbourg, München und Wien.

Friedell, E. (1927–1931) *Kulturgeschichte der Neuzeit* (reprinted 1976, München: dtv). Beck, München.

Irish Tourist Board / Brady Shipman Martin (1988) *Inventory of Cultural Tourism Resources in the Member States and Assessment of Methods Used to Promote Them.* Commission of the European Communities (= *C.E.C. Tourism Study Ref. VII/A-4/1*), Dublin and Brussels.

Lawson, R. (1991) Patterns of tourist expenditure and types of vacation across the family life cycle. *Journal of Travel Research* Spring, pp. 12–18.

Lettl-Schröder, M. (1998) Die Studienreise ist besser als ihr Ruf. FVW-Expertenforum zum Markt für Studienreisen, *Fremdenverkehrswirtschaft International* 1 (January), pp. 26–28.

MacCannell, D. (1992) *Empty Meeting Grounds: the Tourist Papers.* Routledge, London.

McNulty, M. (1993) Developing cultural attractions for the tourists of the 90s – the Irish experience. In: Becker, C. and Steinecke, A. (eds) *Megatrend Kultur? Chancen und Risiken der Vermarktung des kulturellen Erbes.* (*ETI-Texte*, Vol. 1) Europäisches Tourismus Institut (ETI) an der Universität Trier, Trier, pp. 13–22.

Müllenmeister, H. (1993) Studienreisen: Vermarktung des kulturellen Erbes. In: Becker and Steinecke (eds) *Megatrend Kultur? Chancen und Risiken der Vermarktung des kulturellen*

Erbes. (*ETI-Texte*, Vol. 1) Europäisches Tourismus Institut (ETI) an der Universität Trier, Trier, pp. 145–160.

Müllenmeister, H. (1997) Spiegelungen und Vorspiegelungen – Infotainment oder kulturelle Animation. In: Steinecke and Treinen (eds) *Inszenierung im Tourismus. Trends – Modelle – Prognosen.* (*ETI-Studien*, Vol. 3) Europäisches Tourismus Institut (ETI) an der Universität Trier, Trier, pp. 106–117.

Mundt, J. W. (1998) *Einführung in den Tourismus.* Oldenbourg, Munich.

Roth, P. and Langemeyer, A. (1996) Cultural tourism in Germany. In: Richards, G. (ed.) *Cultural Tourism in Europe.* CAB International, Wallingford.

Soyez, D. (1993) Kulturtourismus in Industrielandschaften: Synopse und 'Widerstandsanalyse'. In: Becker and Steinecke (eds) *Kulturtourismus in Europa: Wachstum ohne Grenzen?* (*ETI-Studien*, Vol. 2) Europäisches Tourismus Institut (ETI) an der Universität Trier, Trier, pp. 40–63.

SPIEGEL (1994) SPIEGEL-Dokumentation Geschäftsreisen 1994. SPIEGEL-Verlag, Hamburg.

Steinecke, A. and Treinen, M. (eds) (1997) *Inszenierung im Tourismus. Trends – Modelle – Prognosen.* (*ETI-Studien*, Vol. 3) Europäisches Tourismus Institut (ETI) an der Universität Trier, Trier.

Wells, W. and Gubar, G. (1966) Life cycle concept in marketing research. *Journal of Marketing Research* III, 355–363.

Quotations from German literature were translated by the authors.

Living in Paradise: Youth Culture and Tourism Development in the Mountains of Austria

11

Patricia East[1] and Kurt Luger[2]

[1]Faculty of Tourism, Fachhochschule München, Germany, [2]University of Salzburg, Austria

Introduction

The Alpine Republic of Austria is one of the world's leading tourist destinations. It embraces cities rich in culture with festivals of international fame, spa and recreational tourism in the vanguard of the trend for global fitness and well-being, the Alps with their summer and winter sport attractions, and the alpine foothills in which tourism has not yet reached the stage of full development. The figures speak for themselves: Austria's 8 million inhabitants have a higher per capita income from tourism than any other country – the 1996 figure was 18,430 ATS (Zins, 1996; Österreich-Werbung, 1997) – and tourism contributes roughly 6% of Austria's GDP. 1996 saw 85 million overnight stays registered by some 17 million international guests and approximately 28 million overnight stays by domestic tourists. Notwithstanding this impressive record, the industry is facing serious problems: since the beginning of the 1990s the figures have been declining while visitors' expectations have been moving upscale, and there has been widespread criticism of the negative ecological and cultural effects of tourism. The tourism industry is currently at the centre of a number of controversies.

Tourism is nothing new to Austria. Austrians are used to being a receiving nation, and the huge economic and service sector that has been built up around the industry not only guarantees income but also shapes lifestyles. This article addresses the question of cultural change and the modernization of lifestyles, a process to which tourism is a major – but, it must be remembered, by no means the only – contributing factor. Taking the example of a touristically highly developed mountain region in the Salzburg region which is marketed as 'little paradise', we analyse the situation in which today's young people are growing up, and illustrate the difficulty of steering a course between tradition and modern life.

The Long-standing Tradition of Austrian Tourism

Austria looks back on a long-standing tradition as a tourism host country. By the end of the 18th century, a fashion for travelling had developed among European aristocrats as well as scholars and writers, and a flood of travel reports from that time document the romantic longing for faraway places.

The 19th century saw the emergence of spas as aristocratic tourism destinations, and these were developed around the capital Vienna, in the lake district of the Salzkammergut and in some alpine areas. With the facilitation of travel thanks to the extension of the railway network, and the socio-economic changes which introduced the concept of summer holidays for the bourgeoisie, tourism developed on a larger scale (Brusatti, 1984). In 1890, official tourism statistics were introduced by a decree of the Ministry of the Interior. Growing interest in mountaineering (the Austrian Alpine Association was founded in 1862) and later the rise in alpine winter sports (the Austrian Ski Association was established in 1905) encouraged further growth.

The outbreak of the First World War put a temporary end to the development of tourism, and it was not until the middle of the 1920s that it was able to pick up again. In 1929, almost 20 million overnight stays were recorded, of which 42.9% were visitors from abroad, and Austria boasted a capacity of 168,598 hotel beds and 108,757 privately rented beds. The significance of the industry is reflected in the fact that a National Tourist Board was set up (1923), along with regional organizations in most of the 'Länder' (provinces). A further stimulus to the industry was provided by the construction of a number of cable-cars to transport visitors up the mountains, as well as the introduction of the Salzburg Festival (1920) and the Vienna Festival Weeks (1928), two important cultural attractions.

The worldwide economic crisis of 1929 once more brought a decline in tourism, and Austria was particularly hard hit during the years leading up to the Second World War by financial restrictions on travel imposed by Hitler's Germany, since half of Austria's holidaymakers were Germans. After the annexation of Austria and its integration into Nazi Germany, the 'Kraft durch Freude' ('strength through joy') tourist propaganda boosted the number of German holidaymakers, and the 1929 figure of 20 million overnight stays was again recorded in 1937. However, as the war progressed, tourism declined, and Salzburg, once called 'the district of good nerves', became the 'district of military hospitals' (Kerschbaumer, 1994; Hanisch, 1997).

Tourism Development after 1945

Roughly a quarter of all tourist beds were completely destroyed between 1939 and 1945, but once the war was over, tourism developed into an engine for economic growth and an instrument of reconstruction. In the 1950s, the Marshall Plan and the European Recovery Programme made financial aid in the form of low-interest loans available for building up Austrian tourism, and the western federal provinces of Vorarlberg, Tyrol, Salzburg and Upper Austria were the first to benefit from this (Bischof, 1999).

The repair of important railway lines and roads, as well as the resumption of civil air traffic, paved the way for a rapid development of tourism in the country. Foreign tourism only became possible again in 1947, when the Austrian Government officially decided to promote it, although it was still necessary to get permission from the allied forces to cross the border, and visas were required until 1952. The shortage of food was a further problem: it was only thanks to substantial food aid from the UN that an outbreak of famine was prevented in 1946, and certain foods continued to be rationed in Austria until 1953. Since foreigners were entitled to five times more calories than Austrian nationals, visitors had to be strictly separated from the local people and were only allowed to stay at specially designated hotels. As the new political situation in Eastern Europe meant that there were no longer any tourists from the countries behind the Iron Curtain, the tourism industry focused its attention on guests from Western Europe and the USA (Luger and Rest, 1995).

As a knock-on effect of the German 'Economic Miracle', the 1950s saw the first wave of German outbound holiday tourism, which brought an enormous increase in Austrian tourism figures. With holiday trips moving within the financial reach of an ever-larger section of the population, almost 42 million overnight stays were recorded by the end of the decade. The number of foreign travellers rose continuously, mainly concentrated in the western Länder. In the winter of 1959/60, foreign visitors accounted for 52% of the overnight stays recorded; in the summer of 1960 the figure was 60%. 44% of the visitors were from the Federal Republic of Germany, followed by Britain, the Benelux countries, France, Italy, Switzerland and the USA .

The Perfect Scene: Austria's Image Forged by the Media

The culture industry provided significant support for the tourist sector's efforts to fill Austria's hotel beds. *Heimatfilme* (sentimental films in idealized regional settings) along with popular songs aroused nostalgic associations with good old Austria, and became instruments for media marketing. By 1965, 122 *Heimatfilme* had been produced, with different variations on the same themes, and films for tourists proved to be a lucrative source of income. They were released in all the German-speaking countries and became the most popular form of leisure-time entertainment in the new Austrian Republic (in 1958 alone, 122 million box office tickets were sold). These films not only served Austria's own search for a new national identity, but also promoted Austria in other German-speaking areas. In these films, the scenery, though it served only as a setting or backdrop, was the focal point of a plot which usually turned on a personal destiny, and farming life was idealized and presented from the summer holiday angle. The songs upheld personal happiness and were full of the beauty of the countryside – the wine-growing villages of the Danube Valley, the mountains and lakes of the Salzkammer-gut, etc. A safe and perfect world, staged among contented Tyrolean cows, became a marketable commodity. The *Heimatfilm* helped people to suppress the memory of the Nazi era (in the country village, so it seemed, all was still well with the world) and it accompanied the gradual transformation of the most attractive rural areas into holiday paradises. The countryside began to lose touch with its rural cultural identity as it became the nation's commercial, cultural and tourist attraction (Luger, 1998: 22).

The Hollywood musical *The Sound of Music*, starring Julie Andrews as Maria von Trapp (filmed in and around Salzburg in 1965, on the threshold of the audio-visual age) was the most efficient and cheapest image-making campaign of all times – for Austria and above all for Salzburg and its surrounding countryside. In the first few years after the release of the film, the number of Americans visiting Salzburg doubled. Even today, three out of four tourists still give this film – which is shown frequently on TV in the USA, but is hardly known in Austria itself – as the main reason for their trip. A special 'Sound of Music Tour' takes tourists to the film locations, and a 'Sound of Music Dinner Show', during which tourists could eat traditional food to the accompaniment of some of the catchy songs from the film, proved to be a popular attraction. Thus, Mozart's birthplace, Salzburg, with the house the composer was born in, the old city and the spectacular fortress towering above it, has won its fame as a tourist attraction through its image in the global entertainment industry, and not only through the highbrow Salzburg Festival, which has attracted lovers of classical music and theatre from all over the world for more than 70 years (Luger, 1994: 184).

Over the years, Austria's tourism marketing has integrated all sorts of sights, souvenirs and cultural specialities into its collection of selling points: Tyrolean hats, Viennese coffee-houses, dancing white horses, the Blue Danube waltz, Mozart chocolate balls, mountain peaks – images of Austria have been turned into powerful catchwords and clichés. TV folk music programmes appeal to people's desire to believe in the idyll of an unproblematic, rurally harmonious world, and they enjoy tremendous popularity. Even regional colour and cultural idiosyncrasies often have to be sacrificed so that people will not have any trouble understanding them in other German-speaking areas.

The Privatization of Mobility: Modernization and Cultural Change

The 1960s, with holidays established as part of people's lifestyle, illustrate the way in which the media and the tourist industry can bring about cultural change. This was the decade of eager attempts to remove all barriers, not only in questions of social values and moral concepts, but also in the gratification of long-dreamed-of external contacts. It can be described as the decade in which the lifestyle of most Austrians was noticeably influenced, for the first time, by 'mobile privatization' (Williams, 1973). The term refers to the dichotomy between the search for individual, private freedom and the search for identity within the constraints imposed by society, manifested above all in consumerism, home design and family life. The 'privatization' can be described as a withdrawal into the domestic sphere of the TV-dominated home: mass production and a reduction in the price of appliances, coupled with rising incomes and more demand for convenience and prestige goods led to the TV becoming the characteristic technical acquisition of the decade, and the number of TV households rose from 200,000 in 1960 to 1.4 million in 1970. At the same time, however, technology and the media now offered the possibility of hitherto unimaginable mental mobility, and a chance to take part in events worldwide – something previous generations could only have dreamed. People could now feel that they were really sharing in the advances of the age and participating in the widening of the human horizon. They could experience media events all over the world – space flights, moon-landings and the Olympic Games – and watch how the USA bombed little Vietnam back into the Stone Age.

There had once been a time when an illuminated sailing ship on top of the television set symbolized a longing for faraway places; now it was possible to escape everyday life, not only in one's mind, but in reality, and to break out for a few weeks into the illusion of a holiday dream world (Kos, 1995). The individual radius of activity was extended considerably and the increased motorization of tourist traffic (between 1960 and 1970 the number of cars in Austria rose from 404,000 to 1.2 million) developed into tourism for the masses. The increase in leisure time (the minimum holiday entitlement was extended from 2 to 3 weeks, and weekly working hours were lowered successively to 40) also encouraged this mobility, and Austria saw a collective burst of holidaymaking.

On the one hand, Austrians themselves participated as tourists in the new era of mobility: the typical holiday abroad was a trip to the Adriatic Coast, which had already become popular with the middle class in the 1950s and had now become affordable for the less well-off. At the same time, however, more and more tourists came to Austria, and Austrians became increasingly aware of their position as hosts in a receiving country. Instead of leading static lives, everyone had became mobile, and life was full of comings and goings. The new means of communication, cars and motorways, civil aviation and television brought the hierarchy of near and far into confusion, calling simultaneously for definitions of identities and for adaptation to the new and the foreign.

Austria Today: a World Tourism Champion

While economic development has made it possible for one half of the Austrian population to afford holiday trips, the other half experience tourism mainly from the standpoint of the hosts and is confronted with the enormous intensity of incoming tourism. This has both economic and sociocultural consequences. Within a period of about 40 years, tourism in Austria has become one of the largest sections of the economy. About 6% of Austria's economic output is produced by about 19,000 professional and roughly 40,000 private hosts, providing about 1.25 million guest beds. 150,000 jobs are directly linked to this figure and approximately 400,000 people receive earnings indirectly from it. In Western provinces like Tyrol and Salzburg almost two out of three jobs are either directly or indirectly connected with tourism (Zimmermann, 1991).

Whereas up to the 1970s increasing the number of beds or overnight stays was the main concern, since then more emphasis has been placed on improving stand-ards and the level of comfort. However, the considerable investments made by private hotel owners and landlords have led to an extremely serious state of debt in Austria's tourist industry (Hartl, 1996), aggravated by a fall in tourism figures. In 1992, around 127 million overnight stays were recorded in the Alpine Republic, about three-quarters of which were made by foreign guests; by 1996 the figure had dwindled to only 113 million. The income per capita derived from tourism is higher in Austria than in any other country. With the exception of some island republics, Austria is the most tourism-intensive country in international tourism (Smeral, 1994).

While the summer used to be the most important season – although since the beginning of the 1990s there has been a significant decline in the numbers of German visitors (IPK-International, 1996) – nowdays about 75% of all snow-holidays are taken in Austria, with 50% of the income from tourism coming from the winter months (Zins, 1996: 9). World championships in skiing, the Olympic Games and the victories and places of honour won by Austrian skiers have made the country internationally popular as a winter sports region. Every year people are transported up the mountains about 500 million times by ski-lifts and cable-cars, a fivefold increase since 1972. Since the first drag-lift was built in 1908, the range of technically assisted means of ascent has been continually expanded and modern-ized. In 1952 there were about 44 chair-lifts and 74 drag-lifts; in 1968 there were already over 2000. Today, about 600 main cable-lines (cable-cars and multi-seat chair-lifts) are available and around 2700 drag-lifts guarantee snow and downhill pleasure (Luger and Rest, 1995: 662).

Playing Host: the Sociocultural Effects of Opening up to Tourism

The considerable prosperity which many Austrian regions owe to tourism – some inner alpine villages would presumably no longer be populated were it not for this means of livelihood – has, however, led to changes, for example in the values and attitudes of those concerned and in their everyday culture. It has changed commun-ity life in tourist resorts as well as affecting traditional customs and architecture. Tourism never fails to have an effect on the culture of target regions: the more intensive the contact, the more traditional systems of values are influenced; the more the tourists search for the 'genuine' and 'unspoiled', the greater the disruption of the host's cultural framework. The host inevitably feels obliged, to a certain extent at least, to orient himself towards the expectations and images created by the media and tourism marketers (Kramer, 1997; Hennig, 1997). The local population has to take on the role of host, synchronizing 'backstage' life with the production of tourist facilities and in some ways becoming stereotype 'catalogue Austrians'. Just how the interaction between local landlords and guests has developed in the course of the intensification of tourism has been shown in a comparative pilot study. Whereas in the early stages of a region being discovered, the level of the host's involvement is very high and personal congeniality tends to veil the business side, with increased professionalism the local people prefer to keep their distance, none the less maintaining the image of friendly involvement. Not until the last stage, which can usually be observed in the traditional tourist resorts, do landlords separate private life from business and try to reduce personal involvement to a minimum (Schrutka-Rechtenstamm, 1995).

In the long term, this 'normalization' of business relationships between host and guest may lead to a reduction in turnover, as hospitality, a relaxed atmosphere, culture and direct contact with the local people (a 'home away from home') are precisely the ingredients of an Austrian holiday that guests from outside value. They form the marketable aspects of Austrian identity which dominate the tourist industry's advertising. It is therefore necessary to develop new, sustainable ways of living with tourism – which is not always possible without conflict. As a consequence of mass tourism, people living in the holiday destinations have in recent years become increasingly tired of their guests. Surveys show that the pressure limit has already been reached in many areas, and tourist organizations are now, of necessity, carrying out public relations campaigns in Tyrol, Vorarlberg and Salzburg to demonstrate the advantages of tourism to the local people (Luger and Rest, 1994).

Up to the 1980s, the question of tourism was discussed only with regard to the economic significance of the sector, which was becoming increasingly important to the balance of payments. As a result of this importance, however, criticism of tourism became louder. Sustainability, as a holistic approach to tourism, was discovered, 'gentle tourism' considered a new market niche, and a new concept of tourism, aiming to serve not only the tourism industry but also local people, went on the agenda in the public discussion. The tolerance levels seemed to have been reached and as a consequence of the negative effects of mass tourism, widely discussed in public, demands were made for a gentler and more environment- and culture-friendly form of tourism. At the centre of the debate was the matter of traffic congestion, which had not only been caused by tourism, but also by Austria's sandwich position as a central European transit country. When transit traffic, local traffic and holiday traffic (the individualization of travelling means that now four out of five travellers use their own cars) coincide, this has a negative effect on both travellers and local people: the former have to put up with long traffic jams and the latter with a serious depreciation in the quality of life (CIPRA, 1996).

The Old Life as a Stage Set

Even in a highly modernized and industrialized western country like Austria, the fear that tourism threatens the cultural identity of whole regions leads again and again to emotionally charged disputes. Intercultural contact with tourists, who usually come from urban areas, means that in the primarily rural tourist regions people have to adapt, a kind of service-culture is produced and local culture is integrated into what is offered to tourists. A kind of folklore emerges out of the culture actually lived by the local people, a process which usually infers a loss of culture. There can be no doubt that elements of the traditional civilization – the old life – have been subjected to considerable pressure to modernize and to a process of erosion, whereby tourism is not the only driving force (Luger, 1995). On the other hand, many cultural or folklore activities considered typical of a region have only been generated thanks to the spread of tourism; alongside the revival of old, long-forgotten traditions. Evidence of this is the establishment, or rather re-establishment of numerous associations such as those for national (or local) costumes, customs and rifle clubs, whose 'authenticity' has increasingly been doubted, even by tourist businesses (Kapeller, 1991; Thiem, 1994). Authentic customs are often only kept up by lovers of old traditions and they have little to do with the living, everyday culture of the regional or rural population.

The most noticeable changes in the everyday culture of tourist areas can be found in those places which, in the 40 years since the war, have turned from an economic system based on subsistence farming into a highly developed, tourist-oriented society. At the beginning of the 1950s, about one million Austrians were employed in agriculture; nowdays it is only about 180,000. More than two-thirds of the farming population have to take up some form of casual employment not connected with farming and often not in their local village. Agriculture is increasingly losing economic importance and its contribution to the national income is only about 2.3%. Alpine or mountain farming has changed from a direct, economic form of production to ecologically relevant activities and has produced considerable early achievements for tourism through caring for the countryside (Rest, 1994). The effects of this change in function towards 'landscape gardening' will change the cultural identity of many mountain farmers far more than the encounter with tourism has so far (Bauer *et al.*, 1994).

An identity-changing development is apparent in the present trend in farmhouse holidays and the romanticized and idealized world of farm life it presents. Inventive advertisers have even started to create an artificial Disney Farm World (with dwarf cattle and horses, and other small animals), in which a kind of farm life is presented that, in actual fact, no longer exists. Programmes offer activities such as bread-baking, making farm produce and even trips to mountain pastures and huts that are often no longer in use, as part of the chance to experience life on a farm. In order to be able to do this the farmer's wife must first have attended courses in baking wholewheat bread, spinning wool and so on. The image produced is that of a pre-industrial subsistence farm and, depending on the wishes of the guests, livestock and cultivation are shown in a variety of ways and old farming implements are demonstrated and put to use. Apart from the primary arrangements (bed and breakfast), the product also includes more and more extensive services, which makes demands round the clock on the farmer-cum-landlord. The main pressure of work falls on the farmer's wife, with the farmers themselves in charge of organizing the guests' activities and entertainment (cf. Schrutka-Rechtenstamm, 1994; Rest, 1995).

Changes in Landscape and Lifestyles

Within merely a few decades, a fundamental change has occurred in the landscape of many areas. On the one hand, this is due to developments in agricultural techno- logy and the resulting changes in farming. Corn-growing disappeared from most alpine areas after the beginning of the 1960s. Highly developed tourist valleys show strong tendencies towards urbanization and have almost reached urban population density (Baetzing and Perlik, 1995). The restructuring of the countryside – tourism is often accused of 'eating up' the landscape (Krippendorf, 1984) – is mainly the result of the construction of various tourist infrastructures and tall buildings; but is also due to the spread of housing developments. In the same way, the improve- ments to roads, and the increase in commuter traffic that has followed, have also contributed to this change. The few examples of architecturally sophisticated hotel or tourist buildings in the Austrian Alps were built largely in the period between the wars, but, due to later reconstruction or extension, have lost most of their aesthetic quality. The overuse of the landscape and the ousting of agriculture in the competition for space with tourism present further, much-discussed problem areas in the search for more sustainability in alpine tourism (Mueller, 1994).

This change in landscape is not only reflected in the architectural monotony of the alpine-style architecture (Kos, 1995a). Road and rail connections, car parks, more than 3000 means of conveyance for winter sports and ski-slopes have altered the aesthetic character of the countryside. Changes in structure have also brought about changes in the home. The old parlour, once the room where all those living and working on the farm could get together, has largely become a breakfast room and lounge for guests, and the farmer's family has withdrawn into a kitchen-cum- living-room (Conrad, 1994). The old buildings typical of the region have become a favourite motif in tourist advertising, which concentrates on images which will stimulate the tourist's hopes and anticipation. Consequently, what tourists consider beautiful – the village as a pre-modern setting – often appears to be just an ugly old hut to the local people.

The changes of the last 50 years, the processes of modernization and mobiliza- tion, have largely destroyed the earlier, stable social structures, which were perceived by many as being too restrictive and authoritarian. The modern age has seen the dissolution of traditional lifestyles and identities because of the speed and the per- manence of the changes it has brought about. Living on a knife-edge between tradition and modernity, many people have found themselves changed by tourism into would-be city-dwellers in their minds and lifestyles, and they are trying to catch up with their perceived backwardness in relation to the cities.

Growing up in 'Little Paradise'

The industrialization of society, the development of tourism and the omnipresence of the mass media have brought about changes in the economy, in lifestyles, and in everyday cultural practices. This has led to breaks with cultural traditions and to the formation of new lifestyles, and has instigated an urbanization of the rural scene. The example of the Pinzgau area in the Salzburg Alps, one of Austria's leading tourism destinations with more than a million guests every year, illustrates the effects of this process of transformation on today's youth (Luger and Tedeschi, 1996).

The Pinzgau region is one of the Alpine areas which fits into the popular tourism cliché of a rural paradise *à la Sound of Music*. It is one of the many regions that has seen its economic orientation switch from alpine agriculture to tourism, which is now its most important economic sector and employs 60% of the work-force. What does this mean for the young people growing up there? Nearly 40% of the population of 80,000 are under 25 years old. Far from being the rosy-cheeked boys and girls of the Heidi-cliché that still forms a cornerstone of tourism marketing, the young people of Pinzgau are affected by social change, economic problems, and the psychological stress of modern life, and like the youth in the cities they try to escape into the illusion of 'easy living' with alcohol, the disco-theque, and new American sport fads which constitute their 'weekend nonconform-ity'. While living in the foothills of the only mountain national park in Austria (the Hohe Tauern National Park), they have developed a music taste which follows the global trends: techno, rave, pop, rock and heavy metal. Under the surface of this 'fun generation', however, many of them are dissatisfied, resigned, depressed, and latently violent, and they reject many aspects of conventional social life; and as in every generation conflict, the older generation looks on in despair.

A flashback to 1955: the whole of Austria was celebrating the republic's regained independence and neutrality, and the strains of the waltz could be heard from all the country's ballrooms. A youth survey conducted the same year revealed that a third of Austria's young people gave Boogie Woogie as their favourite dance: 40% of the working-class young already mastered it, and 50% of the rural youth were learning it. Parents and teachers were horrified, seeing decency and morality threatened by jeans, T-shirts, leather jackets and this new form of physical expres-sion with its disregard for taboos. The cinema was top of the list of leisure pastimes in those days before the advent of the TV age, and many of those who were growing up at that time will remember it as the scene of their first furtive attempts at approaching members of the opposite sex. The motor car still filled mountain-dwellers with delight, and nobody felt that the number of tourists was getting out of hand: the whole of the federal state of Salzburg only recorded some four million overnight stays a year, and these welcome guests were transported up the mountains by 80 ski lifts. Today, more than 40 years later, the tourist industry registers 22 million bed-nights – half a million of them visitors from Great Britain – and has become the federal state's largest economic sector. More than 700 lifts and cable cars have been constructed for the pleasure of the recreation-seekers, some of them with direct motorway access in order to optimize convenience. The cinema has lost its special status, and in its place both young and old now go for communication via the television screen – today's most popular leisure activity (Hoffmann and Luger, 1997).

These changes have not failed to make their mark on the local populations in tourism destinations. Above all, the young people now grow up in completely different circumstances. Parents find it hard to come to terms with their children's need for greater intensity of experience, and, like parents 40 years ago, they think that the western world is on the brink of an apocalypse. Yet it was they themselves – as the then younger generation – who blazed the trail for a process of modernization that plunged their villages into a frantic struggle to move with the times, and they themselves who spurred on this development with their youthful enthusiasm. An examination of youth culture presents a particularly clear picture of social and cultural change, since in general young people are 'early adopters' and pick up fastest on new currents, thus representing a society's cultural avant-garde (Luger, 1991). In the case of the Pinzgau region, the picture illustrates how the urbanization of rural areas finds its expression not only in architecture or mobilization, but also in the minds of the rural population.

City-dwellers in the Mind

The Pinzgau youth have grown up with tourism and have had holiday guests around them all their lives. They all share a pragmatic attitude to tourism in general, whose economic advantages are widely perceived to outweigh the disadvantages: tourism provides jobs and income. The fact is that in most cases there is no alternative. The overall picture of the young people working in tourism is of a two-class society, those whose parents own businesses in the industry, and those who are working as ordinary employees. Not surprisingly, the young people who work in their parents' businesses tend to be more optimistic about their chances of making a career in the tourism industry than those who are employed without any family ties. They also claim to feel a greater sense of job satisfaction through cultivating more-intensive personal contact with the guests. The young employees, on the other hand, are more directly affected by the fact that frequent staff changes in tourism businesses and the extremely high degree of seasonal work make it difficult to establish long-term friendships at the workplace. At the same time, these employees suffer more from the long working hours in the hospitality industry, and the necessity of working at weekends and on bank holidays, which leave them too little time for friends and family. (A strong contrast can also be observed here with the young people in the region working outside the tourism industry, for example as craftsmen, who maintain close personal relationships to colleagues both during their working hours and in their leisure time.) Young people in their parents' tourism businesses are very consumer-oriented in their leisure time: 'shopping' is one of their main leisure activities, beside sports and going out in the evenings, and their idea of a holiday is often a long-haul trip to an exotic destination. In contrast, the young employees set their sights on more-modest destinations closer to home.

Feelings about the visitors tend to be determined by the pragmatic attitude that, as a host, one has to be hospitable to one's guests: 'I can't complain about the tourists because we live off them, it's as simple as that!'. Once again, the young people working in their parents' businesses more often feel that they benefit from the intercultural exchange – although there is seldom any contact outside the context of the actual holiday situation – and the young people rarely show any genuine interest in gaining deeper insight into the lives of the guests. At the other end of the spectrum, some view the tourists as arrogant outsiders:

> tourists only think of themselves, they're demanding and ignorant, they come here for a week and live it up, and think they own the place and don't care what happens to us when they've gone . . . ' or 'they think they can order us around and that we should be honoured that it's our place they've chosen to come to, and we have to treat them with kid gloves.

Some young people feel personally disadvantaged when tourists are given preferential treatment, and because they are also hit by tourist-induced price rises in shops and in the bars and discos.

The young people of the more tourist-intensive parts of the Pinzgau do not attach much importance to maintaining local customs and traditions, most of which have ceased to have any function beyond being a tourist attraction or a public holiday which families and friends can use to get together. In the areas where there is less tourism, however, young people are much more aware of their old traditions and the cultural patterns of their villages, and attach importance to maintaining them within the local circle without turning them into marketable tourism products.

Trouble in Paradise

Although a lot of these young people dream of living somewhere where there is 'more going on', they are not often really willing to move away from home because they do not want to give up their ties to family and friends. They hope that things will change for the better, especially that more leisure activities will be made available to them. The discotheque is the clearest symbol of the desire to break out and negate the social constraints of the village community, and young people are prepared to drive up to 80 km to get to their favourite venue. In their minds the cities are where real life is happening, and they want to feel that they too are following the city-style scene in their leisure time.

When it comes to alcohol, the young people have not moved so very far away from their parents' culture; nobody needs to worry about future beer sales in the Pinzgau region. A quarter of them drink alcohol on a regular basis, and the number who get drunk regularly is well above Austria's average. In a lot of rural areas alcohol is a major problem, although many claim that they are not only drinking away their problems, but drinking because they like the drink. Alcohol, and increasingly designer drugs – which are also being imported and consumed by tourists – heighten pleasure besides suppressing negative experiences. Young people are particularly susceptible, with so many things in their everyday lives that make them feel inadequate, and so much that needs compensating for – a lack of family ties and security, problems at school, no job prospects. Deviation from social norms and escape into drugs increasingly present themselves as ways of getting away from it all.

Beside the strong trend towards the individualization of the private sphere and the emphasis on distinction, young people get together in cliques, short-lived social groupings of the like-minded with no commitment. As a postmodern form of passing relationships, these cliques have in some ways complemented or even replaced clubs. Although half the young still belong to clubs (especially sports clubs), which, like village public life, tend to be male-dominated, club life no longer offers the support framework and close network of social ties which was once typical of country life. Indeed, in many cases this old form of security is no longer something that young people are attracted to.

The New Youth Discourse

As rural and farming ways of life increasingly develop into urban lifestyles, village communication and social structures have undergone a change of meaning. Just like in the cities, numerous forms of youth culture have sprung up in the country with distinguishing features such as outward appearance, identification with particular symbols, or particular forms of behaviour and sets of values – a development following in the wake of increasing social pluralism and a decline in the validity of traditional cultural conventions and behavioural norms. Additional new, looser patterns of orientation have emerged to give young people a sense of security in this phase of their lives, which is dominated by a feeling of permanent irritation. Increasing importance is attached to socialization within the peer group, a kind of 'self-education' in groups and cliques within the framework of the youth scene. Role models and life perspectives propagated through the media have partially eclipsed or even replaced traditional ideas. The process of growing up and breaking away from the parental home is one that is increasingly shifting its focus to the sphere of pleasure-oriented leisure and a search for meaning there. With today's alliance between the media and the consumer world, youth culture is a very marketable commodity and young people are key consumers in the new market (Larkey, 1993).

At the same time, improved vocational training has led to new expectations in the region, such as the demand for the chance to get adequate employment; most highly-qualified young people have to move outside their home region to find work that corresponds to their qualifications. Young people often find that the older generation has little understanding for their needs. In contrast with the urban young, there are severe deficits in the infrastructure for young people in the country areas, for example with regard to the opportunities for peer group contact and communication: there are hardly any youth centres, and far fewer extracurricular forums in schools or through community-run youth work than in urban areas.

For a long time, no heed was paid to youth culture in the rural areas, and all the attention of local policy-makers was directed towards tourism development. It took a number of scandals in the drug scene, individual tragedies which demonstrated the underlying social problems, some headline stories pointing to the degeneration of the age of prosperity, and pressure from active youth organizations to wake local politics up to the necessity of reopening the political dialogue with the young.

On the basis of the first study on the young people in the Austrian Alps (Luger and Tedeschi, 1996), the 'Jugendprojekt Pinzgau' (Pinzgau youth project) was initiated two years ago by the youth department of the Salzburg regional government, together with a number of youth organizations that had been actively involved in youth work but had until then received no financial support from the state. Funding was made available for facilities for young people, in particular for leisure activities, employment of apprentices, further vocational training, support for underprivileged children, and prevention of drug abuse. Youth forums were set up, skating facilities built, and a youth conference held with workshops and exhibitions on a variety of sociopolitical issues. A drug-prevention project was set up and an employment scheme initiated for the unemployed young. Above all, it has been recognized that today's generation conflict is governed by a new set of values, and that far from being out of control – as in every generation conflict, this is the perception of the older side – the young people value family ties, reliability and helpfulness, and want to assert themselves and enjoy career success. The new component is that they also feel they have the right to enjoy life more intensively – following the example set by the tourists they see in their midst pursuing pleasure and seeking new fun experiences as they switch out of the problems of life and look down on the world from the mountain tops.

For all its international aspirations, its hook-up to the global tourism industry, the modernization of rural life, the cultural change, the millions of visitors from all over the world – the world-famous ski resort Saalbach/Hinterglemm with its 3000 inhabitants registers some 2 million overnight stays annually, second only to Vienna – despite all this development towards urban modernity, the Pinzgau region has remained a rural alpine region which offers a high degree of leisure and recreational possibilities. Not all the policy-makers have taken in exactly what has happened in this process of modernization, and when it comes to addressing the problems of the young, many put up the stubborn resistance sometimes attributed to the character of the alpine peoples. However, many have recognized the need for action and have put the youth question high on the political agenda.

The change in the system of values set in motion by the process of social transformation has altered the way the different generations live together. This fact must be recognized and accepted, and a new pact must be negotiated between them. In the rural communities – and the research on the Pinzgau region surely speaks for others as well – the age of unquestioned authority is past. This may make young people difficult to deal with, but if the older generation gives them their chance to go through with their own development and does not try to rob them of their future, then they too will benefit, and will one day feel more confident about handing over the house, the hotel, the sports club and the mayor's office into younger hands.

References

Baetzing, W. and Perlik, M. (1995) Tourismus und Regionalentwicklung in den Alpen 1870–1990. In: Luger, K. and Inmann, K. (eds) *Verreiste Berge – Kultur und Tourismus im Hochgebirge*. Studienverlag, Innsbruck, pp. 43–80.

Bauer, W., Rest, F. and Schweighofer, C. (eds) (1994) *Sind die Bauern noch zu retten? Über die Zukunft einer alpinen Kultur*. Kulturverein Schloß Goldegg.

Bischof, G. (1999) Der Marshall-Plan und die Wiederbelebung des österreichischen Fremdenverkehrs nach dem Zweiten Weltkrieg. In: Bischof, G. and Stiefel, D. (eds) *80 Dollar: 50 Jahre ERP-Fonds und Marshall-Plan in Österreich 1948–1998*. Ueberreuter, Vienna, pp. 133–182.

Brusatti, A. (1984) *100 Jahre oesterreichischer Fremdenverkehr. Historische Entwicklung 1884–1984*. Wiener Verlag, Vienna.

CIPRA (Commission Internationale pour la Protection des Alpes) (1996) *Mythos Alpen*. CIPRA, Vienna.

Conrad, K. (1994) Tourismus und alpine Baukultur. In: Poettler, B. and Kammerhofer-Aggermann, U. (eds) *Tourismus und Regionalkultur*. Verein für Volkskunde, Vienna, pp. 277–284.

Hanisch, E. (1997) *Der Gau der guten Nerven*. Pustet, Salzburg.

Hartl, F. (1996) Finanzierung, Investition und Verschuldung im Tourismus. In: Weiermair, K. (ed.) *Alpine Tourism: Sustainability Reconsidered and Redesigned*. Conference Publication, Innsbruck, pp. 55–71.

Hennig, C. (1997) *Reiselust: Touristen, Tourismus und Urlaubskultur*. Insel, Frankfurt.

Hoffmann, R. and Luger, K. (1997) Tourismus und sozialer Wandel – Strukturelle Rahmenbedingungen. In: Hanisch, E. and Kriechbaumer, R. (eds) *Salzburg – Geschichte der österreichischen Bundesländer seit 1945*. Böhlau, Vienna, pp. 168–209.

IPK-International (1996) *Sommer-Urlaub Oesterreich: Study of the German Market*. IPK, Munich.

Kapeller, K. (1991) *Tourismus und Volkskultur*. dbv-Verlag für die Technische Universität Graz, Graz.

Kerschbaumer, G. (1994) *Tourismus im politischen Wandel der 30er und 40er Jahre. In: Haas, H., Hoffmann, R. and Luger, K. (eds) (1994) Weltbühne und Naturkulisse – Zwei Jahrhunderte Salzburgtourismus*. Pustet, Salzburg, pp. 120–128.

Kos, W. (1995) *Eigenheim Oesterreich. Zu Politik, Kultur und Alltag nach 1945*. Sonderzahl, Vienna.

Kos, W. (1995a) Imagereservoir Landschaft. Landschaftsmoden und ideologische Gemuetslagen seit 1945. In: Sieder, R., Steinert, H. and Tálos, E. (eds) *Oesterreich 1945–1995. Gesellschaft, Politik, Kultur.* Verlag fuer Gesellschaftskritik, Vienna, pp. 599–624.

Kramer, D. (1997) *Aus der Region – Fuer die Region. Konzepte für einen Tourismus mit menschlichem Mass.* Deuticke, Vienna-Munich.

Krippendorf, J. (1984) *Die Ferienmenschen.* Orell Füssli, Zürich.

Larkey, E. (1993) *Pungent Sounds: Constructing Identity with Popular Music in Austria.* Peter Lang, New York.

Luger, K. (1991) *Die konsumierte Rebellion. Geschichte der Jugendkultur 1945–1990.* Österreichischer Kunst- und Kulturverlag, Vienna.

Luger, K. (1994) Salzburg als Buehne und Kulisse. Die Stadt als Schauplatz der internationalen Unterhaltungsindustrie. In: Haas, H., Hoffmann, R. and Luger, K. (eds) (1994) *Weltbühne und Naturkulisse – Zwei Jahrhunderte Salzburgtourismus.* Pustet, Salzburg, pp. 176–187.

Luger, K. (1995) Kulturen im Veränderungsstress. In: Luger, K. and Inmann, K. (eds) *Verreiste Berge – Kultur und Tourismus im Hochgebirge.* Studienverlag, Innsbruck, pp. 19–42.

Luger, K. (1998) *Vergnügen Zeitgeist Kritik. Streifzüge durch die populäre Kultur.* Österreichischer Kunst- und Kulturverlag, Vienna.

Luger, K. and Rest, F. (1994) Vom Massentourismus zum sanften Reisen. In: Haas, H., Hoffmann, R. and Luger, K. (eds) (1994) *Weltbühne und Naturkulisse – Zwei Jahrhunderte Salzburgtourismus.* Pustet, Salzburg, pp. 200–210.

Luger, K. and Rest, F. (1995) Mobile Privatisierung. Kultur und Tourismus in der Zweiten Republik. In: Sieder, R., Steinert, H. and Tálos, E. (eds) *Oesterreich 1945–1995. Gesellschaft, Politik, Kultur.* Verlag fuer Gesellschaftskritik, Vienna, pp. 655–670.

Luger, K. and Tedeschi, C. (1996) *Gratwanderung zwischen Tradition und Modernität.* Akzente Eigenverlag, Salzburg.

Mueller, H.-R. (1994) The thorny path to sustainable tourism development. *Journal of Sustainable Tourism* 3, 131–136.

Österreich-Werbung (1997) *Jahresbericht 1996.* Österreich-Werbung, Vienna.

Rest, F. (1994) Das leichtverdiente Geld. Über die Beziehung zwischen Fremdenverkehr und Landwirtschaft. In: Haas, H., Hoffmann, R. and Luger, K. (eds) (1994) *Weltbühne und Naturkulisse – Zwei Jahrhunderte Salzburgtourismus.* Pustet, Salzburg, pp. 160–168.

Rest, F. (1995) Kulturelle Identitaet und transkulturelle Heimat. In: Luger, K. and Inmann, K. (eds) *Verreiste Berge – Kultur und Tourismus im Hochgebirge.* Studienverlag, Innsbruck, pp. 81–94.

Schrutka-Rechtenstamm, A. (1995) Einfluesse des Fremdenverkehrs auf die Alltagskultur im Alpenraum. In: Cantauw, C. (ed) *Arbeit Freizeit Reisen. Die feinen Unterschiede im Alltag.* Waxmann, Münster-New York, pp. 151–160.

Smeral, E. (1994) Tourismus 2005. *Entwicklungsaspekte und Szenarien fuer die Tourismus- und Freizeitwirtschaft.* Überreuter, Vienna.

Thiem, M. (1994) Tourismus und kulturelle Identität: die Bedeutung des Tourismus für die Kultur touristischer Ziel- und Quellgebiete. *Berner Studien zu Freizeit und Tourismus* vol. 30, Berne.

Williams, R. (1973) *Television, Technology, and Cultural Form.* Fontana Press, Glasgow.

Zimmermann, F. (1991) Austria: contrasting tourist seasons and contrasting regions. In: Williams, A. and Shaw, G. (eds) *Tourism and Economic Development.* Belhaven Press, London–New York, pp. 153–172.

Zins, A. (1996) *Reiseausgaben im Österreichischen Tourismus.* Oesterreichischer Wirtschaftsverlag, Vienna.

Conclusion
Demographic Change, Climatic Change and the 'Smart' Consumer: Influences on Tourism in the Western Europe of the 21st Century

Richard Voase

University of Lincoln, Lincoln Campus, Lincoln, UK

Introduction

The diverse material in the foregoing chapters can be interpreted as evidence of, at the broadest level, a shift from an 'old' to a 'new' tourism. This shift, which has been identified in the first chapter as a manifestation of the cultural transition from the modern to the postmodern, has involved fragmentations in the spatial and temporal distribution of vacational tourism. Established destinations such as seaside communities have encountered problems; new destinations such as post-industrial urban centres and rural regions, have emerged from improbable beginnings. These changes have been variously driven, and on occasions impeded, by political and economic considerations as dominant influences; they have been fuelled by increased levels of education within the western European population, as much as by increased levels of discretionary income and increased holiday entitlements. The consequences have included a plethora of sociocultural impacts on local identities, as communities and their proprietary lifestyles become annexed to the diversified view of what constitutes a tourist product. The paradigm set out in the first chapter for the arrangement and interpretation of the material has been the PEST analysis, accompanied by an assemblage of cultural theory. The purpose of this concluding chapter is to adopt a forward-looking perspective, by complementing the existing material with an outline appraisal of three additional influences. The first of these is demographic change; the second is climatic change; and the chapter will conclude with some observations on the emergence or otherwise of the so-called 'smart' consumer.

Before embarking on this discussion, it is important to apply a caveat. There

© CAB *International* 2002. *Tourism in Western Europe: a Collection of Case Histories*
(ed. Richard Voase)

are research organizations which make it their full-time business to analyse the present and forecast the future: the UK's *Henley Centre for Forecasting* and *Travel and Tourism Intelligence* are examples, as is *Reiseanalyse* in Germany. What follows does not aim to emulate the efforts of organizations such as these. Rather, this concluding chapter offers a summary of the demographic and climatic factors, and a particular cultural factor, which may prove to be determining influences on western European tourism, and tourist destinations, in the next 30 or so years. The examples are primarily drawn from the United Kingdom, but the intention is to raise model issues which can usefully be explored in respect of the consumer culture of any European country. If at the end of this chapter a certain level of complexity is apparent, and if more questions have been raised than answered, then the chapter will have fulfilled its intended purpose.

Demographic Change

The population of Europe is growing older. The tendency toward smaller families, complemented by improvements in healthcare, are leading to a substantial increase in the elderly population. Projections by the European Commission have suggested that, by the year 2025, in excess of 100 million Europeans – one third of the projected population – will be over 60 years of age, representing an increase over the present figure of over 50%. Over the same period, there will be a decline in the number of citizens of working age, and of children and teenagers. A trebling of the number of people aged 80 and above will place particular demands on the infrastructure needed to cope with their needs (Bates, 1996). Caution must be exercised inasmuch as demographic projections are based on assumptions about births and fertility, mortality and migration, which may prove inaccurate. What is more, such projections do not take into account unanticipated cultural or biological factors. For example, fertility rates in developed countries are influenced as much by cultural as by biological factors; birth control is practised widely within the European population. A cultural shift in favour of larger rather than smaller families would be expected to alter projections. Similarly, disease epidemics can be unanticipated biological factors. A discussion of demographics published in the late 1980s speculated on the likely consequences of an AIDS epidemic in Europe (*Marketing*, 1989). Although this disease has taken a substantial hold on populations in parts of Africa, Europe is (at the time of writing) relatively unaffected; the worst speculations of the late 1980s proved in practice to have not come true. However, there is much current speculation within the United Kingdom of the likely effects of the disease known as new-variant CJD, the brain disease which is thought to have an incubation period measured in decades rather than years. It is thought to result from the consumption of meat infected with the cattle disease known as BSE during the 1980s. Whether victims will be numbered in the hundreds, or in the hundreds of thousands, is too early to say. Interestingly, this author wrote with some confidence 6 years ago, based on official information available at that time, that BSE posed a 'negligible risk' to human health: a salutary lesson in treating official statements with caution! (Voase, 1995: 154).

However, our present purpose is to discuss the extent to which demographic changes may influence patterns of tourism, and tourist destinations, in Europe. It can be said, with some certainty, that the proportion of older people will increase significantly: a so-called 'greying' of the western European population will occur. Bates' interpretation of the European Commission's projections is that the meeting of the needs of these 'grey' consumers, and in particular those aged over 80 years who may treble in number, will increasingly dominate social and family life. It is also anticipated that the trend of migration for retirement purposes from northern Europe to more-agreeable climates in southern Europe, in particular from countries such as Britain and Germany to Spain, would continue and accelerate (Bates, 1996). This is based on the assumption that southern Europe will continue to remain climatically attractive, and that such moves will remain economically attractive. Later in this chapter it shall be suggested that the assumed constancy of the climate cannot be relied upon; and if southern European economies continue to develop and local costs of living increase, the economic attractiveness of southern Europe as a retirement destination may itself lessen.

However, it is important to remember that age and financial importunity do not necessarily accompany one another. Many of the elderly of western Europe will benefit from occupational pensions, from generous state pensions (generous in some countries, but not all), and by inheritance from their own parents. In the United Kingdom in particular, where some two-thirds of homes are owner-occupied (Boycott, 1997), the inheritance of owned properties by offspring in their middle years provides capital assets which can be liquefied into substantial funds. The vision of the former prime minister, John Major, of wealth 'cascading down the generations' was shown to be accurate when a firm of probate specialists produced data showing increases in inheritances in England and Wales. In 1992, the average inheritance was £68,000 and one in six estates was worth more than £100,000. It was estimated that the value of property passed on between 1992 and 2000 would be in excess of £24bn (Davison and Bradberry, 1992). For the purpose of comparison, this was the equivalent of all spending on tourism by UK residents in 1992. Thus, an increase in migration, fuelled by wealth, from northern Europe to southern Europe, could be anticipated. Indeed, in the late 1990s, one-fifth of the land and 45,000 houses on the Spanish island of Mallorca were said to be in German ownership (Hearst, 1998). Not unnaturally this can be the cause of social as well as economic impacts on the host community, just as surely as, for example, earlier waves of migration within the United Kingdom from the urban centres to the coast have created idiosyncratic demographic profiles in seaside resorts.

The ageing population is the most conspicuous anticipated demographic change, but this should not obfuscate the search for other significant changes which may impact on European tourism. For example, within the United Kingdom, a glance into the domiciliary habits of young persons in the age range 20–30 years presents an intriguing picture. In the late 1970s, 370,000 UK citizens lived alone as owner-occupiers; this had risen to 1 million by the late 1990s. Fascinatingly, most of this increase was not accounted for by elderly individuals outliving their partners, but by young people in their 20s and 30s: there were six times as many single (i.e. not married and not cohabiting) people in this age group who lived alone in their own property (Boycott, 1997). This picture becomes even more intriguing when we learn that, in the late 1990s, nearly a third of young men aged 20–35 lived with their parents, compared with only 25% 20 years earlier (Furedi, 2001). Clearly the picture can expected to differ from country to country, but, as a snapshot of one example, this glance suggests a growing number of young people unengaged by the financial responsibilities of marriage and cohabitation, whose discretionary income and discretionary time may well be attracted toward travel, and whose enquiring dispositions fuelled by increasing levels of education may direct them to it. Indeed, at the time of writing, very recent data suggest that 20% of 16–24-year-olds in the United Kingdom spend in the region of £3000 per annum on travel (Furedi, 2001). So, using the kind of data briefly exposed in the above paragraphs, demographic change and patterns of tourism and tourism-related migration can be linked.

Climatic Change

The key climatic issue currently facing world governments is that known as 'global warming'. In essence, this involves an acceleration of a general and gradual heating-up of the Earth's atmosphere by the effects of carbon dioxide and other gases emitted from motor vehicle engines and industrial processes. The consequence is the creation of a shield which limits the escape of warmth from the Earth; hence, 'global warming'. While the precise effects are still to some extent unknown, many experts became convinced, from the mid-1990s onwards, that real consequences would ensue from these effects. The comment in an early study that 'the development of entirely new patterns of recreational activity' could be one of the consequences of accelerated global warming (Kemp, 1990: 158) somewhat understates the full implications: another early study concluded that those regions most vulnerable to change were those which were 'arid and marginal', which would include the Mediterranean coastlands of southern Europe (Leggett (ed.), 1990: 127). The purpose here is to summarize possible consequences for western and southern Europe, based on recent research.

Agnew and Viner (2001) suggest the following consequences of global warming for the regions of western and southern Europe. Generally speaking, coastal resorts in south-eastern Europe, principally in Greece and Turkey, may experience an increased incidence of extreme heat, represented by days above 40°C becoming increasingly common. The south-western coasts may also experience increased temperatures: while the levels of discomfort in Spain may not rival those in Greece and Turkey, September temperatures in the middle of the present century may rival the current temperatures experienced in July. Of greater concern is perhaps the likelihood that parts of Spain will become a suitable habitat for malaria-carrying mosquitoes. Winter tourism would also be affected: lower-altitude resorts in the European

Alps would see their snow cover eroded; in Scotland, snow cover may virtually expire. The melting of polar ice caps and expansion of the warming seas could cause serious inundation in countries such as the Netherlands. Within the United Kingdom, the north and north-west could be expected to become warmer and wetter, the south and south-east warmer and drier. The coastal resorts of southern England would find themselves equipped with a climate increasingly agreeable for beach holidaymakers; while industries such as farming would need to cope with arid conditions and, perhaps, seek to introduce and grow new kinds of crops (McKie, 1996).

However, it may be premature to draw the conclusion that the visitation of these destinations for vacational purposes will be radically and adversely affected by these anticipated climatic changes. The reason is that the enjoyment of the environment can be argued to be a social construct (Macnaghton and Urry, 1998: 19–20), in which humankind makes natural adversity the subordinate to cultural desire. Present-day tourism is replete with examples of this. For example, the dramatically increased incidence of skin cancer amongst western European populations, the consequence of some 30 years' excess vacational exposure, has not resulted the abandonment of the beaches of the Mediterranean. Although studies in Australia (a population of primarily European origin) have suggested that the fashionability of deep suntans appears to have reduced, the symbolic value of the tan as a signifier of health and happiness remains undiminished (Chapman *et al.*, 1992). In the United Kingdom, Coupland and Coupland's (1997) analysis of the discourse of suntanning as represented in the printed media suggested that the dangers of excess exposure were subordinate to the citizen's duty to consume the sun, while it made its fleeting domestic appearance. The recommended compromise was labelled 'healthy tanning', an uneasy balancing act involving the use of creams and tactical 'covering-up'. Similarly, very satisfactory sun holiday packages are being sold to Europeans for destinations in the hottest parts of the world, such as the Persian Gulf, where culture in the form of air conditioning in buildings and vehicles is deployed to overcome the excesses of nature. It is not unreasonable to expect that such a solution, deployed comprehensively in Greece, Turkey and Spain, would work as effectively. Similarly, an established trend in tourism, identifiable since the 1970s, has been an increased emphasis on active rather than passive leisure pursuits, and an accelerating interest in the natural environment (Euromonitor, 1992: 3). Over this period, the enjoyment of mountain regions such as the Alps has already begun to diversify. Given the gradual nature of climatic change, it is not unreasonable to posit a strategy of change for ski resorts which, finding themselves increasingly prevented from offering the ski experience, may re-position themselves as a different kind of vacational environment. Perhaps most convincingly, it is useful to remember that the enjoyment of the sea and the beach is, itself, also a social construct. Until the beginning of the 19th century, the sea was a place to be avoided, or bathed in for purely curative purposes. Romanticism instigated the construction of the sea and its coastline as aesthetic objects to enjoy and consume (Inglis, 2000: chapter 3). This social transformation was completed with the development of railways, which offered the capacity to transport urban populations *en masse* to the coast to enjoy the seaside as leisure/liminal zone (Urry, 1990: chapter 2).

The 'Smart' Consumer?

The discussion on social construction leads, neatly, to the third and final topic for this chapter. Is it possible to speculate on the qualitative nature of tourist consumption as it may appear in the coming decades? A useful starting-point may be to examine identified trends from a decade ago, in the early 1990s, and consider the extent to which they can be shown to be valid. Martin and Mason (1993: 34) wrote of a 'shift in emphasis from passive fun to active learning' and, though writing principally about visitor attractions, suggested that their interpretation was relevant to a much wider field of consumption. Euromonitor, as cited earlier, was making similar comments around the same time (Euromonitor, 1992: 3). Subsequent data relating to the active exercise of imagination and initiative, as opposed to passive consumption, seem to indicate that these projections were well-founded. The reading of books is perhaps one indicator worthy of examination, given that to read is a proactive mental activity requiring the deployment of intellectual skill. In 1996, in the United Kingdom, data showed that two-thirds of adults had read books in the 4-week period prior to official survey, compared with a little over half 20 years earlier (ONS, 1998: 214). This is perhaps not surprising when one considers that the number of titles published or re-issued has proliferated, from 64,000 titles to 95,000 between the years 1990 and 1995 alone (PSI, 1997: 48), and the proportion of adults claiming to have bought books over the same 5 year period rises from 62% in 1990 to 71% in 1995 (PSI, 1997: 69). However, data from the public library service adds an intriguing qualitative twist: while loans of adult fiction fell over the same period, loans of adult non-fiction, and of children's books, increased (PSI, 1997: 69). Again, this need not surprise, when it is considered that levels of education have risen dramatically over the same period. In the United Kingdom in the mid-1990s, the proportion of employees in intermediate non-manual jobs in possession of a degree was higher than the proportion of degree-holders amongst managers and employers (ONS, 1998: 95): representing, arguably, the entry into the workforce of increasing numbers of university graduates, by the turn of the century accounting for 30% of all school leavers. Indeed, across Europe as a whole, OECD data shows, between 1990 and 1996, no exception to increased enrolments in tertiary education in a range of European countries. In Finland, France, and Italy, this increase was of the order of 25%; in Ireland and Norway, closer to 50%; in the United Kingdom, 75%; and in Portugal, 300% (Marshall, 2001).

To provide a contrast with book-reading, television viewing perhaps represents the apogee of passive, as opposed to active, consumption. The last two decades have witnessed an explosion of televised output: in the United Kingdom, between the years of 1985/86 and 1991/92, average weekly broadcast hours increased from 477 h to 632 h for terrestrial channels alone. This represents an increase of 30%, without taking into account the proliferation of satellite and cable television channels over the same period (PSI, 1993: 14). Intriguingly, over a comparable period, British people actually started watching *less* television: from an average 27.1 h per week in 1985, to 25.2 h per week in 1994 (PSI, 1996: 79).

The attempted resolution of this apparent paradox is a research interest of the author and is the object of present (Voase, 2001) and future investigation. For the present, it is proposed that the starting point for resolving the paradox is to query the nature of 'active' and 'passive'. The accepted meaning of these terms, or one of them at any rate, was elegantly challenged by the journalist Francine Stock in a newspaper article (Stock, 1997). Citing an address given by Sir Nicholas Goodison, chairman of the National Art Collections Fund, she expanded on Sir Nicholas' suggestion that in the 'interactive museum', the term 'interactive' is a misnomer: the operator of the interactive exhibit is essentially accessing pre-programmed responses and as such, the 'activity' is essentially passive. Stock uses the term 'binary culture' to describe the 'two-lane highway of the interactive system' and analyses the outcome thus:

> The drawback of the interactive, audio-visual 1990s museum is that it can limit rather than extend the imagination. Every tableau, every video display, every screen journey is charted territory. Someone has mapped out the way ahead so carefully that you can only go forward or back in their steps. Lateral thought is out. Collections left largely to themselves can be a fascinating source of greater mystery and adventure . . . let's abandon this popular cultural imperialism and put the mystery and mysticism back into museums. (Stock, 1997)

Two pieces of research into museum and gallery visitors appear to support the view that museum visitors can be trusted to deploy their imaginations. Liddiard's detailed interviews with 200 museum visitors revealed that many respondents were highly active in constructing meanings from the material they encountered, and reflected critically on their experience. In particular, more than half believed that there were aspects of topics which the museum did not want to display. Interestingly, Liddiard reports that these results confounded the views of a number of museum professionals, who seriously underestimated the ability of their visitors to 'read' the material and generate their own meanings (Liddiard, 2002). Similarly, Linko's (2001) research involved the analysis of autobiographical accounts of experiences of either producing or viewing visual art. The results suggested that respondents integrated cognitive and emotional responses at a complex level, confounding the widely-believed notion that the contemporary subject lacks the ability to experience, enjoy and articulate genuine aesthetic sense and emotion.

Perhaps the principal flag-bearer for the contrasting people-as-dupes thesis is the French social philosopher, Jean Baudrillard. His view of television is one of an informational medium where the objective is the consumption of the form rather than the content: '(The message of TV) . . . is the message of message consumption . . . the total dominance of a system of reading over a world now become a system of signs' (Baudrillard, 1990: 89). The essence of his argument is that sign-value has eclipsed use-value in contemporary consumption, which leads Baudrillard to this bleak corollary:

All the great humanist criteria of value, the whole civilization of moral, aesthetic and practical judgement are effaced in our system of images and signs. Everything becomes undecidable, the characteristic effect of the domination of the code, which everywhere rests on the principle of neutralization, of indifference. (Baudrillard, 1993: 9)

Liddiard's and also Linko's research cited earlier suggests that the 'principle of indifference' is not quite the pandemic that Baudrillard would have us believe. Nevertheless, it has to be remembered that the field of tourist consumption is, to coin a cliché, a very broad church. It is a mistake to assume that all visitors to a destination are culturally competent, with a Foucauldian eye for the ocularly consumable. This point was made by Christopher Holloway in a conference paper 5 years ago. He pointed out that the defining characteristic of tourists deposited in a strange city may be more accurately defined as 'tourist daze' than 'tourist gaze'. They have a limited notion of where they are and what they are looking at (Holloway, 1995: 80). This echoes a point made by Daniel Boorstin, writing several decades ago about the 'lost art of travel', and observing that his fellow Americans whom he encountered on international flights had little idea of where they were going, or why (Boorstin, 1963: 99). This notion was supported by a wonderfully neat piece of research done a year or two ago by one of the author's undergraduate students. Curious to discover how much of her home town of Windsor was ingested by tourists during their visits, she showed a list of named visitor attractions to tourists and asked them to indicate those which they either had visited, or intended to visit, during their time in Windsor. The most-mentioned, not surprisingly, was Windsor Castle, a private home of the British Royal Family. The second most-mentioned, intriguingly, was the Jorvik Viking Centre, located 300 miles away in the City of York (J. Dovey, Heritage tourism: the tourist-historic town. Unpublished undergraduate dissertation, University of Lincolnshire and Humberside, 1998, used with permission). These tourists were for the most part from overseas, initially based in London but with a touring itinerary which would take them to stay in other historic cities, and they visited Windsor on a day-trip. They knew that they would encounter certain well-known visitor attractions during their total stay, but relating what to where, and when, was puzzling and confusing: the 'tourist daze' in action. Whether a tourist is an active or passive consumer, a practitioner of the 'gaze' or a subject of the 'daze' depends very much on context, and on the meanings ascribed to these terms.

Conclusion

Projected demographic change can be expected to influence patterns of European tourism. This may include the acceleration of patterns of tourism-influenced migration, for residence purposes, of retired populations from north to south. In more subtle ways, links may be posited between the increase in single-living amongst the younger population, and increasing incidence of their participation in tertiary education, and participation in travel experiences broadly referred to as 'new' tourism: the seeking out of new destinations and visitor experiences linked to cultural and intellectual experience, as well as recreation. Projected climatic change may, or may not, influence the fortunes of certain regions: increased heat may lead to exacerbated levels of physical discomfort in southern Europe, and decreased snow cover will demand diversification policies on the part of low-altitude ski resorts. However, past history, present theory and the evidence of the contributions in this volume suggest that environments are socially constructed, and consumed on that basis. If populations enjoy a socially-induced desire to visit a region, the means of adaptation will be found. The response to increased incidence of skin cancer, which has not led to the desertion of warm-climate beaches, is offered as evidence for this.

There is also this question of the emergence of the 'smart' consumer. The tentative proposition was that the meaning of the terms 'active' and 'passive' may require definition: the 'interactive' museum can be argued to be the deliverer of an essentially 'passive' experience; similarly, crowds of tourists visiting cultural destinations can be equally in a passive 'daze', as practitioners of an active 'gaze'. An anecdote may help to reconcile these positions: a televised documentary, seen by the author shortly before writing these lines, featured a family which had been asked to experiment with a new system which offered an enormous menu of televised output mediated via telephone lines into their home. What was interesting was not so much the technology, but how the family 'consumed' the output, and the words they chose to describe the experience. The father had developed a 'passion' for natural history documentaries; the son's 'consuming interest' was a 1980s soap opera, made and broadcast before he was born. Faced with a proliferation of opportunities, the consumers combined a process of highly active choice with passive consumption. This of course is the essence of the use of the World Wide Web: a process of choice which is in a real sense highly active, but which accesses pre-prepared data: in the second sense, passive.

The experience of 'new tourism' is in many ways a parallel experience. Even the most apparently ardently active and adventurous of 'new' tourists are in a sense passive consumers, as Munt concluded from his detailed study:

> The practices of travellers are best conceived within a 'cult of individualism' . . . though it is deeply ironic that they are largely indistinguishable from each other by virtue of their discourse, dress codes and the informal 'packages' they follow through travel guides. Whole regions have become travel *circuits* (in popular travel discourse, 'doing' South East Asia, Central America, and so on) . . . (Munt, 1994: 114)

The demand for individualistic tourist activity is met by the commodification of niche travel opportunities. The act of choosing may be active, the travel experience itself may be physically and intellectually active, but the end result is the accessing of a pre-programmed packaged experience: essentially passive. In this sense, the new tourist is both smart, and passive. It is the desire to escape from 'traditional' passivity which has led, arguably, to the emergence of new and improbable destinations, and the desire to avoid some old ones, as the cases in this volume ably demonstrate. As levels of education and individual wealth continue to increase, it is difficult to avoid the conclusion that the search for the as-yet-undiscovered, and the avoidance of the over-familiar, will continue to be the driving force behind the new tourism. The 'new' western European tourist has been described as a seeker of a state of pre-modern contentment (Selwyn, 1996: 2; Voase, 1999), a Utopia where change and ambition are redundant. Like the *Utopia* described by Sir Thomas More in 1516, it is to be found nowhere.

References

Agnew, M. and Viner, D. (2001–forthcoming) Potential impacts of climate change on international tourism, *International Journal of Tourism and Hospitality Research* (accepted).

Bates, S. (1996) Europe faces a grey future. *Guardian*, 5 March.

Baudrillard, J. (1990) *Revenge of the Crystal*. Pluto Press, Leichhardt, NSW.

Baudrillard, J. (1993) *Symbolic Exchange and Death*. Sage, London.

Boorstin, D. (1963) *The Image, or What Happened to the American Dream*. Penguin, London.

Boycott, O. (1997) England's single households boom. *Guardian*, 9 May.

Chapman, S., Marks, R. and King, M. (1992) Trends in tans and skin protection in Australian fashion magazines, 1982 through 1991. *American Journal of Public Health* 82 (12), 1677–1680.

Coupland, N. and Coupland, J. (1997) Bodies, beaches and burn-times: 'environmentalism' and its discursive competitors. *Discourse and Society* 8 (1), 7–25.

Davison, J. and Bradberry, G. (1992) Inherited millions release 'cascade of wealth'. *Sunday Times*, 3 May, p. 5.

Euromonitor (1992) *The European Travel and Tourism Marketing Directory*. Euromonitor, London.

Furedi, F. (2001) You'll always be my baby. *Times Higher Education Supplement*, 23 March, p. 19.

Hearst, D. (1998) Majorcans fight losing battle as invading Germans put their mark on the island. *Guardian*, 25 July, p. 16.

Holloway, C. (1995) The tourist as streetwalker: gaze or daze? *The Urban Environment: Tourism*, conference paper. South Bank University, London.

Inglis, F. (2000) *The Delicious History of the Holiday*. Routledge, London.

Kemp, D. (1990) *Global Environmental Issues: a Climatological Approach*. Routledge, London.

Leggett, J. (ed.) (1990) *Global Warming: the Greenpeace Report*. Oxford University Press, Oxford.

Liddiard, M. (2002) *Making Histories of Sexuality and Gender*. Cassell, London.

Linko, M. (2001) The longing for authentic experiences: the subjective meaning of visual art for museum audiences and amateur artists. In: Ernst, K., Halbertsma, M., Janssen, S. and Ijdens, T. (eds) *Taking Stock: Trends and Strategies in the Arts and Cultural Industries*. Barjesteh and Co., Rotterdam.

Macnaghten, P. and Urry, J. (1998) *Contested Natures*. Sage, London.

McKie, R. (1996) Here is the forecast for 2030. *Observer*, 17 March, p. 28.

Marketing (1989) *Marketing Guide 3: Demographics*, 5 January.

Marshall, J. (2001) Vision of lifelong learning put at the heart of OECD target. *Times Higher Education Supplement*, 6 April, p. 11.

Martin, B. and Mason, S. (1993) The future for attractions: meeting the needs of the new consumers. *Tourism Management*, February 1993, 34–40.

Munt, I. (1994) The 'other' postmodern tourism: culture, travel and the new middle classes. *Theory, Culture and Society* 11, 101–123.

ONS (Office for National Statistics) (1998) *Living in Britain: Results from the 1996 General Household Survey*. The Stationery Office, London.

PSI (Policy Studies Institute) (1993) *Cultural Trends* 17, 5 (1).

PSI (Policy Studies Institute) (1995) *Cultural Trends* 25, 7 (1).

PSI (Policy Studies Institute) (1996) *Cultural Trends* 25, 7 (1).

PSI (Policy Studies Institute) (1997) *Cultural Trends* 26, 7 (2).

Selwyn, T. (ed.) (1996) *The Tourist Image: Myths and Myth-Making in Tourism*. John Wiley and Sons, Chichester.

Stock, F. (1997) I collect things, therefore I am a human being. *Guardian*, 21 May, p. 17.

Urry, J. (1990) *The Tourist Gaze*. Sage, London.

Voase, R.N. (1995) *Tourism: the Human Perspective*. Hodder and Stoughton, London.

Voase, R.N. (1999) 'Consuming' tourist sites/sights: a note on York. *Leisure Studies* 18 (4), 289–296.

Voase, R.N. (2001) The imagination rediscovered: cultural consumption, postmodernization and the future for live drama. In: Ernst, K., Halbertsma, M., Janssen, S. and Ijdens, T. (eds) *Taking Stock: Trends and Strategies in the Arts and Cultural Industries*. Barjesteh and Co., Rotterdam.

Index

Figures in **bold** indicate major references.
Figures in *italic* refer to diagrams, photographs and tables.